A PUBLIC SERVANT'S VOICE

Through the Words of the First Woman Clerk for the Privy Council of Canada

Jocelyne Bourgon

Can ideas from the past help to invent a better future? In this book, part memoir and part guide, Jocelyne Bourgon explores this central question through the representation of her noteworthy career and professional life.

A Public Servant's Voice presents Bourgon's reflections on her time in government. As the first woman clerk for the privy council of Canada, secretary to cabinet, and head of the public service from 1994 to 1999, Bourgon brings an unprecedented perspective to public administration and public sector reform. She reflects on decades of work in the public sector and the field of public administration, in Canada and abroad. This book covers her career from her first days as a public servant to creating *A New Synthesis of Public Administration* to face the challenges of the twenty-first century. Along the way she played a key role in the Charlottetown negotiations, helped bring Canada a decade of fiscal surplus, launched initiatives to strengthen the public service, and worked with peers around the world.

Providing a public service perspective on events in Canada in the late twentieth century as seen through the life of one public servant, this book is more than a memoir. Instead, it speaks specifically to those who are willing to take on the heavy burden of serving their fellow citizens and provides vital insights for the future of Canadian governance.

The Honourable JOCELYNE BOURGON, PC, OC is the founding president of Public Governance International and president emeritus of the Canada School of Public Service. She had a distinguished career in the public service, including as the first woman secretary to cabinet for federal-provincial relations under Prime Minister Mulroney's government and the first woman clerk for the privy council of Canada under the government of Prime Minister Chrétien.

THE INSTITUTE OF PUBLIC ADMINISTRATION OF CANADA SERIES IN PUBLIC MANAGEMENT AND GOVERNANCE

Editors:
Peter Aucoin, 2001–2
Donald Savoie, 2003–7
Luc Bernier, 2007–9
Patrice Dutil, 2010–18
Luc Juillet, 2018–

This series is sponsored by the Institute of Public Administration of Canada as part of its commitment to encourage research on issues in Canadian public administration, public sector management, and public policy. It also seeks to foster wider knowledge and understanding among practitioners, academics, and the general public.

For a list of books published in the series, see page 239.

JOCELYNE BOURGON

A Public Servant's Voice

Through the Words of the First Woman Clerk for the Privy Council of Canada

UNIVERSITY OF TORONTO PRESS
Toronto Buffalo London

Toronto Buffalo London
utppublishing.com
Printed in Canada

ISBN 978-1-4875-7475-8 (paper)
ISBN 978-1-4875-7531-1 (EPUB)
ISBN 978-1-4875-7489-5 (PDF)

Library and Archives Canada Cataloguing in Publication

Title: A public servant's voice : through the words of the first woman clerk for the Privy Council of Canada / Jocelyne Bourgon.
Names: Bourgon, Jocelyne, author
Series: Institute of Public Administration of Canada series in public management and governance.
Description: Series statement: Institute of Public Administration of Canada series in public management and governance | Includes bibliographical references and index.
Identifiers: Canadiana (print) 20250301172 | Canadiana (ebook) 20250301253 | ISBN 9781487574758 (paper) | ISBN 9781487574895 (PDF) | ISBN 9781487575311 (EPUB)
Subjects: LCSH: Bourgon, Jocelyne. | LCSH: Canada – Officials and employees – Biography. | LCSH: Public administration – Canada. | LCSH: Civil service – Canada. | LCSH: Administrative agencies – Canada. | LCSH: Canada – Politics and government – 20th century. | LCGFT: Autobiographies.
Classification: LCC JL75 .B695 2026 | DDC 351.71–dc23

Cover design: Greg Jorss
Cover image: Photo by Lindsey Gibeau

The manufacturer's authorised representative in the EU for product safety is Mare Nostrum Group B.V., Doelen 72, 4831 GR Breda, The Netherlands.
Email: gpsr@mare-nostrum.co.uk.

We wish to acknowledge the land on which the University of Toronto Press operates. This land is the traditional territory of the Wendat, the Anishnaabeg, the Haudenosaunee, the Métis, and the Mississaugas of the Credit First Nation.

University of Toronto Press acknowledges the financial support of the Government of Canada, the Canada Council for the Arts, and the Ontario Arts Council, an agency of the Government of Ontario, for its publishing activities.

Canada Council for the Arts
Conseil des Arts du Canada

Funded by the Government of Canada
Financé par le gouvernement du Canada

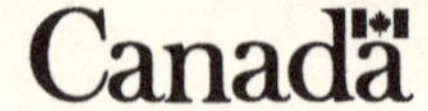

For Xavier

Contents

Acknowledgments

It took a long time to convince myself to undertake this project and to collect my personal archives. As always, I surrounded myself with remarkable people who made the project enriching.

As President of Public Governance International (PGI), I have long drawn on the skills and talents of master's degree and PhD students, hiring some each year. This approach gave me the pleasure of working with young, brilliant, and committed people from Canada and abroad. They infused every project with their energy and creativity.

In the summer of 2023, I hired two students to collect and organize my personal archives and relevant public documents: Justin Fiacconi, master in political science, and Corin Tentchoff, a PhD student in political science, both from Carleton University. Over the summer, they expanded the collection of speeches and research documents I already had, finding records I did not know existed, recovering documents I was surprised were still available, filling the gaps about events I vaguely remembered. They helped me see that there was something worthwhile to be drawn from the vast number of documents I had generated over the years; something from the past was worth sharing with today's public servants.

At the end of that summer, *Corin Tentchoff* became my research partner for the preparation of this book. I could not have had a better partner. He has a phenomenal ability to dig up information. His eye as an editor, his curiosity, his willingness to serve as a sounding board for ideas, and his skill at revealing the richness of our collection are remarkable. This manuscript owes much to his rigorous work. *Michel Bilodeau* is my partner in life and in crime. He believed in the importance of this book long before me. He patiently and critically read through the drafts that emerged as the project moved through various phases. At first, the project was simply to prepare short papers to accompany the transfer of my archives. Progressively, it blended memories, lessons learned, and probing questions about the future. This book owes much to his patient reviews and suggestions.

Others played a key role at various times. I discussed the idea of this book with Professor Luc Juillet, associate professor of public and international affairs at the University of Ottawa, in August 2023. He encouraged me to see it through and put me in touch with Daniel Quinlan, Senior Acquisitions Editor, University of Toronto Press. Professor Juillet's encouragement meant a lot to me, but I was still doubtful about the value of the project.

Three people reviewed the manuscript before I decided to submit it to University of Toronto Press: *Taki Sarantakis*, President of the Canada School of Public Service; *Mark Jarvis*, PhD Public Administration, University of Victoria and senior executive in the Public Service of Canada; and Professor *Tim Mau*, Political Science, University of Guelph. Their comments and encouragement convinced me of the usefulness of this effort for future public sector leaders and for a range of audiences. It took almost a year before I felt that the manuscript was worthy of being presented to the University of Toronto Press. *Daniel Quinlan* was a most supportive publishing partner for the last phase of this project that transformed a manuscript into a book in the hands of readers. And so, this project is coming to an end. But not quite just yet.

Having done the hard work of remembering, gathering, collecting, organizing, documenting, narrating, and writing about ideas and events that have guided my practice over fifty years, I now want to do more thinking, more sharing, and maybe some writing about the public service of Canada at this juncture. People in government today are serving in a more dangerous and challenging time, and they deserve all the help we can give them. Some old ideas are worth remembering and sharing, and some new practices are worth challenging and revisiting. The question is: has the past something to offer to public sector leaders today? Can a public servant's voice from the past help public service leaders set the public service of Canada on a trajectory to serve in 2025 and beyond? This may be my next project.

A PUBLIC SERVANT'S VOICE

Introduction

I joined the public service of Canada in 1973. A summer student job became a career: manager, deputy minister, the country's first woman Clerk of the Privy Council, President of the Centre for Management Development, Ambassador. After leaving the public service, I continued to dedicate myself to the field of public administration, in Canada and abroad. In 2009, I created Public Governance International (PGI) to pursue my passion for government, governance, and the role of the public sector in society.

In 2023, I started collecting my documents for their transfer to and safe keeping by Library and Archives Canada (LAC). In the process, I realized how valuable these records are. The public records on many issues are lacking a public service perspective, even about events and changes that have shaped the public service as an institution over the years. I also realized that, valuable as they are, my records need context to be useful and need a narrative about the aspirations and ideas behind the changes I was involved in or initiatives that I led.

Colleagues I consulted suggested that the transfer of my documents to LAC should be accompanied by a selected number of essays to guide future readers and researchers. This was a useful suggestion. It was with this in mind that I began drafting short essays to bring a *public service perspective* to initiatives launched during my time in the public service of Canada and in which I had a direct involvement.

As the work progressed during the course of 2023, the project became more ambitious. The question became: what can be learned from the past that may help invent a better future? *A Public Servant's Voice* is meant to help bring some lessons forward. This is a memoir in a way, but not just a memoir. It is written as a practical book, reflecting on the past to help inform the future. It is a collection of pages of history in the life of the public service of Canada, history as personal experience exemplified by personal stories. It has no claim to be an exhaustive history of the public service. It is limited to issues and topics for which I hold personal documents. It is based on publicly available documents. It highlights some of the changes that have taken place and provides a perspective that may be relevant to future public sector leaders searching for avenues to prepare the public service for what lies ahead.

Throughout the book, I have used references less in the classic academic way than as a guide through my records: a way to link discussion to the documents I am providing to Library and Archives Canada, to help future researchers navigate these records, and to let readers know where to go for additional context and for more of my thinking. One does not need to read the records – the book stands on its own – but it works in tandem with the records, each supporting the other. Since the time I served as deputy minister and Clerk of the Privy Council, there has been a rich and ever-growing literature tied to many of the topics I discuss, including but nowhere near limited to Donald Savoie's *Governing from the Centre* and later works, Ian Brodie's *At the Centre of Government,* Alasdair Roberts's *The Adaptable Country*, and many more. These were not the focus for citation because they did not exist at the time. When academic work is cited, it is generally because it either influenced my thinking *at the time* or provides important context.

Part 1 covers my early years in the public service of Canada – the making of a public servant and a manager. Looking back, I constantly see the marks they left on how I've approached theory and practice alike for decades to come. Chapter 1 covers my entry into the public service and my becoming a public servant. Chapter 2 covers over a decade of rising through the ranks of the public service, becoming a manager, learning to manage large and complex organizations and serving at the centre of government. The chapter discusses the growing challenges facing Canadian public service managers today.

Part 2 covers my years as deputy minister. Chapter 3 covers my first deputy minister position: Deputy Minister of Consumer and Corporate Affairs. Here, I explore the relationship between minister and deputy minister, and a third actor that has taken a growing place between them: a network of political staff. More broadly, I look at the erosion of ministerial authority. Chapter 4 covers the Charlottetown Accord and the constitutional reform effort of 1991–2, a process I was deeply involved in as Associate and then Secretary to the Cabinet for Federal-Provincial Relations. It draws attention to the need for effective ways of managing the federation. In chapter 5, I draw lessons from a short stay at the Canadian International Development Agency that ended prematurely owing to a major reorganization, and my return to Transport as DM. This was my last assignment before becoming Clerk of the Privy Council.

On 28 March 1994, I became Canada's first woman Clerk of the Privy Council, Secretary to the Cabinet, and Head of the Public Service. Part 3, chapters 6 through 11, explores this phase of my life, from starting as Clerk to moving on into the Canadian Centre for Management Development. In chapter 6, I share my views about the position of Clerk, its role and place within a Cabinet system of government. The role of the Clerk at any time is shaped by the Prime Minister in office and the circumstances prevailing at the time. Mine was a time characterized by chronic deficit and debt, and a public service battered by years of budget cuts and expenditure reductions.

Chapter 7 focuses on the steps taken to eliminate a sizeable deficit and regain Canada's fiscal sovereignty: Program Review. Building on past work at Transport Canada, Public Service Renewal Minister Marcel Massé and I proposed an approach to replace the across-the-board cuts combined with staffing/salary freezes that had been used extensively before.

The national unity crisis of 1995 is the subject of chapter 8. It dominated the government agenda that year. With sovereigntist movements again on the rise in Quebec and in the Prairies, Canada may face equally challenging circumstances in a not too distant future

Chapter 9 is about the Head of the Public Service, a new title that had only just been introduced. As Head of the Public Service, I needed to focus on the stewardship of the public service, preserving and strengthening it even as it underwent cuts and downsizing. I sought to preserve its core capacities and build them up stronger.

Chapter 10 covers the public service reforms I shepherded on three fronts – *Citizens First*, an effort to build citizen-centred service; the *Policy Research Initiative*, a project to preserve and build up a cross-cutting policy capacity; and *La Relève*, an effort to prepare public servants and public service leaders for the challenges ahead.

On 18 January 1999, I stepped down as Clerk to become the President of the Canadian Centre for Management Development. In many ways, this was a continuation of my work as Clerk, particularly as Head of the Public Service. Chapter 11 is about the transition itself, and CCMD's effort to build the public service learning organization – from coast to coast to coast.

As the CCMD became the Canada School of Public Service, it was time for me to take a new step. Part 4 covers my years as an international public servant. Chapter 12 situates my years as ambassador to the OECD in the greater context of my international activities dating back to my time as Clerk. It explores the development of ideas through exposure to a diversity of contexts, through preparing keynote addresses, and working with others around the world.

In 2006, I was invited to give the Braibant lecture, a keynote that marked a turning point in my work. It led to a major international research project to craft a theory of public administration for the twenty-first century, the *New Synthesis of Public Administration*, the subject of chapter 13. The project involved preparatory literature reviews, presenting work in progress, bringing a network of experts from several countries together, theorizing, and testing the results in practice around the world. An improbable consensus was reached. The key insights were published in 2011 and 2017.

Chapter 14, as a conclusion, brings me back to Canada where it all began. The second quarter of the twenty-first century is poised to be more dangerous than the first. The work of public sector leaders is more challenging than ever. The challenge today is to ensure that Canada will be among the few countries that will successfully navigate through an accelerating period of change and that Canada is well positioned to prosper in the future. It is also to ensure that the public service of Canada is and will remain fit for the problems ahead.

No one owes Canada and Canadians a prosperous future. This is never a forgone conclusion. From one generation of public servants to the next, the challenge is to put Canada on a trajectory leading to a better future. The chapters about how this will be achieved in the future are not yet written. They belong to people in office today and those who will join the public service of Canada in the years to come. For those who came before, sharing what they have learned is one way of extending a helping hand to those who accept the heavy burden of serving their fellow citizens. These pages of history are one contribution.

***

This book was sent to University of Toronto Press for publication in the fall of 2024 before the results of the presidential election in the United States of America were known and before the resignation of Prime Minister Trudeau in January 2025.

I chose not to rewrite any of the chapters because the text as written before these events bears an important lesson: many of the challenges Canada is facing in the early days of 2025 have been in the making over a long period of time. A lot was already known that we chose to ignore or that was left unattended. What remained unknown was the scope, scale, and speed of change once a *point of inflexion* is reached.

Now we know.

PART 1

The Public Servant

1 Discovering Public Service

Public sector leaders are not separate from the challenges they face and the context where they are called upon to serve. Their ideas and past experiences shape the way they think, frame issues, invent solutions, and take actions.[1] In that sense, my formative years in the public service played a key role in how I understood my role as public servant, Deputy Minister, Clerk of the Privy Council, and later President of the Canada School of Public Service and Ambassador.

I joined the public service of Canada by accident during the summer of 1973. I was recruited as a summer student in an "ES-1D" position ("D" standing for "Development" – a training position) by the Department of Transport. No one in my family had worked in the public service. I had no particular view, either good or bad, about the role of the public sector. I needed a job for the summer to support myself come the fall to finish a master's degree.

Some people will search all their life for something they feel passionate about. I found what would become the passion of my professional life by accident in the summer of 1973. I could not believe that the public service of Canada could be interested in hiring *someone like me*.

That summer, the Department of Transport (MOT) hired someone with no prior experience in the subject matter but keen to learn. The department had recruited a large number of veterans at the end of the Second World War. It had also been welcoming to highly skilled immigrants who came to Canada to escape the war raging in their country, build a new life, and offer their children a better future. These people knew the business; they knew about planes, boats, and rail. MOT at the time had a hierarchical and almost military style of management. It was male dominated and unilingual English speaking. And yet, it was recruiting a young woman, unilingual French with a bachelor's in biology and half an MBA, with no relevant knowledge of transport. *They were risk takers.*

That year, I discovered the public service. My project, working with four other students, was to develop an airport planning model adapted to the needs of remote communities. It was a discovery at multiple levels. MOT had a more modern technology infrastructure than the infamous punch card computer system I was familiar with at the University of Montreal. It was possible to write programs on desktop computers to analyse the functioning of airports to project incoming and departing flights, the movements of boarding and deplaning passengers, and the transfer of cargo.

However, my most important discovery was not at the technical level. Every week, our supervisor held a briefing session with the students. These sessions did not contribute much to our project (I do not think he knew much about computers), but his teaching was invaluable. He taught us about his pride in serving Canada and the importance of our work because it made a difference in the life of Canadians. Our project mattered because the life of people in remote communities depended on the lifeline of access by plane for all their needs. His family had moved from Poland in the 1950s. For him, there was no greater pride than to work for the public service of Canada and no higher calling than to serve Canadians. His teaching was about Canada, public service, and being a public servant.

I was hooked. A public service career provided the unbelievable opportunity to get invested in issues that had not yet been solved. If one came up with some practical ideas, they might even be tried! People like me could make a difference in the life of fellow Canadians in faraway places whom we might never meet.[2] Awesome!

The prospect of a public service career resonated with me. It combined a drive for learning and trying new things with a deep sense of purpose. That summer, I discovered that I was born to be a public servant.

At the end of the summer, I was offered a permanent position, an offer that I enthusiastically accepted. This was an interesting time at MOT. The department was planning new airports in Mirabel and Pickering, and an overarching National Airports Plan was in development. Canada had been negotiating the world's largest bilateral air agreement with the United States, finally signing it in May 1974. The department produced a new policy framework to address pollution and issues related to the energy crisis in 1975.[3] There is never a dull moment in government.

MOT's workforce was changing. A generation was retiring, and another was taking over. In the mid-1970s, the newcomers were young, they had university degrees, and they were eager to use the new technologies emerging at the time. MOT was a welcoming place for university graduates; I was one of them.

Canada and its public service were changing as well. The newcomers to the public service in the 1970s were different. Unlike their parents, they had not experienced two world wars and the Great Depression. They were born in a "free" world that would enjoy an unprecedented period of growth and peace. They were more idealistic than their parents; they aspired to build a better world. A new generation was on the move. May 1968 and protest against the Vietnam war were part of their formative years. In Canada, the rise of a nationalist movement in Quebec, McGill français, and the 1980 referendum drew inspiration from similar sources. Citizen expectations of government were changing, and a more vocal citizenry was emerging.

In the public service, the cohort that came in the early 1970s, of which I was one, progressively moved through the ranks, reaching more senior positions in the 1990s. They would oversee the expansion of Canada's social safety net in the 1970s and 1980s, introduce structural reforms, open Canada to the world in the mid-1980s, and eliminate a sizeable deficit in the mid-1990s. That cohort shared the same passion as their predecessors, but they brought different ideas about the public service.

People are not born public servants; they become public servants. For everyone who joins the public service, there is at some point in time a "*passage obligé*." Is this a job like any other? Or is this a job like no other, exclusively dedicated to serving the public good and the collective interest? This choice has deep consequences. This is when public sector employees become public servants. The job is not for everyone, but this choice makes a world of difference.

Serving a Public Purpose

Public servants serve a public purpose. That perspective shapes every action, decision, and intervention thereafter. Serving a public purpose is broader than the position one holds, the program one administers, or the services one provides. Serving a public purpose shifts the focus from the transactional level to a strategic level; every action is intended to build a better future and/or improve human conditions. Serving a public purpose inevitably leads to working across boundaries to generate viable solutions. From a public purpose perspective, food inspection is not just a stamp of approval; it is about public health and the branding of Canadian products in the international market. Increasing health spending is not just a financial transaction; it is one lever that might be used to achieve better health outcomes. An intervention that does not yield better societal results signals the need to rethink thc approach and explore how a different mix of actions may generate better public results in the circumstances. Serving a public purpose and generating public results of value for society is the yardstick that reveals the contribution of government to society.

Serving a public purpose connects public servants to one another and the public service to citizens. A public service career is not for the faint of heart. It is hard at times to put the public interest above self-interest or group interests. Public servants have a duty of loyalty to the democratic institutions they serve and accountability to ministers for the delegated authority they exercise. *Serving Canada and Canadians is the most fundamental principle around which all other ideas or values must be reconciled in the public service.*

At the time I joined the public service of Canada, we were discovering what it means to be a public servant through practice and over time. Public servants progressively learned about the covenant of the public service, the functioning of the Canadian model of Cabinet government, and parliamentary democracy. Practice taught us about the importance of ministerial authority, the framework laws that constrain the exercise of power, and the extent of their management prerogatives. By the late 1980s, public sector managers could count on the support of the Canadian Centre for Management Development, and much later on the Canada School of Public Service, to develop their management and leadership skills.

In essence, public servants *were apprentices* learning through practice with minimal theoretical and academic training support. The approach worked reasonably well then, but it is doubtful that it will be adequate in the future.

Then and Beyond

Each generation of public servants is different. It serves in a different context and is confronted by different circumstances.

People who joined the public service of Canada in the 1970s were born in the "free world." These countries had a number of common characteristics: a commitment to freedom never perfectly achieved but as a collective aspiration, the recognition of human rights, a society governed by the rule of law protecting individual rights and ensuring equality under the law, a preference for a market-based economy, and democratic principles to ensure that all had a voice in the governance of their country.

People who joined the public service of Canada in the 1990s grew up in an even "freer" world. That generation witnessed the fall of the Berlin Wall (1989), the disintegration of the USSR (1991), the reunification of Germany, the creation of the European single market (1993), and the expansion of Europe and NATO. Some came to believe that the trajectory of the modern world was inexorably towards a blend of democratic principles, market economy, and social solidarity. For a time, it was easy to forget that the fundamentals for a liberal democratic society need constant attention and that the quest for freedom and equality is never over. Progressively, attention shifted from a societal and collective perspective to a more individualistic and identity-based focus. After all, a global economy would ensure prosperity, and the digital revolution would ensure access to the knowledge of the world and promote democracy. For a short time, the Western world had an optimistic and even utopian view of the world trajectory. Events would soon reveal that peace, prosperity, freedom, and rights should never be taken for granted.

People joining the public service in 2025 will serve in a *more dangerous world* than their predecessors, and in many ways *a more challenging world.*

Globalization is shifting in reverse; protectionism is on the rise again. Illiberal societies are flourishing. Democratic societies are challenged from the outside by authoritarian regimes and from the inside by pressures to erode the principle of equality of all under the law that made it possible to govern a diverse human society. Toxic extremism is expanding, propelled by social media, and polarization leads to uncompromising positions.

People serving in the second quarter of the twenty-first century are facing a convergence of existential threats – of which climate change is only one. They will serve without the benefit of the protective shield of international conventions that contributed to an extended period of peace and global growth. A world of *realpolitik* governed by the rule of the jungle is very different from a world governed by rules.

They will serve without the protective shields that nature's ecological systems provided. Human activities are eroding nature's protective shields. At this juncture, there is no evidence that the digital economy, with its heavy demand for energy, will be any less damaging than the industrial economy.

People joining the public service in the second quarter of the twenty-first century are natives of a digital world. They know that technological innovation generates new opportunities and new risks for society. They will need to manage technological innovations such as AI, bioengineering, and geoengineering to capture their unprecedented potential while preventing new existential threats for humanity.

Eighty thousand people joined the public service of Canada between 2019 and 2024[4] during and in the aftermath of the COVID-19 crisis.[5] Their work experience during the first few years of their career was radically different from that of their predecessors. They worked from home, spending much time online with limited direct interactions with their colleagues and supervisors.

New approaches will be needed to ensure that people working from home some of the time, in the office some of the time, and online most of the time *become public servants*. Proactive actions will be needed to ensure that they discover the importance of their role beyond the job they hold and the unit that pays their salary; to ensure that they appreciate the fullness of their responsibilities as members of the public service of Canada serving Canada and Canadians.

Learning as you go, as was done in the past, will not be good enough to prepare future public servants for what lies ahead. It will require a public-service-wide effort to enrol and bring on board new recruits from the day of their joining the public service and to support them as they move through the ranks. Public servants will need ongoing support to gain an appreciation of the fast-changing international, economic, political, technological, and environmental landscape. Technology makes it possible to line up some of the best scholars and thought leaders the country has to offer in order to support their learning and development. The centre of government and public sector leaders will need to figure out new ways of ensuring that public servants gain an appreciation of the shared values, principles, and conventions that underpin their mission.

I would venture to say that parliamentarians also need support from the day of their election or appointment; to understand the institutions they have a mission to defend, and to stay apprised of emerging risks and opportunities that Canada is facing in an accelerated period of change.[6]

What do we need to do to ensure that Canada will be among the countries that will successfully navigate this period of change and prosper in the future? Canada will need more than an apprenticeship system to prepare public service leaders. It will need people able to serve in unpredictable circumstances and to address increasingly complex issues – with the will and capacity to invent solutions and to make them happen.

2 A Public Service Manager

I joined the Department of Fisheries and Oceans (DFO) in 1975. I was happy at MOT, but I was ready for a change. I wanted to learn about other parts of Canada and other domains of activity. One of the advantages of a public service career is that it offers an inexhaustible diversity of experiences.

I discovered that public service employees could take charge and manage their own careers. The public service of Canada offered the amazing possibility of lateral transfers across departments. It was also possible, at that time, to apply for positions at a higher level and in other departments. Vacancies were posted (with actual posters on the wall) with a qualification profile and an area of competition. It was up to the employees to apply for the jobs they were interested in if they felt they were qualified. If they met the requirements, they could be granted an interview – and then, let the best one win. This approach suited me fine. The merit principle, on balance, helped ensure that highly qualified individuals filled positions. It ensured transparency about the qualifications required for the positions, and the Public Service Commission encouraged interdepartmental mobility.

Like the last ten to fifteen years, this was a period of growth in the public service and one of rapid turnover due to retirement. There were ample opportunities for people interested in getting a diversity of experience. By the end of the 1980s, budget cuts and staffing freezes would takc a toll on interdepartmental mobility. This is a situation the public service of Canada will most likely experience again in the coming years; the budgets of 2023 and 2024 have already announced a number of rounds of cuts that will probably be followed by more stringent measures.

Serving Canadians: Fisheries and Oceans

I applied and was offered a position as marketing analyst at Fisheries and Oceans Canada (DFO). Shortly after, I was asked to take charge of the

Intelligence Division in the same branch; this was my first experience as a supervisor. The members of my team, all four of us, were responsible for gathering, tabulating, and distributing monthly data about catches and production from fishing zones across Canada. This was based on an elaborate manual data collection system of catches per vessel and production per plant. I would not swear by the accuracy of the data, but this was the best there was at the time.

It was the twentieth anniversary of the Intelligence Division. To mark the event, my team and I decided to prepare a publication looking at trends over twenty years;[1] the division was rich with data but poor in analysis. Preparing this report was an occasion to improve the analytical skills of the team. The publication was well received and attracted some attention by senior management. To my astonishment, in the course of gathering my archives, we found a copy of this report on the DFO website.

The initiative was small, in the scheme of things, but instructive for me as a newly appointed supervisor. One key takeaway was that there is always room for innovative ideas and there are always enough resources around to try new things if one is committed to it.[2] Second, innovative ideas can be initiated anywhere and at any level. They do not come fully formed from the top down. Most innovative ideas are generated at a much lower level.[3] Finally, an important lesson was that there is no need to ask for permission when acting within one's authority and within the organization's mission.[4] I did not realize it at the time, but these ideas would later shape my approach as a manager and would stay with me as I moved through the ranks. I would later develop these ideas more fully in the context of La Relève and the New Synthesis Initiative.[5]

My husband and I moved to Quebec City in 1977. I was hired as *Director of Planning, Quebec region,* for the same department (DFO). For the first time, I was working in French. That was a discovery, and it did much to build my self-confidence. One is always more brilliant in one's own language, and since I learned English as an adult, I will never achieve the level of fluency I would have liked.

The Quebec region was a great management school for me. Progressively, I was given responsibility for all corporate services including finance, human resources, corporate services, and communication. This was an opportunity to learn about the framework laws of the public service of Canada, ranging from the Public Service Employment Act to labour relations, from the Financial Administration Act to access to information and privacy legislation, and so on. I studied the framework laws of the public service as well as the laws specific to the responsibilities of the Department of Fisheries and Oceans. This was time well spent.

Public service managers operate within constraints: the constraints of their delegated authority, the constraints of the resources allocated to them, and the constraints of the laws. It is important for managers to understand the legal constraints in order to exercise their authority to the fullest and preserve their management prerogatives.[6] DFO had sweeping authority; management prerogatives were another story. There were enough control mechanisms around to tie the best-intentioned managers in knots.

Time and time again, as I grew through the ranks, I was told, "You can't do this," when in fact this was not the case. I kept asking, "Show me where the law says that?" Managers need to know the extent of their authority to use it to the fullest, to protect it and to resist pressures from those who are intent on curtailing their management prerogatives. This is not mischievous or due to ill intention. There are tensions between line managers and staff units, departments and central agencies. Each one has a role to play; one is primarily concerned about getting things done and fulfilling a public mission, others are primarily concerned about compliance and risk avoidance. It is not "*let* managers manage," but "bring back the managers!" that is most needed. The lesson is: do not let anyone usurp your authority.

There is a world of difference between a legal requirement and a corporate policy. No one is above the law, and public servants, more than any other citizens, have a duty to uphold the law. An administrative policy is not a law. It is the interpretation of a given organization at a given time about "how things will be done here." Two sets of corporate policies are particularly important for public service managers: Treasury Board policies as the employer and departmental policies as the legal entity with delegated ministerial authority. The problem is that these policies accumulate over time. New ones are added without rethinking or re-engineering what was there before. Departments averse to blame tend to add new layers of controls each time a problem emerges instead of dealing with the issue on a micro scale.[7] Progressively, corporate policies become dysfunctional and sometimes outright contradictory.

There is a need for a dynamic review process for keeping control mechanisms in check. A periodic assessment of the cumulative effect of corporate policies is essential. This is the responsibility of the Treasury Board Secretariat. No new corporate policy should be added without a prior look at the existing ecosystem to ensure that all the pieces fit together. Managers should be encouraged to challenge corporate requirements that limit their capacity to fulfil their mission – corporate policies can be improved, and that is everyone's responsibility.

The challenge is to ensure that managers' authority is commensurate with their responsibility for managing large and complex public organizations and fulfilling their mission of serving Canada and Canadians. The challenge is also to ensure that the people in managerial positions are able and willing to exercise a high level of responsibility. *Management is not for everyone.*

Public service managers who do not defend their legal authority shortchange the potential of their team. This is the situation when more could be achieved if managers exercised their legal authority to the fullest. This is also the case when people neither elected nor accountable are allowed to make decisions directly or indirectly, thus eroding ministerial authority and undermining the professional public service.[8] This trend has taken on more importance in recent times.

From my time as a young manager at DFO, I developed the habit of reading the laws relevant to my department, something I frequently recommended to newly appointed executives over the years.

After three years, I became Director of Fisheries Operations. This involved running a number of programs ranging from fish inspection to small craft harbour development, scientific research programs, habitat and resource protection, and more. Above all, it involved working with fishers and their communities, an aspect of the work I enjoyed most.

In October 1981, I became Regional Director General, managing two hundred plus employees. I was the first woman regional DG at the Department of Fisheries and Oceans. People working in regional offices exercise more responsibility than their peers at the same level in headquarters. There were (and still are, I believe) built-in inequalities in the classification system. On the other hand, people working in regional offices enjoy more freedom of action and flexibility than their counterparts in headquarters; this was most enjoyable.

Over a five-year period, I discovered that I enjoyed management and was good at it. It combines serving a public purpose with access to levers and resources to achieve results. I had gained experience in staff positions and line operations. Both aspects contributed to my development as a manager, but I had more to learn about public policy making and leading change.

The Quebec regional office was underdeveloped and underfunded compared to the Maritime or the Newfoundland regional offices as a result of Canada's two-hundred-mile zone extension.[9] The Quebec region was dependent on others for patrol activities in the Gulf and along the Gaspé Peninsula. The scientific team was small but dynamic. The regional team lacked resources, but not ideas.

The management team scraped up some resources here and there to prepare fisheries development plans for the Quebec region, starting with the Gaspé Peninsula. The department was kept informed of this initiative. It did not show much interest but had no objection to the regional team taking this on. This was all the team needed to get the work underway. Sometimes a nod is all that is needed.

People in headquarters had a macro view of the industry but a limited knowledge of the industry at the local level. That is normal, but it means that the ideas with the best likelihood of success on the ground were likely to take shape where these ideas needed to take hold.[10] This was an important insight that will stay with me over the years. Fishery officers knew every fishing boat, its captain, its crew, and even their families. They were living in the communities. They knew the processing plants, their management, and the working conditions of the employees. This granularity of knowledge was inaccessible to people working in headquarters with a concern for the overall health of the fishing industry. We worked with people with the best knowledge of fisheries in the Gaspé Peninsula, Québec North Shore, and the Magdalen Islands.

The industry was in serious difficulty. It could be viewed as a long chain with weak links at every step, from resource management to transformation and market development. Canada has one of the world's great natural fisheries resources and is located at the doorstep of the United States, one of the largest markets in the world – yet fishermen, boat owners, processors, and shareholders were struggling to earn a decent return. The fishing industry had sustained communities along the shore for years but did not ensure their prosperity.

Fisheries development plans required rethinking a long chain of interrelated results.[11] For profitability to improve, quality needed to improve to yield higher prices. The fish landed and products leaving the plants needed to be of a higher grade. Plants needed to reduce their costs by lengthening their season of operation. The race among fishermen for the largest share of the quota needed to be curbed by exploring different licensing systems, like a boat quota. Furthermore, the Quebec region had a fragmented system of split jurisdictions maladapted to the changing reality and mobility of the fishing industry in and out of coastal zones.

Some modest improvements could be implemented by taking actions at the regional level, and they were. This enhanced the credibility of the regional office with the industry. It built a sense of common purpose among employees and the management team. Even so, many ideas exceeded the capacity of the regional office, but *ideas have a way of finding their way.*

In January 1982, Prime Minister Pierre Trudeau announced the creation of the Kirby Task Force, known by the name of the chair, Michael Kirby, to explore "how to achieve and maintain a viable Atlantic fishery industry, with due consideration for the overall economic and social development of the Atlantic provinces."[12] To this day, I consider this report to be a remarkable achievement. It was the best piece of public policy work I had seen, and it changed my view about public policy making. It is not about long-winded papers generated by policy analysts working in relative isolation. Public policy making is an exploratory process to invent solutions that work in practice to yield a better future.[13] It is not the exclusive prerogative of people out there in policy branches; it is within the reach of public servants at all levels. I forever dropped the idea that public policy work was not for people like us running programs and delivering services to Canadians in a regional office.[14] *Policy work is what we had been doing all along; we just had not dared to call it by its name.*

The Kirby task force, a small team of people, generated in nine months an ambitious report and pragmatic recommendations. It brought together a holistic perspective of the issues, a comprehensive plan, and powerful arguments as to why actions were needed. The Kirby task force report was supportive of the policy work we had done, and it went where the management team did not dare to go. It recommended that "the assumption of full management responsibility by the federal government should also entail increasing federal fisheries visibility in the province through, for instance, establishing a research centre in the lower St. Lawrence area."[15]

At the time, Marc Lalonde, Minister of Finance, was looking for actionable projects to encourage regional development, not studies or research initiatives but projects ready for implementation. The Quebec Regional Office had a plan and we had the support of the industry. There was a sudden interest in the work we had done over the years. The Honourable Pierre De Bané, newly appointed Minister of Fisheries and Oceans on 30 September 1982, had a particular interest in the Gaspé Peninsula; a window of opportunity was opening. We had done our homework and we had ideas to put forward.

The coming together of practical ideas and the political will to bring about change can transform the course of events. The public service has a special responsibility for generating ideas. However, ideas, even good ones, may only go so far without political support.[16] Ambitious public policy ideas require ministers willing to use the political capital they have earned through an electoral process to bring about changes they judge worthy of public support. The coming together of ideas and political will transforms ideas into a reality that citizens experience collectively as members of society. This is a defining characteristic of public administration and an important lesson for public administrators.[17]

Minister De Bané provided the political impetus. By the time I left, the development plans for the Gaspé Peninsula, North Shore, and Magdalen Islands had been approved. The Quebec Region had received its first patrol vessel, *le Pierre Fortin*. L'institut Maurice-Lamontagne, a world-class marine biology centre in Rimouski, is the proud legacy of a recommendation by Michael Kirby and of the efforts of the Hon. Pierre De Bané.

There are no windows of opportunities for organizations or people that have nothing to propose and no ideas to put forward. The most important constraints to bringing about change are often the limits of our own imagination.[18] The most critical factor in ensuring the success of a policy idea is the staying power of a team of people willing to shoulder the change and to see it through to the end. The announcement of a new policy lasts a day; the results generated by the successful implementation of a powerful idea last for years to come.

I learned that the best knowledge about a public policy issue often resides close to the issue. I also learned that nothing much can stand in the way of a team committed to bringing about change. Government priorities provide an

Figure 1. DFO Quebec Area Director Bourgon and the Hon. Pierre De Bané, Minister of Fisheries and Oceans, 1982. Courtesy of the Government of Canada, originally from *Entrefilets* 3, no. 2 (October 1982), used with permission.

impetus for change. But they cover a small fraction of the work done by the public sector. A political impetus for change needs to be supplemented by a "*leadership of proximity*" to capture the best available knowledge and generate innovative ideas deserving of ministerial attention.[19]

For five years, I served with an exceptional team of people united by a common sense of purpose. To this day, I am proud to call them my friends. It was a most rewarding and formative work experience.

Serving Ministers: Regional Industrial Expansion

I returned to Ottawa in the spring of 1983, my family by that time including a five-year-old boy getting ready to start school in an entirely new environment.

In March, I joined the Department of Regional Industrial Expansion (DRIE) as Director General, Food and Consumer Products. The team spirit I had experienced in the DFO regional office was not always on display at DRIE. There were reasons for that.

Regional Industrial Expansion was a department in flux, undergoing a major reorganization – one of many. In 1969, the Department of Regional Economic Expansion (DREE) was formed to alleviate economic disparities between regions, with a particular focus on Eastern Canada. Alongside it, the Department of Industry was merged with the Department of Trade and Commerce to form the Department of Industry, Trade and Commerce. After a policy review in 1972, DREE progressively developed a more national focus by working with all provinces through federal-provincial partnership agreements. Overlap and duplication ensued. In 1982, in an effort to streamline economic assistance programming, Regional Economic Expansion (DREE) was merged with a portion of Industry, Trade and Commerce (ITC) to form the new Department of Regional Industrial Expansion (DRIE), with Trade handed off to External Relations under the Minister of International Trade. The new DRIE was to support economic development in all regions of Canada, particularly those in greatest need.[20]

Perpetual reorganizations do not help to develop cohesion and achieve a common sense of public purpose. From 1983 through 1985, the formation of the new department was at the top of DRIE's agenda. This included, in addition to reorganization, negotiating and signing new Economic and Regional Development Agreements with the provinces and territories, working towards a national tourism strategy, and encouraging innovation and technological development.[21] When I joined in 1983, the department had not yet internalized the many changes brought about by successive reorganizations and frequent mandate changes.

Organizations are living systems. They need time to align individual contributions, develop a common sense of purpose, and ensure that all the parts work synergistically. From that time, I have gained a healthy caution about reorganizations. They are costly and disruptive and drain organizations of their life energy for years to come.

This assignment gave me the opportunity to work at a more senior level. The department was populated with some of the most brilliant people I had met. The Hon. Ed Lumley was a brilliant, energetic, and engaging minister. Bill Teschke, Deputy Minister, and Gordon Ritchie, Associate Deputy Minister, were second to none. All three were most generous to the new person on the block coming from a regional office with no senior experience in headquarters or central agencies. I had worked with ministers before, but DRIE was in a different league. It was the most important microeconomic department headed by a powerful and experienced senior minister.

At DRIE, DGs and other officers briefed the minister directly. This is a good practice that allows officials to have a greater sense of responsibility for their files and to gain experience briefing ministers. Briefing Minister Lumley was an intimidating experience at first. The official responsible would be called into a vast boardroom where the minister was surrounded by the most senior officials of the department sitting around a long table. After a concise presentation of the issue, the person presenting would be questioned by the minister and others. Some senior officials asked questions to improve decision making, and others to show how smart they were. This was not unique to DRIE. I observed similar behaviours in interdepartmental meetings. I learned to hold my own and not to easily accept being interrupted.

Being "different" makes a person more visible for better or for worse ... if briefing the minister goes badly, it reinforces the view that others might be better qualified; if it goes well, it attracts attention and brings visibility. I did not have the profile of the people around the table; I got plenty of visibility.

Minister Lumley had a wonderful sense of humour. Bill Teschke was nothing but supportive of the new kid on the block, and Gordon Ritchie, fluently bilingual, was happy to assist whenever I stumbled in English. I admired them.

On Teschke's suggestions, I joined the Board of Directors of Canada Mortgage and Housing Corporation (CMHC) and the Federal Business Development Bank (FBDB), and later the National Film Board (NFB). This helped me learn about corporate governance. Associate Deputy Minister Ritchie asked me to represent the department on an interdepartmental committee dealing with the restructuring of the Atlantic fishery industry. DRIE was playing a key role in the financial restructuring of the fish-processing firms. This was right up my alley. It was my first experience with interdepartmental committee meetings with central agencies. It was also a learning experience.

The fishing industry was shutting down as fish stocks, one after another, were depleted. The largest companies, including Fishery Products International, National Sea Products, and Pêcheurs-Unis du Québec, were close to bankruptcy and needing financial restructuring.

I was impressed by the powerful response of the government of Canada to mitigate the impact of the crisis. I was also amazed at the limited knowledge of the situation at the centre of government. This was an issue that affected the livelihood of thousands of people across the Atlantic provinces, and ministers needed advice. At the centre of government, there was no shortage of resources and capabilities, but there was a shortage of knowledge. Except for some senior people at the Department of Fisheries and Oceans and key members of the Kirby Task force, I was suddenly one of the most knowledgeable persons in town about a crisis that was mobilizing government attention. I had visibility and something to say – a powerful combination.

Governing entails making decisions with imperfect knowledge. That is understood. However, it also requires early detection, course correction, and early interventions in order to prevent what is preventable, mitigate risks, and protect the most vulnerable in society. These capabilities had obviously been lacking. The experience left me wondering about the role of the centre of government and central agencies to anticipate and act proactively to prevent crises.[22]

Serving First Ministers: Federal-Provincial Relations

The opportunity to learn more about the role of the centre of government emerged in the spring of 1985. Gérard Veilleux, Secretary to Cabinet for Federal-Provincial Relations, asked me to take charge of the economic portfolio at the Federal-Provincial Relations Office (FPRO).

Working in a central agency does not play to my strengths, but at some point, I needed to get central agency experience to become a more experienced public service manager. This was as good a time as any. The FPRO's primary areas of expertise were national unity and constitutional affairs. On economic and trade issues, its role was complementary to the Privy Council Office, providing information on the federal-provincial dimensions of issues going to Cabinet. Easy enough, I thought … except that this time was different.

Early in his mandate, Prime Minister Brian Mulroney committed to hosting annual First Ministers' Conferences (FMC) on the economy and a series of FMCs on Aboriginal constitutional matters. First Ministers' Meetings (FMM) on the Canada-USA negotiations were soon added to the mix.

My team and I (all five of us) were tasked with preparing First Ministers' meetings on the economy and the Canada-USA negotiation. Over a few years, this small team organized three FMCs on the economy (February 1985, November 1985, and November 1986), several FMMs on the Canada-USA trade negotiations (too many to enumerate), and some FMCs on Aboriginal constitutional matters (April 1985, March 1987).

Federal-provincial relations was not a domain I was familiar with. I found that First Ministers' gatherings were a strange instrument for managing a federation as diverse and complex as Canada. They are not mandatory. They have no legal authority, no formal decision-making power, and no permanent infrastructure to advance preparatory work on behalf of First Ministers. Consensus, if reached, may be undone without consequences as a result of an election or simply because someone changed their mind. There is no rigorous mechanism to monitor the implementation of federal-provincial agreements and no recourse if nothing is done. Premiers may or may not meet in advance of a First Ministers' meeting to develop a shared position. The most frequent point of convergence among premiers is to agree that more unconditional federal funding is needed. This delinks funding decisions from accountability for results and it does not create an impetus for achieving better results.

To this day, the Canadian federation lacks mechanisms for co-decision and coordination when sharing responsibilities is needed for progress. Canada lacks mechanisms that may be found in other federations, let alone the kind of mechanisms created over fifty years to encourage decision making among the member countries of the European Union. Irregular and ad hoc structures that lack strong secretariats to help prepare and don't lead to firm, trackable commitments are of only so much use.[23] Other states have crafted systems with stronger secretariats and more regular and consistent meetings, such as the Australian National Cabinet.

The lack of federal-provincial machinery did not prevent Canada from achieving a high level of development in the past, but it may constrain future prosperity. Issues are becoming more complex, thus requiring synergistic actions at multiple levels. Some of the consequences are becoming more visible. It is the case in the health sector, where Canada spends more than most countries to accomplish less than most. It is manifest in the difficulty in making progress on climate change. It is on display in areas where long chains of interrelated results at the federal, provincial, and municipal levels are needed to bring about a viable solution. This is the case for the interrelationships between immigration, housing, labour force management, and social integration.

An increasing number of issues cannot be addressed through the lens of exclusive jurisdiction. Sooner or later, Canada will need to invent its way to make shared decisions, encourage shared knowledge, and learn and act collectively. The alternative is for Canada to face an increasing number of systemic failures when a convergence of actions at multiple levels is needed. Canada in that sense has unfinished business.[24]

There was much to think about, but not much time. My team and I were busy. After some preparatory work in 1985, the Canada-USA Free Trade negotiations formally began in 1986. The negotiation was entrusted to the Trade Negotiation Office (TNO), headed by the formidable Simon Reisman and the no less formidable Gordon Ritchie as Deputy. The TNO was separate from the Department of External Affairs' trade branch, headed by Minister for International Trade Pat Carney, who had played a lead role in dismantling the much-maligned National Energy Program.

First Ministers were meeting *in camera* in the Cabinet room on Parliament Hill, where Simon Reisman and Gordon Ritchie would give them an update on the latest negotiations and challenges ahead. The symbolism of First Ministers meeting in Council *in camera* in the Cabinet room was powerful. It also once more illustrated the lack of mechanisms for the management of the Canadian federation. I was responsible for preparing these meetings with Alan Nymark, a respected colleague and member of the negotiation team. His assistance was invaluable. It was a privilege to attend First Ministers' meetings as Assistant Secretary to Cabinet and note taker. After multiple rounds, the negotiators reached a tentative agreement in October 1987. It was signed by Mulroney and Ronald Reagan on 2 January 1988. The Canada-US Free Trade Agreement (CUSFTA) would not have been possible without the leadership and resolve of the Prime Minister.

Brian Mulroney was a transformative leader. I had the chance to watch the Prime Minister of Canada and the Premiers in action. PM Mulroney was recognized as a gifted negotiator. His approach combined rallying people willingly and building pressure.[25] His leadership was prominent during the annual First Ministers' Conferences on the economy. It is my view that Prime Minister Mulroney single-handedly educated the public about the debilitating effects of the ever-increasing deficits and debts prevailing until the mid-1980s. With charts in hand and camera rolling, he explained to Canadians how this situation was crowding out much-needed investments and shortchanging future generations.

He introduced the Goods and Services Tax reform and negotiated the Canada-US free trade agreement. Neither was popular at the time. The PM took on both challenges despite the lack of public support and despite the political risks they entailed. He kept Cabinet and caucus united, even at the worst of times. These initiatives laid the basis for reforms in the mid-1990s that would ultimately lead to the elimination of the deficit and that contributed to Canada's prosperity.[26]

I learned about the importance of the role of the Prime Minister, clarity of purpose, setting a course, making choices, and a willingness to spend one's political capital to achieve results. These are the key ingredients to shape an ambitious *governing agenda*. I also learned about the danger of agenda overload and the limits of society's capacity to absorb changes. Governing is a search for a delicate balance to steer society forward while maintaining a reasonable level of public support.[27] The combination of the national unity debate and major structural reforms was straining Canada's social fabric.

At a professional level, I learned about the importance of networking and working with multiple departments at once. Time and time again, I called on departments to help prepare First Ministers' Meetings, to provide briefing material or propose ideas that could be put forward. I acquired a good knowledge of the Deputy Ministers' community and built personal relationships with most.

In retrospect, this was an enriching experience. Besides First Ministers' meetings, I attended all the meetings of the Cabinet Committee on the Economy. There was not a day climbing the stairs on Parliament Hill to attend a Cabinet Committee meeting when I did not feel pride in Canada's public institutions and respect for the men and women running for office to serve their country. It is an honour and a privilege to see public institutions up close and to contribute to their functioning, no matter how modestly. I was left wondering how the "centre of government" could better serve Cabinet, the most important decision-making forum in the country. I felt there were ambiguities between power, institutional authority, and personal responsibilities. I would forge clearer ideas on these topics in the coming years.

A Master Class: Energy, Mines and Resources

After two years at the centre of government, I was eager to go back to a line department. I made it known, and to my surprise, a number of Deputy Ministers approached me to join their departments. Leaving proved more challenging than I had expected.

Paul Tellier suggested I take a Deputy Secretary position in the Privy Council Office (PCO); he was very gracious when I indicated that I had spent enough time in a central agency for my liking (if not for a lifetime).

The Deputy Clerk had a different view. Jack Manion had a distinguished career. Before becoming Deputy Clerk, he had been Secretary of the Treasury Board from 1979 to 1986, and before that Deputy Minister for Immigration. We were from different generations and had some differences of views about the management of the public service, although there was never any disagreement between us about the importance of the public service as an institution. His view about senior personnel was that, when asked, one must obey. My view was that as long as I was an Assistant Deputy Minister I would make my own career decisions. I chose to join the Department of Energy, Mines and Resources (EMR) as Corporate Policy Assistant Deputy Minister. It was inconceivable for some that I would refuse promotions to join EMR. I had chosen to work for Arthur Kroeger, one of the best Deputy Ministers in town.

Things between the Deputy Clerk and me became a little more complicated a year later when I declined a Deputy Minister position. I was not being capricious; I honestly felt that it was not the right time to leave EMR. Jack famously said that, with such an attitude, "you will never become a Deputy Minister." I was fine with this and never regretted my decision. We both laughed about this a few years later.

Over the years, my advice to people moving through the ranks was to think twice before accepting an Order in Council appointment because you forgo a degree of freedom. If asked, listen to what is asked of you. Don't be capricious – after all, we are here to serve. Then decide what is right for you in your life at that time.

My assignment at EMR was a master class about the role of Deputy Minister. EMR is a science-based department with a proud history. The Geological Survey of Canada predates Confederation and has played a prominent role in the development of natural resources in Canada, especially the western provinces. It stood alongside EMR's main technological research and development branch, the Canadian Centre for Mineral and Energy Technology (CANMET), which focused on meeting the needs of partners in resource and energy industries.

At the time I was there, energy policy was dominating the agenda. EMR was playing a major role in negotiations for several oil megaprojects, including the Hibernia oil field development project, for which a statement of principles was signed in 1988. Under discussion as well were the Lloydminster upgrader, the OSLO oil sands project, and a pipeline to Vancouver Island. While negotiating megaprojects with industry partners, the department was attempting to shape a broader federal policy on megaproject assessment and financing. Arthur Kroeger, the Deputy Minister, was playing a prominent role in all these negotiations. He was a wonderful coach and I owe much to him. Through this assignment, I gained a better knowledge of western Canada. I developed a deep admiration for the entrepreneurship of the oil and gas industry and the innovative spirit of the western provinces.

This assignment ended up being a master class in the management of the political-professional interface. It was well known that the relation between the Minister, Marcel Masse, and the Deputy Minister was challenging. Deputy Ministers work "at pleasure." This expression generally means that the Crown reserves the right to terminate their service, with or without cause. But "serving at pleasure" works both ways. If the tensions that occasionally emerge between Ministers and Deputy Heads are not managed with care, a government could lose key people when they are most needed. Efforts were made to ease tensions by building stronger communication between my office as Corporate Assistant Deputy Minister (ADM) and the Minister's office. Luc Lavoie, the Deputy Chief of Staff, understood and respected the role of the public service, and I respected his role – that made collaboration easy. We worked to ensure close collaboration between the Minister's office and the department and to avoid misunderstandings. Luc Lavoie kept PM Mulroney informed of the situation, and I kept Paul Tellier, then Clerk, informed.

In a difficult relationship between Minister and DM, the DM does not have the upper hand, but DMs are not powerless either. The Clerk plays a key role in these situations to detect and ease tensions as early as possible, to ensure that the government can pursue its agenda while making sure that the public service retains the talent to fulfil its mission. I admired how a skilful Clerk, Paul Tellier, managed complex interrelationships between the PM, the Minister, and the Deputy Minister. The Minister went on to serve as Minister for Communication and later for the Department of Defence. The government continued to benefit from the services of an experienced Deputy Minister for years to come. Arthur Kroeger left EMR in 1988 and went on to serve as Deputy Minister of Employment and Immigration until his retirement in 1992. At the request of PM Mulroney, he would later play a key role in running a series of *Renewal of Canada Conferences* in the aftermath of the failure of the Meech Lake Accord.

By the end of 1989, I had served in headquarters, at the regional level, and in a central agency. I had staff and line, policy, and service delivery experience. I had worked with ministers and served a Cabinet committee. I had served a

Prime Minister and First Ministers. Unknowingly, my stay at EMR was the end of my formative years as Assistant Deputy Minister.

Then and Beyond

Assistant Deputy Ministers serve at the apex of the professional non-partisan public service. They are appointed under the Public Service Employment Act and as such enjoy special protection. Deputy Ministers, on the other hand, are appointed by Order in Council. This signals that they enjoy the confidence of the Government of Canada. At the time, most Deputy Ministers were Deputy Heads under the law. They were the channel through which ministerial authority was delegated to a department.

In recent years, there has been a significant increase in the number of Order in Council appointments in the public service and also in the number of people remunerated as Deputy Ministers even though they are not Deputy Heads. I do not think this is wise. The proliferation of Order in Council appointments is not without risks; this practice runs the risk of undermining the importance of the role of ADM.

My journey convinced me that for public sector leaders to be prepared to serve at the highest level, they need a diversity of experience. During my time as Clerk, I brought forward a number of initiatives to provide future public service leaders with a diversity of experience. A program for policy analysts offered rotational assignments in the Privy Council Office, the Department of Finance, and the Treasury Board. New corporate programs were created to accelerate the development of executives from directors to director general levels (EX-01 to EX-03). A family of corporate programs encouraged a progression from management training to supervisors, middle managers, and executives. People were encouraged to put their names forward for competitions to pre-qualify as Assistant Deputy Ministers.

That was then, however, and this is now. What needs to be done to ensure that senior public servants acquire the breadth of knowledge and experience to serve with confidence at the highest level in the public service of Canada and in a period that is both more dangerous and more challenging than before?

The public sector needs to learn faster, anticipate better, course-correct quickly, and adapt to changing circumstances. Agility, creativity, and adaptive capacity are some of the characteristics needed in public organizations. How this will be achieved in the Canadian context remains to be seen. Much effort in recent years has focused on building healthy workplaces, ensuring that the public service reflects the society it has the mission to serve, and accommodating individual needs and circumstances. These efforts must be framed in the broader context of building the capacity of the public service to fulfil its mission now and in the future. Serving Canada and Canadians is the core principle of the public service and *the centre of gravity* against which all measures must be articulated. Without clarity of purpose and a solid foundation, the public service is at risk of eroding its capacity to fulfil its most fundamental mission of serving Canada and Canadians at all times and in yet unforeseen circumstances. From the outside looking in, it feels at times as if the public service is losing sight of its core mission, being pushed in many directions without a strong centre of gravity.

There is a need for frank discussions and an unvarnished assessment of the recent trajectory of Canada's public service. Is it moving towards better services to Canadians? Better advice to government? Is the public service getting its fair share of the best talent in the country and the skills of critical importance to fulfil its mission? Is it able to compete for talents at the highest levels and in the most critical domains? Does it display a drive to excellence? Does it display the anticipative capacity, and the adaptive capacity, needed to face some of the challenges ahead? In short, is it *fit for these times*?

I, for one, believe that the public service is capable of a frank and fearless assessment of the situation it is in and that senior public service leaders are able to speak frankly about the course corrections needed. An outside commission of inquiry, frequently suggested, is not without downsides. It takes time, commissioners have no responsibility past tabling a report, and it would run the risk of disempowering the senior ranks of the public service who must *own* the solution and lead change.

Course corrections are indeed needed. They may come from inside through thoughtful and courageous actions or be brought about by the strong winds of change that are rising outside. My advice to the public service, for what it is worth, is *heal thyself*, but do it fast.

At issue is the relationship of trust between the public service, citizens, and elected officials. Recent breakdowns in service delivery and a troubling number of corruption cases have created doubt about the capacity of the public service to heal itself.[28] This is a dangerous trend. It may lead to death through a thousand cuts (a situation the public service experienced before), the politicization of the public service, or other equally unwise outcomes.

The state of the public service as an institution should be a matter of concern for all political parties, all parliamentarians, and all Canadians. There are no well-performing countries without well-performing public institutions and public organizations.[29] Who will want to be a manager in the public service of Canada in the future and what are we prepared to do to support them? Part of the answer is to ensure that the public service is *manageable* to start with and not just *hospitable.* This requires clarity of purpose and an uncompromising commitment to excellence in serving Canada and Canadians.

A case could be made that managers leading an ambitious change agenda to improve quality and productivity and encourage innovation are facing a more challenging environment than before. The obstacles to dealing with poor performance are overwhelming. Complaint mechanisms for employees are many, but the support systems for managers are weak or lacking.

Accepting a management position in the public service should not be an act of heroism. Who will dare to take a management position to ensure that the public service of Canada remains one of the best in the world and a source of pride for Canadians? This may ultimately depend on the support given to managers as agents of change in the next few years.

PART 2

The Deputy Minister

3 Becoming Deputy Minister: Consumer and Corporate Affairs

I became Deputy Minister of *Consumer and Corporate Affairs* (CCA) in 1989 under the leadership of Paul Tellier, then Clerk, and the Government of Prime Minister Brian Mulroney. I thought I had died and gone to heaven.

Paul Tellier was an energetic leader. He spoke his mind with conviction and expected people to do the same. I was comfortable in this environment. Speaking truth to power does not begin with fearless advice to ministers but with frank discussions among colleagues on difficult and conflicted topics. Tellier encouraged collective problem solving, an approach I supported in my practice.

A Partnership Like No Other

The relationship between Minister and Deputy Minister plays a central role in the functioning of the Canadian system of ministerial responsibility and accountability. It also plays a key role in the functioning of Canadian democratic institutions. In Canada, it is possible for people with no prior experience in government to run for office because they aspire to serve and represent their fellow citizens. People do not need to be rich or closely connected to political elites, unlike in the USA, where the power of money plays a crucial role. They do not need to have served at the local or provincial levels before running for office at the federal level, as in some European and Asian countries. Ministers are often not groomed by being given increasing responsibilities over many years, as is the case in some countries. They have full ministerial authority from the day of their appointment, and no safety net. While there are notable exceptions, elected officials in Canada generally serve for relatively short periods of time.[1]

A Canadian citizen today may be elected tomorrow and become a minister the day after in a portfolio where they may have no prior knowledge. The Canadian system is designed to make this possible. This means that departments

Figure 2. The first day as Deputy Minister of Consumer and Corporate Affairs, 1989.

must be prepared to welcome a newly appointed minister, anticipate risks, and prevent mistakes as ministers learn the ropes of the office, discover their department, and forge an opinion about what they will want to accomplish at the helm of the department. Central to the success of this delicate phase is the role of the deputy minister. This is why it is unwise to have newly appointed ministers assisted by newly appointed deputy ministers. Careful planning generally avoids creating such situations that are inherently risky for ministers.

Deputy ministers have their own way of working with ministers, the result of a combination of prior experience and personal style. My approach has evolved over time, but the fundamentals have remained essentially the same. Ministers play many roles: they are responsible for a department, serve on parliamentary committees, play an active role in their riding, and represent their constituency in Ottawa. They may also have special responsibilities in their political party as organizer or fund raiser or in another capacity. It is important to gain an appreciation of the time a minister is able to dedicate to their department. This helps to manage the minister's time wisely and to shape an agenda commensurate to their aspirations.

There are some rules of engagement I like to discuss early with the minister I serve. I have been able to manage most departments with one extended working session per week with the minister in normal circumstances, but I am happy to take as much time as the minister wishes. In the midst of major reforms, more frequent meetings might be needed. I expect to have immediate access to the minister if I request it – some things cannot wait – but I will not abuse this privilege. I may ask to see the minister privately on matters of particular sensitivity; on other occasions the Chief of Staff is welcome to attend. If the department makes a mistake, I will be quick to recognize it, inform the minister, and take action.[2] I will provide advice orally or in writing on all matters relevant to the department; my advice is to the minister and no one else. The department will not take responsibility for information provided outside of official departmental channels. Once a decision is made, I will ensure that actions are taken to implement it quickly and competently. There will be no doubt about the loyalty of the department to ministerial decisions.

Leaving administrative matters aside, the main task is to assist the minister in shaping an ambitious agenda. Generally, I do not ask newly appointed ministers about their priorities for the department. It is preferable that they form an opinion as they discover their department, the issues, challenges, constraints, and opportunities. A key role of deputy ministers is to help ministers shape the most ambitious agenda they aspire to lead. Why would history remember this minister as one of the most important ones in this department? What will be different because this minister was in office at that time? How will the proposed agenda lead to a better future for Canada and Canadians? Generally, it does not take much time for ministers to shape an agenda that resonates with them. This in turn focuses departmental actions and helps ensure coherence.

Working with Harvie Andre first and then Pierre Blais, the Department of Consumer and Corporate Affairs set an ambitious path. Both ministers were very political. They were active in their political party and more than willing to use their political capital to move the agenda forward. The government of PM Mulroney at the time was shaping a "Prosperity Agenda."[3] In December 1991, Minister Blais released CCA's strategic plan. CCA was the *Department of the Marketplace.*[4] It embarked on a program to modernize the framework laws governing the Canadian market space, from bankruptcy to competition, from copyright and patents to consumer protection. On top of its enforcement work, CCA carried out an extensive legislative reform agenda. It had just finished modernizing the Competition Act. And now, alongside laws such as the Textile Labelling Act and the Consumer Packaging Act, it undertook to overhaul the Bankruptcy Act, the first major revision in over two decades.[5]

CCA played “a pivotal role in maintaining Canada’s competitiveness,”[6] but signs of potential trouble were ahead. The view was that “if the current trajectory continues, the standard of living of Canadians seems destined to fall behind. Yet there is nothing inevitable about this outcome: Canadians have in their own hands the power to change it.”[7] Thirty-five years later, this document sounds surprisingly prescient. The topic of Canada’s competitiveness and the Canadian standard of living is resurfacing again as a concern.

Some managers are of the view that there is no need for departments to spend much time setting strategic directions that may be overtaken by events. I do not share this view. I have engaged the management team of every organization I have led over the years in a strategic planning exercise. The benefit of a plan is not to generate a paper; it is to *think ahead* and to develop a common sense of purpose. No one is hostage to a plan, but having one helps people to be aware when circumstances warrant deliberately departing from it. It avoids drift. It helps people at all levels to align their contributions and to exercise judgment about what is worthy of priority attention.[8]

The Canadian system of responsible government entails a special relationship between a minister, the source of ministerial authority, and a deputy minister responsible for the exercise of delegated authority. This is central to the Canadian system of Cabinet government for the exercise of power and accountability to Parliament.

I realize as I am drafting these notes that many factors are transforming this special relationship. Talking about her relationship with Prince Charles, Princess Diana famously said, “There were three of us in this marriage, so it was a bit crowded.”[9] Similarly, the relationship between minister and deputy is a little crowded at this time.

Exempt Staff: A Change of Degree or a Change of Nature?

The system of ministerial responsibility was designed for a direct interface between elected officials serving as ministers and the professional public service. Some scholars have asked whether this bilateral relationship has become a trilateral relationship in light of the expanding role of political staff in ministers’ offices and the Prime Minister’s Office. The question is important and has many ramifications.[10]

At first, a limited number of political staff was responsible for supporting ministers in their political and partisan activities. This included support and liaison with the riding, party politics, fundraising events, ministers’ speeches not related to the mandate of the department, liaison with other elected officials, caucus meetings, and the like. These people are “exempt” from the obligations imposed on the professional non-partisan public service so as to enable them to provide ministers with services “the public service cannot provide”[11] because they are political in nature. These activities were expected to "complement" rather than duplicate the professional, expert, and non-partisan advice and support provided by the public service.[12] This was the theory, and it was still roughly accurate at the time I served as Deputy Minister and then Clerk. But is it an accurate reflection of the current reality? There are reasons to doubt it.

Over time, the number of exempt staff has increased, and the scope of their activities has expanded. This change happened incrementally without much consideration of whether it was just a change of scale or if it amounted to a fundamental transformation of Canada's governing system.

All Prime Ministers have contributed in some ways to the expanded reach of exempt staff. Lester Pearson had one formal political advisor in 1963. Cabinet approved an explicit policy advisor title in ministers' offices in 1978 under P.E. Trudeau. Brian Mulroney expanded the Prime Minister's Office and introduced deputy-minister-equivalent pay for the newly named Chief of Staff position. Jean Chrétien allowed his policy advisor to deal directly with Finance and thus bypass other ministers and the PCO during his third term. Paul Martin expanded the policy role of his office and allowed political advisors to attend Cabinet and caucus meetings that had been the exclusive preserve of elected officials till then. Stephen Harper introduced a formal system of written advice with a PMO overlay on all Privy Council notes to the Prime Minister.[13]

In the last ten years or so, the changes have been *institutionalized* in ways that may amount to changing the governing system of Canada. To start with, the number of exempt staff has grown rapidly. Based on the Ethics Commissioner's reports, there were 815 exempt staff subject to the Conflict of Interest Act in September 2024[14] compared to 381 in 2016.[15]

Exempt staff that were once dedicated to assisting ministers with their political responsibilities are now operating as a network of political staff that spans across the public service, anchored around the Prime Minister's Office. In short, they operate increasingly outside and beyond ministerial authority as conventionally understood. The network sometimes speaks on behalf of the Prime Minister, sometimes acts on its own initiative to explore ideas that might be of interest to the Prime Minister or the governing party, and, in some cases, may act on behalf of third parties.

There is no doubt that the network of political staff under the leadership of the Prime Minister's Office exercises growing influence. This is an extension of the governing political party inside every public organization. It gives rise to a concern about the capacity to maintain a non-partisan public service serving every political party in an even-handed way. Scholar Jonathan Craft provided an interesting taxonomy of the expanding role of this network, including providing direct advice (buffering), filtering and choosing what advice not to bring in (bridging), shepherding an idea through the system (moving), and shaping departmental proposals (shaping).[16]

Most commentaries about the expansion of political staff have focused on the issue of centralization in the Prime Minister's Office. I wonder if this is not missing a more important issue: are we witnessing a transformation of Canada's governing system of ministerial authority that is at the heart of Canada's system of responsible government? Are we witnessing the progressive politicization of the professional non-partisan public service?

The reality of modern politics is that most attention is focused on the Prime Minister. Social media and the 24/7 news cycle mean that the Prime Minister plays a key role in getting their political party elected. This reinforces the loyalty of ministers to the Prime Minister to whom they owe their election and their position.

The Prime Minister of Canada has a lot of power, and relatively more than in other federal systems. No one doubts that the PM can set the government agenda. This is as it should be. Prime ministers can get their way when they are committed to a result and in particular in areas where they are expected to play a prominent role, such as in foreign affairs, federal-provincial relations, or the overall fiscal framework. That said, ministers have constitutional and legal authority over all matters assigned to them by law for the department(s) they are responsible for.

There are signs of erosion of ministerial authority. First, ministers have lost control of their political office. Ministers used to surround themselves with a few people they trusted to assist them with the ridings and other political matters. Today, the Prime Minister's Office has the final choice of each Chief of Staff. Martin's PMO limited ministers' discretion in hiring. Harper went further and formalized the role of PMO in Treasury Board Guidelines. The formal veto power of the PMO remains in the current 2011 *Policies for Ministers' Offices*.[17] In a way, ministers exercise their authority under high surveillance by unelected officials.

Second, ministers have progressively lost direct access to the Prime Minister. I know that this was not the case under PMs Mulroney and Chrétien. While I was out of the country when Prime Minister Harper was in office, accounts indicate that he preferred a process driven by briefing notes over in-person briefings to advance files and take decisions.[18] Under PM Trudeau, ministers are likely to be referred to the PMO Chief of Staff or other members of the office when they ask to see the Prime Minister.[19]

Third, some practices have progressively limited ministers' flexibility. Mandate letters are one example. They were initially introduced to signal the need to make progress on horizontal issues requiring a high degree of interdepartmental coordination. They have become instruments to micromanage ministers and departments, significantly reducing their flexibility and capacity to adapt to emerging circumstances. Ministers and departments spend time tracking and reporting on a list of commitments flowing from an electoral platform that was crafted years earlier. Future governments may be well advised to put an end to this practice. As the complexity of issues and the velocity of change are increasing, governments need to be able to adapt to fast-changing circumstances and course-correct when needed.

There are also signs of erosion of the Canadian system of Cabinet government. Few ministers are aware of the full extent of their constitutional authority. The Prime Minister has the authority to form a Cabinet, to appoint and remove ministers, but once they are appointed, ministers are personally responsible for exercising the authority assigned to them by law. This is the essence of the Canadian system of ministerial responsibility and accountability to Parliament. Ministers are collectively responsible for Cabinet decisions. Decisions made outside the Cabinet system undermine the collective responsibility of ministers and Canada's Cabinet system of government. There were always cases when a Prime Minister would make a commitment and say "make it so." There were instances where the Prime Minister might say "leave it to me" after hearing all sides in a Cabinet meeting. But a Cabinet system of responsible government was not designed to "paper decisions" that were made in backrooms, even with the blessing of the Prime Minister. There are too many known cases of budget decisions that were made in discussion between exempt staff without the involvement of the responsible ministers.[20]

The erosion of ministerial authority translates into an erosion of departmental capacity. A separation of policy decisions from implementation consideration leads to repeated failures and declining public confidence in the capacity of government to get things done.

Six or eight hundred political exempt staff are daily generating demands on departments. Is this wise? International comparisons are difficult to make, but it is worth noting that this is many more staff than in the United Kingdom with its population of sixty-nine million people.[21] It is a reasonable assumption that exempt staff are not all focusing on political activities that cannot be performed by the public service. In fact, much of the work political staff do in Canada is performed in the UK by non-partisan civil servants.[22] There is no evidence that the practice of politics in Canada has much improved in the recent past. I have not seen signs of improved political relations between government and opposition parties, between the House and the Senate, or between the Prime Minister and the caucus or Premiers' offices. So, if not politics, *what are all these people doing?*

Political advisors operate as a extension of the governing political party inside government, in a space that escapes scrutiny; that amounts to "a black hole of accountability."[23] Their sheer number makes it impossible for ministers to credibly claim awareness of their actions – and more dangerously, possible for ministers to credibly claim a *lack* of awareness. This undermines parliamentary oversight, as a number of cases have demonstrated when advisors had a prominent role in controversies.[24] Canada is not alone facing this issue.

Similar concerns have been raised in the United Kingdom, Australia, and New Zealand.[25]

I have worked with exceptional Chiefs of Staff: Derek Burney and Hugh Segal under Prime Minister Mulroney, and Jean Pelletier under Prime Minister Chrétien. The issue is not about the calibre or commitment of individuals. *The issue is about the exercise of power on behalf of Canada and Canadians.*

The authority of the state in a democratic society should not be exercised in the shadows by people who are not elected or accountable. A time when democratic governments are being challenged by illiberal states and authoritarian regimes, a time when democratic principles are in flux south of the border, is no time to allow any doubt about the health of democratic institutions in Canada. A Canadian answer to ensuring accountability for the exercise of power in Canada deserves attention. A professional non-partisan public service is one that at all times is deserving of the trust of all political parties.

4 Canada Is Calling: The Charlottetown Accord

Deputy ministers, like ministers, have individual responsibility for the department they lead and a collective responsibility for the well-being of the public service and for supporting government priorities.

In the early 1990s, national unity was high on the government agenda. The Meech Lake Accord was signed on *3 June 1987*. It initially generated some enthusiasm, but the excitement was short lived. A year later, the Accord was in trouble. The Right Honourable Pierre Trudeau attacked the agreement; Frank McKenna, the newly elected Premier of New Brunswick, had "grave concerns"; Premier Garry Filmon, who was running a minority government in Manitoba, had problems moving the constitutional resolution ahead; and Premier Clyde Wells "was open to rescind" the Newfoundland resolution.

The expectation that a solution would be found to ratify the Meech Lake Accord in time was vanishing. The accord would die a natural death on *23 June 1990* unless a solution was found. This situation was an illustration of the lack of mechanism I had witnessed before. A hard-won unanimous consensus involving all Premiers and the Prime Minister of Canada had no binding value.

The deputy minister community was increasingly worried. Paul Tellier called a deputy minister retreat in the spring of 1990. The question deputy ministers kept asking was … what if it fails? Deputies are not pessimistic by nature, but they are trained to explore every possible avenue. A strategy with no fall-back position may end up causing more harm than good. The ultimate responsibility of the government of Canada is to keep Canada united, to protect and defend the rights of all Canadians. No answer to the question Deputy Ministers kept asking was forthcoming and the lack of answer was cause for concern. Till the end, the government worked on the assumption that the Meech Lake Accord would get through. The unfolding events would demonstrate the danger of a one-sided strategy.

The Annus Horribilis of 1990

Lucien Bouchard, a Quebec nationalist recruited by Prime Minister Mulroney, resigned from Cabinet on 21 May 1990. His departure fragmented the Conservative party as he was followed by a number of Quebec MPs, forming the Bloc Québécois.

In a last-minute effort to save the Meech Lake Agreement, First Ministers worked on a companion document outlining a program for future constitutional negotiations on a broad range of topics including Senate reforms and Aboriginal self-government. After a week of intense negotiations, an agreement was reached on 9 June 1990.

All Premiers committed to "use every possible means" to achieve ratification by 23 June 1990; some were more committed than others. Manitoba could not vote before the 23rd for procedural reasons. Premier Wells adjourned the Newfoundland legislature without submitting the resolution to a vote. The Meech Lake Accord died on 23 June 1990, unleashing a major national unity crisis.

To the sense of betrayal that prevailed in Quebec as a result of the patriation of the Constitution in 1981–2 was now added a sense of rejection for what were deemed to be the minimal demands of the federalist Quebec government of Premier Robert Bourassa. It did no good to argue that seven out of ten legislatures had approved the accord. The country was exhausted by years of existential drama. It was more divided than ever and there was no solution in sight.

To lower the temperature, Premier Bourassa launched several initiatives. The *Allaire Commission* recommended changes to federal-provincial jurisdiction in twenty-two areas. Under the recommendations of *the Belanger-Campeau Commission*, the National Assembly adopted a law that would require a referendum either on a Canada-Quebec proposal or on sovereignty no later than *26 October 1992*. A line had been drawn. The clock was ticking again.

The government of Canada, for its part, launched a number of initiatives, including the *Citizens' Forum* (November 1990), the *Beaudoin-Edwards Committee on the Amending Process* (December 1990), an *Ad Hoc Committee of Ministers on National Unity*, and *six DM Task Forces* (January 1991). I served on a number of them. There was much agitation but, as far as I could tell, not much traction.

By the end of *May 1991*, the government of Canada was in no position to present a proposal for a "Canada Round" of constitutional discussion. And yet, the government announced that its proposals would be made public in *September 1991*.[1] There were only a few months left till the release of the proposals and barely a year till the next referendum; this was not mission impossible, but close to it.

Serving at Pleasure

I was happy at Consumer and Corporate Affairs (CCA) and would gladly have stayed there for many years. This was not to be. I became Associate Secretary to the Cabinet for Federal-Provincial Relations for the Canada Round of negotiations in *June 1991*.

For many reasons, some professional and others more personal, this is not an assignment I wanted. For one, I did not feel qualified for the job. I do not have a legal or constitutional background. I had not been part of prior constitutional negotiations and therefore had no knowledge of the minefields; I did not know the ideas that had been tested and previously rejected and those that might be helpful to build a consensus. Knowledge of the subject matter is important.

Second, I feared that this challenge would be too emotionally charged for me. I was born and raised in Quebec. I identified with the need for a "quiet revolution" that toppled a patriarchal way of governing that had dominated in Quebec. I was part of the first generation of students going through CEGEP, which democratized access to higher education. As noted earlier, I came of age with May 1968, McGill français, the protests against the Vietnam War, etc. National unity and the place of Quebec in the Canadian federation are emotionally charged topics that have divided families and friends in Quebec for generations.

I was also afraid of the consequences for my family, with a teenage son and a husband in a challenging job of his own. I argued that, surely, the government of Canada could find someone with a more relevant background. This was not the time for an inexperienced leader like me. My arguments did not convince Paul Tellier. As a last resort, I asked to speak directly to Prime Minister Mulroney. This was most unusual. Normally, deputy ministers would ask to see the PM only in the most exceptional circumstances, like being asked to do something unconscionable or illegal. I felt strongly that I should at least try to prevent the Prime Minister from making a terrible mistake. Tellier accepted my request readily. I should have been suspicious. The PM listened carefully. In the end, he argued that I was not the best judge of who could lead this work and that I "should trust the judgment of others," in this case the Clerk and the PM. Furthermore, he argued that the so-called experts I was talking about had not prevented the difficult situation the country was in. *Je ne pouvais que m'incliner,* but I was not convinced.

At dinner that night with my family, I was rehashing all the reasons why I was the wrong person for the job. My son was thirteen years old at the time. He listened and asked, "What does it mean for us if you take this on?" "It means that I won't be here much and by the time it is done you will be fifteen." "Oh," he said as the information was sinking in. The next morning, over breakfast, he said, "Go ahead, we'll manage." My heart sinks when I think of this. My son had the last word. Later that day, I informed Paul Tellier that I was ready. From that time until March 1993, I did not see much of my family.

In the span of a career, senior public servants can expect that their commitment to serving will be tested many times. Canadians have no idea how difficult this might be at times. The expression "glass cliff" was not known then, but it might have been an able description for how I felt.

The Canada Round

One of my guiding principles is to deal with the circumstances as they are, not as I would wish them to be. For the past months, constitutional proposal planning had not gone smoothly. The *Citizens' Forum,* chaired by Keith Spicer and assisted by eleven prominent Canadians, tabled a report on 27 June 1991. It recommended another process but made no recommendation on the substance.

A *Special Joint Committee on the Constitutional Amending Process* – the Beaudoin-Edwards Committee – was set up on 17 December 1990. In its 20 June 1991 report, it recommended something akin to the Victoria formula with four regional vetoes. The report was dead on arrival, as British Columbia, Alberta, and Newfoundland objected.

The Ad Hoc Committee of Ministers on National Unity dealt with federal-provincial issues as they emerged but had made no progress at defining a federal position on constitutional renewal.

The Right Honourable Joe Clark was appointed Minister responsible for Constitutional Affairs on 21 April 1991, and I joined FPRO in June 1991. There was no time to rehash what might have been done in the preceding year. There was no approved content and no approved outline for a Canada round proposal. The office had commissioned numerous academic research papers; most concluded that more research was needed. *There were three months left before the government-set deadline.*

My team and I mapped out week by week all the Cabinet decisions needed to meet the Prime Minister's deadline. The Cabinet committee on national unity, chaired by Clark, met nine times over the summer. Ministers worked under an extremely tight timeline. This inevitably created tensions. Ministers had the difficult task of reconciling conflicting views and striking a balance between different philosophical and ideological positions. Adding to the complexity of the exercise and the workload, the Cabinet committee meetings were held in Ottawa, Winnipeg, Niagara-on-the-Lake, Quebec City, Charlottetown, and Iqaluit.

By the end of August 1991, the Priorities and Planning Committee, the full Cabinet, and the PM were fully engaged in finalizing the proposals. My team and I were drafting on the go without much time between Cabinet meetings. Without in any way taking away the merit of ministers serving on the Cabinet committee, the proposals owe much to the exceptional contribution of Deputy Ministers who brought forward innovative and courageous ideas to modernize the Canadian federation. The work of the Departments of Finance, Justice, and Employment and Immigration was particularly important. The ideas put forward by Fred Gorbet (Deputy Minister of Finance) to discipline the use of the federal spending power are noteworthy. In September 1991, the government released its program for constitutional change in "*Shaping Canada's Future Together: A Proposal.*" The fact that ministers were able to achieve a consensus is a tribute to their commitment to national unity.

The proposals were not as elegant as one might have liked and there were loose ends, but this was the best that could be done in the time available. It gave me comfort that Gordon Robertson described the proposals as "the most comprehensive proposals put before the Canadian public in the entire history of our constitutional discussions."[2] Over and above the issues discussed in the Meech Lake Accord, the proposals covered issues such as a reformed Senate, Aboriginal self-government, changes to the division of powers, mobility rights in the Canadian economic union, discipline on the use of the federal spending power, and so on. They included some innovative ideas for the management of a highly decentralized federation.

The proposals were released on time, but without any advance work to prepare the way for their release. They at least showed the government of Canada's seriousness in launching a "Canada Round" of constitutional negotiations. The work during this period reinforced my conviction that many of the most innovative ideas rest with departments, if only they are given a chance to bring them forward. A Cabinet system of government performs at its best by harnessing the best the public service has to offer together with the political will to bring about change.[3]

As a manager, I do not like working in a crisis mode; some people do. I see it as a measure of success to think ahead, anticipate and prevent the preventable so that there is more energy left to deal with unpredictable challenges.[4] One can only speculate about what could have been accomplished if the work had started a year earlier.

Now, it was time for parliamentarians to do the heavy lifting. The proposals were tabled in the House of Commons by Prime Minister Mulroney on 24 September 1991. The proposals were immediately referred to a Special Joint Committee on a Renewed Canada (SJC). The committee was asked to produce its report by the end of February, leaving very little time for federal-provincial discussions. Deputy Minister of Finance Fred Gorbet, Deputy Minister of Justice John Tait, and I spent five days explaining the proposals, answering the questions of parliamentarians, and providing additional information to assist them. In spite of our best efforts, the SJC was off to a bumpy start.[5]

Fearing that the committee might be unable to produce a unanimous report in time, the government launched a parallel public consultation process. Five three-day national conferences were organized under the auspices of independent organizations in Halifax, Calgary, Montreal, Toronto, and Vancouver. Arthur Kroeger was appointed Constitutional Conferences Coordinator. Eminent Canadians, including Gordon Robertson, Rosie Abella, Yves Fortier, Peter Lougheed, Monique Jérôme-Forget, and others, contributed to these events. The conferences were well run. They revealed goodwill across the country and produced a "fragile consensus" among those who attended.[6]

All this work did not prevent the SJC from running into difficulties. Fractiousness resurfaced as the committee struggled to complete its report by the end of February 1992. The government served notice that the SJC report, known as the Beaudoin-Dobbie report, was not its final position on constitutional reforms. The Quebec national assembly voted to disapprove of the SJC report on 11 March, and on 18 March it voted in favour of a boycott of the multilateral process. This proposition by the Parti Québécois prevented Premier Bourassa from being part of the solution. The Parti Québécois' preferred outcome was for the Canada Round to fail, thus opening the way for a referendum on separation that would be held by Robert Bourassa, a federalist Quebec Premier.

The Multilateral Negotiation Process

At the invitation of the Prime Minister, on 12 March 1992, a ministerial meeting was held in Ottawa at the Lester B. Pearson Building, chaired by Joe Clark. Four provinces were represented by their Premiers – Ontario, Newfoundland, Nova Scotia, and Prince Edward Island. Attendees reached an agreement to prepare, on a "best effort" basis, a consensus package of constitutional amendments by the end of May 1992.[7] This was less than six months before Quebec's 26 October deadline for a provincial referendum on either a proposal or independence.

There was an elaborate network of constitutional experts in the country at the time. Some had been involved in prior constitutional negotiations since Pearson's in 1968. They knew each other. Many had published extensively on the subject and most had dedicated their careers to constitutional negotiations. The 12 March 1992 meeting signalled that there was an opportunity to re-engage the constitutional machinery that had been dormant since the patriation of the Constitution. There were Multilateral Meetings on the Constitution (MMC) for Ministers, a Continuing Committee on the Constitution (CCC) of Deputy Ministers, a federal-provincial coordination group of officials, and four working groups.[8]

My team was responsible for supporting all these meetings, preparing proposals, identifying areas of consensus, and capturing the main decisions. The work was unrelenting, consuming an inordinate amount of energy. Ministers met in Halifax on 8–9 April, Edmonton on 29–30 April, St John's on 6–7 May, Vancouver on 11–13 May, Montreal on 20–2 May, and Toronto 26–30 May 1992.[9] Participants were optimistic that a comprehensive package could be turned over to First Ministers by 31 May.

In reality, the government of Canada was not in control of the negotiation process. Some were of the view that the government could call off the multilateral process if it was not reaching a consensus and table its own set of proposals to meet the Quebec deadline. On 15 May 1992 the government of Canada tabled its referendum legislation. Personally, I did not think that a unilateral proposal was a viable option. The provincial governments had invested too much time and political capital to let the government of Canada go at it alone. No agreement would mean a referendum on separation. The Parti Québécois and the Bloc Québécois would make sure of it. That much was clear.

The only way to avoid another national unity crisis was for all to succeed or fail together. This meant achieving a unanimous agreement with eleven governments, three territorial governments, and four national Aboriginal associations. *No one could be left behind.*

On 26 May 1992, I started to chair a team with five or six delegations to prepare a "rolling draft" of the consensus to date. This formed the basis of what would become the *"Consensus Report on the Constitution."* It was clear that a consensus paper would not be ready by the end of May. There had been much progress in several areas, including on Aboriginal self-government, but some major issues remained outstanding. The MMC resumed its meetings in Ottawa on 9 June 1992, and on 11 June, ministers concluded that they had made as much progress as possible, although they had not reached a consensus on three major issues: Senate reform, the amending formula, and expanding section 121 of the Constitution for a common market. Senate reform was the most contentious issue. *It was time for First Ministers to get involved.*

All through the ministerial meetings, the Prime Minister was kept informed. Paul Tellier and I had regular meetings with the PM, the Minister, and the PM's Chief of Staff, Hugh Segal. On 24 June 1992, the PM indicated publicly that Parliament would be reconvened on *15 July 1992*[10] and that he would table either an agreement or a federal proposal. From that point on, there are conflicting views about events.

The Pearson Accord

The PM called an informal meeting of First Ministers on 29 June 1992 at Harrington Lake. Paul Tellier and I were the only officials on site. It is noteworthy that the Prime Minister did not shut down the multilateral process that day. If he had, this would have left fifteen days to prepare a proposal for tabling on 15 July. Instead, it was agreed that the Premiers would meet on 3 July in Toronto without the Prime Minister. The purpose of the meeting was to seek an agreement on Senate reform.[11] Minister Clark was invited as an "observer"; I accompanied him, and if I recall correctly, I was the only official on site. This meeting would prove to be an important turning point. Group dynamics unleash powerful forces.

Premiers started to coalesce around an equal Senate model. Premier Bob Rae, Ontario, had softened his objections. On many occasions, Premier Rae had influenced the course of events during the constitutional negotiation. He personally attended all ministerial meetings instead of delegating this role to his minister. He had consistently expanded the scope of the discussion and pushed for more players to come to the table. He was committed to the Aboriginal self-government agenda and contributed to making progress in this area. He was now signalling a willingness to support institutional changes that, at first glance, were not aligned with the interests of Ontario, since the province would go from twenty-four to eight senators. His calculus was not obvious, but his signal was received loud and clear by the other Premiers. A window of opportunity had emerged for a triple-E Senate.

It was agreed to reconvene in Ottawa in the Pearson building on 6 July. The meeting went on all day and was extended into the following morning. A crucial moment occurred when Premier Rae signalled that he could support an equal Senate. He had been in communication with Premier Bourassa, who had signalled that he would not object to an equal Senate if other demands were met. Mr. Clark had also been in communication with Premier Bourassa, and he conveyed the same information. This information was of crucial importance. Premiers were unanimous that *in no circumstances would Quebec be isolated.*[12]

The Pearson Accord was reached in the absence of the Premier of Quebec and the Prime Minister of Canada on 7 July 1992. Prime Minister Mulroney had reasons to think that the Premiers of Quebec and Ontario could never agree to an equal senate. The agreement proved otherwise.

Premier Rae and Minister Clark consistently indicated that they acted on the understanding that Premier Bourassa could support an equal Senate. Whatever the case, the challenge now was to bring Quebec to the table so that Premier Bourassa could speak for himself, be heard without intermediaries, and be part of a unanimous agreement before the deadline of 26 October 1992.

The Prime Minister convened Premiers to an informal meeting at Harrington Lake on 4 August 1992. Premier Bourassa could credibly end his post-Meech-Lake boycott of First Ministers' meetings, since the Pearson Accord was going much further than the Meech Lake Accord. Exceptionally, the territorial and Aboriginal leaders were not invited to this meeting.[13] The purpose of the meeting was to assess if there was enough flexibility all around to address the outstanding issues. Discussions would resume only if all Premiers agreed to participate. It was understood that the negotiations would produce a political accord, not a legal text. The meeting was inconclusive.

A second informal First Ministers' meeting at Harrington Lake was scheduled for 10 August. In between, the Prime Minister and Minister Clark met with territorial and Aboriginal leaders on 5 August. This was a delicate moment. Premier Bourassa was approaching the deadline for a Quebec referendum process. A special meeting of the Quebec Liberal Party was scheduled on 29 August.[14] If Premier Bourassa failed to present a constitutional reform proposal, under Law 150, a yes/no referendum on sovereignty should be held.

At the conclusion of the 10 August meeting, Minister Clark announced that a First Ministers' Meeting with territorial and Aboriginal leaders would take place within the next ten days.[15] It was clear to all that the standard of success was unanimity. There was no room for anything else. No one could be left behind.

The Charlottetown Accord

During the first phase of the Canada Round of constitutional negotiations, Tellier and I worked very closely. Tellier started to progressively distance himself in 1992; he was preparing to leave the public service. On 1 July 1992, I became

23 août, 1992

Cher Jocelyne,

Je ne veut pas laisser passer les moments historiques que nous avons vécus ensemble au cours des derniers jours sans t'exprimer mes sentiments.

D'abord, je veut t'exprimer ma gratitude pour ton appui de tous les instants, la qualité de ta gestion, la sagesse de tes conseils et la sureté de ton jugement.

Ensuite, j'aimerais t'exprimer mon admiration pour le dévouement et le talent que tu as consacrés au dossier (même si tu détestes le sujet, ce qui n'a jamais paru).

Enfin je veut te dire combien j'ai véritablement aimé travailler avec toi. Ton sourire, ton air parfois espiègle, ta spontanéité et ta féminité sont des atouts que j'ai appréciés à tous les instants. Je me rappelle avec chaleur les moments de gaité que nous avons connus même durant les périodes les plus difficiles.

Durant mes 25 ans dans la fonction publique dont 13 comme sous-ministre, j'ai croisé un certain nombre de gens exceptionnels. Tu n'as rien à envier à personne.

Merci pour tout.

Over to you...

Sincères amitiés

P

P.S. Je te souhaite d'être heureuse.

Figure 3. Letter from former Clerk Paul Tellier, 23 August 1992.

Secretary to the Cabinet for Federal-Provincial Relations reporting to the PM. I was the only federal official in the room with the PM and First Ministers during the most crucial phase of the negotiation.

The 18–22 August FMM was the first formal constitutional negotiating session with all First Ministers since the June 1990 failure of the Meech Lake Accord. I attended all the private sessions, sometimes accompanied by one provincial official, Jack MacDonald.

Institutional reforms were at the heart of the Charlottetown Accord. A number of proposals were at play. The House of Commons would substantially improve representation by population. This would address a democratic deficit as population grew across Canada and in particular in the Western provinces. This change would be alongside a constitutional guarantee that Quebec representation in the House would never fall below 25 per cent.

The Senate would be equal, elected, and effective, a true House of the provinces. The Accord was proposing a profound transformation of the governance of Canada and putting forward a model for the management of its relations with First Nations. It was proposing a transformation of the governing system of Canada, the place of Quebec in the federation, and a system of Aboriginal governments. This was groundbreaking.

A follow-up meeting was scheduled for the week of 24 August 1992. Some Quebec officials described Premier Bourassa as being in a weak position during these negotiations.[16] What I witnessed was quite the opposite. The Premier was commanding respect and skilfully achieving significant gains for the Province of Quebec, including support for a 25 per cent constitutional guarantee for the representation of Quebec in the House of Commons.

However, I had concerns. I had periodically briefed the Quebec delegation during the ministerial negotiations to keep officials informed of progress and to facilitate their eventual return to the table. As the negotiations were picking up momentum, the tone, cordial at first, became more tense. The briefing session on 2 June was noteworthy: as an agreement was becoming a serious possibility, behaviours changed. Officials displayed the most aggressive behaviour I had ever witnessed among professionals in the exercise of their functions. I am not a shrinking violet. I have seen aggressive behaviour in many instances before and since, but this was beyond bounds. I left the meeting with the feeling that some of the most senior advisors of Premier Bourassa might have been hoping that the negotiations would fail – thus forcing his hand to hold a referendum on Quebec independence. This was purely speculative on my part, so I kept my doubts to myself. From time to time during the last critical days I wondered if Premier Bourassa was not holding similar concerns.

The Charlottetown Accord was reached on 28 August 1992. It enjoyed the support of all ten provinces, three territories, and four national Aboriginal associations, as well as all political parties in the House of Commons: a major achievement in itself.

Figure 4. The last lines in the last day of the Charlottetown Accord negotiation, 28 August 1992. Front row, left to right: Bob Rae, Clyde Wells, Brian Mulroney, Ovide Mercredi, Robert Bourassa. Back row: Donald Cameron, Jocelyne Bourgon, Benoît Morin.

On that day, First Ministers decided to run a referendum on the basis of the political Accord without a legal text, feeling that such a text would not be necessary. *This was a mistake.*

The House of Commons, with a vote of 233 to 12, approved the legislation for a national referendum on the Charlottetown Accord. The referendum, officially proclaimed on 17 September 1992, would take place on 26 October – thirty-nine days after writs were issued.

The 1992 Referendum

Initially, the Accord's reception was good, but problems soon emerged. A conversation between two senior members of Premier Bourassa's delegation was leaked. Premier Bourassa was portrayed as unable to defend the interests of Quebec. The expression "on s'est écrasé c'est tout"[17] became famous. This declaration took almost everybody by surprise, but sadly not me. Professional public servants must loyally serve elected officials in a democratic system. If they are unable to do so, they may ask to be transferred to a less demanding position or they may resign. On the matter of loyalty there is no grey zone.[18] Premier Bourassa had endorsed the Charlottetown Accord and played a key role in shaping the final agreement. The incident was damaging for Premier Bourassa, for all First Ministers, and for the reputation of professional non-partisan public servants.

Jacques Parizeau led a Quebec coalition opposing the Charlottetown Accord. He was joined by the RH Pierre Trudeau on 1 October 1992. Premier Bourassa was in the situation of defending the agreement against federalists led by P.E. Trudeau and sovereigntists led by Jacques Parizeau. Politics makes strange bedfellows.

It took only a few weeks for First Ministers to realize that they could not defend the Accord without a legal text. On *10 September 1992,* I pulled all the delegations back together to begin legal drafting to give effect to the unprecedentedly broad political Accord. The people most knowledgeable about every word and detail of the Accord were locked in a room doing legal drafting rather than being available to assist First Ministers during the referendum campaign.

The legal text was released on *9 October*. This was a gargantuan effort that was only possible because of the exceptional contribution of John Tait and Mary Dawson, Deputy Minister and Associate Deputy Minister, Justice Canada. But by then it was too late. The Charlottetown Accord was rejected in a national referendum on *26 October 1992* by a majority of Canadians in a majority of provinces. There was no drama. A strange kind of calm settled in. First Ministers had met the deadline but missed their rendezvous with history.

The clock that had been set by the legislative assembly of Quebec had left no time to explain to Canadians the content of the most complex constitutional accord since Confederation. With no time to form an opinion, Canadians felt that *the status quo had a much better taste*. An opportunity had come and gone.

Prime Minister Mulroney campaigned till the very last day. He had used much political capital and gone to great personal effort to bring Quebec into the constitutional fold "with honour and enthusiasm."[19] Once the verdict was known, the Prime Minister expressed the view that losing on a unanimous proposal was preferable to losing a referendum on the separation of Quebec. It may be so, but preventable mistakes had been made, and a high price had been paid. Future public service leaders must learn from these events, because history tends to repeat itself.

Who Believes in Federalism?

I think Canada has reached the end of a long cycle of mega-constitutional negotiations that has been going on since the first constitutional conference in the 1950s with Louis St Laurent: in the late 1960s with Lester Pearson, in the 1970s and 1980s with Pierre Trudeau, and the 1980s and 1990s with Brian Mulroney. Each failed attempt left the country more divided. It may be wise to leave the Constitution to rest and learn to work with it.

Canada has had an unhealthy obsession with constitutional changes. At the same time, not enough attention was given to the management of a highly decentralized federation like Canada. The Canadian federation still needs to invent a way of facing complex issues requiring cooperation across multiple boundaries, at home and abroad, and generate viable solutions. Who believes in federalism enough to invest time and energy to give Canada the system and practices it needs to face the challenges ahead?

There are no mechanisms or institutional arrangements in place to support such work. First Ministers may talk and even agree, but there are no mechanisms to protect decisions achieved at great cost, even if unanimously. Canada has no cooperative mechanisms that compare to those of the OECD for shared learning among member countries. It has none of the mechanisms used to promote cooperative policy work, as in Australia or Germany. It has no tradition of joint policy reviews, as in the European Union, to accelerate members' learning. Canada needs to invent its approach to federalism in the twenty-first century. The issue is not about centralization versus decentralization, but about making progress in areas that require the coming together of multiple governments, each one with their respective authorities, tools, and capabilities.

This is not an insurmountable task. It is a challenge well worth the attention of future public sector leaders. I find it ironic that in the time it took to reach the Meech Lake Accord and the Charlottetown Accord and then to see both fail, European countries successfully reached an agreement on an Economic Union and a common currency.

National unity issues will never go away. They are and will remain an everyday concern for the government of Canada. But unity is not achieved by putting words in constitutional law. It is achieved by building the collective capacity to share and create a better future together. This means building the capacity for collective knowledge, collective learning, and collective actions to advance a common purpose – even in the face of ideological and political differences.[20]

Most of Meech and many other issues could have been achieved through non-constitutional means, as was done later under Prime Ministers Chrétien, Harper, and Justin Trudeau. Change is possible without bringing the country to the brink. Constitutional negotiations are not the answer to the complex issues governments are called upon to address, from climate change to population migration to homelessness and poverty alleviation. These issues require working across multiple boundaries and bringing multiple agents together.

Figure 5. Photograph of Bourgon and the Right Hon. Brian Mulroney, 1992, signed by the latter – a memento of years of working together.

A good strategy should give as much consideration to success as to failure. It should have a reasonable prospect of achieving the desired public policy outcome while leaving the parties no worse off in case of failure. Negotiation strategies for the patriation of the Constitution, Meech, and Charlottetown were all lacking. The first was designed as a war game, the second had no exit strategy, and the third had no reasonable chance of success. There are plenty of lessons to go around.

Moving On

This assignment was difficult and even painful at times. But … I gained a lifetime's worth of constitutional experience. As a non-lawyer, I got my badge of honour in constitutional law when on the last day, after I proposed some wording to address a concern between Robert Bourassa and Ovide Mercredi, Clyde Wells asked me, "How did you get such a fine legal mind?" I replied, "By studying biology" – the study of what causes living systems to behave the way they do. We had a good laugh, but I was only half joking.

I learned more about the country and about First Nations. I had the privilege to get to know the First Ministers and Aboriginal leaders and to admire their commitment and resolve: the wisdom of Joe Ghiz, the energy of Frank McKenna, the dignity of Ovide Mercredi, the serenity of Rosemary Kuptana, the unique skills of Brian Mulroney, the courage of Robert Bourassa, and the unstoppable commitment to inclusiveness of Joe Clark and Bob Rae. It was a once in a lifetime experience.

After the 1992 referendum, my priority immediately shifted to finding jobs for the employees who had worked so hard over the months. Once again, the response of the Deputy Minister community was heartwarming. Within a month or so, FPRO was back to its original size and employees had been offered new jobs. The Canadian negotiation team ended up being a training ground for officials who would later serve at more senior levels in the public service, like Janice Charette, Michael Wernick, Suzanne Hurtubise, and Scott Serson, to name but a few. To everything there is a silver lining. For my part, I wanted nothing more than to go home with my family.

5 From CIDA to Transport

I became *President of the Canadian International Development Agency* (CIDA) in March 1993. I had not fully recovered from two years on the road and the many sleepless nights during the Charlottetown negotiations, but this appointment was a match made in heaven. I was most grateful to Prime Minister Mulroney for the chance to serve at CIDA.

CIDA was an agency under pressure and facing many uncertainties. Like other aid agencies around the world, it faced accelerating global changes. The Cold War had just ended, and a new technological revolution was starting to show its potential. CIDA had been undergoing a strategic management review for far too long, and organizational changes had been under discussion for years. Like all other departments and agencies, it had experienced multiple spending cuts that necessitated closing down programs. In just a few months in 1993, CIDA went through major changes in leadership, losing Senior Vice-President Douglas Lindores, getting a new Minister, Monique Vézina, and getting a new President.[1]

CIDA employees had a deep sense of mission and public purpose. Many employees had grown through the ranks from junior positions to senior levels. They had knowledge and expertise in all aspects of their work and were rightly proud of their accomplishments. I felt at home, and the employees were responding well to my leadership. There were managerial problems, but nothing that could not be solved. The strength of a place like CIDA was the drive and motivation of its employees.

In 1993, PM Mulroney was preparing to leave and trying to ensure a smooth transition at the helm of the Progressive Conservative party. Kim Campbell took over as leader on 13 June 1993, and was sworn in as Prime Minister on 25 June. My assignment to CIDA ended that day.

I was out of the country at a meeting of international development agencies when I was informed of the change that would be announced the next day. I flew back to Ottawa to attend a Deputy Ministers' meeting that had been called by the Clerk to brief deputies on a massive reorganization of the public service of Canada.

Leaving aside the wisdom of the reorganization, I could not condone the manner. The decision to move ahead with a shuffle of Deputy Ministers at the same time as a major government reorganization and a major shuffle of Ministers was questionable and was leaving Ministers exposed. Deputy Ministers were redeployed to new positions in unprecedented numbers. Overnight, forty-three ADMs had lost their jobs, a 17 per cent reduction in the number of Assistant Deputy Ministers, and nothing was in place to manage their layoff or redeployment. "By accident," the shuffle was especially harsh for women Deputy Ministers. They were being demoted or moved aside. I was the lucky one, since I was being "promoted" to a bigger department. This made sense only for people who judge the importance of a department by the size of its budget rather than its contribution to society.

The DM shuffle was going beyond what was needed to support the reorganization. For instance, CIDA was not affected by the reorganization and yet I was moved to a new department. The reorganization did not affect Transport Canada and yet the Deputy Minister was shuffled out in the middle of sensitive negotiations.

I had been at CIDA for only a few months. I considered such an early transfer to be disrespectful of CIDA's employees. I was furious and made it known. My view was and remains that the operation displayed no concern for the well-being of the public service and no respect for public servants. The handling of the reform did nothing to enhance the reputation of the Privy Council Office, a new Clerk, and a new Prime Minister. The agitation across the public service was such that Prime Minister Campbell called a meeting of the Deputy Ministers who had been most vocal, me included. She made it clear that the DM shuffle was added at the very last minute on the advice of the PCO; she later mentioned this in her memoir.[2] Her gesture was appreciated, but the harm was done. The meeting was civil. Politics is not kind to women; Deputy Ministers were not about to add to the difficulties faced by a newly appointed Prime Minister and the first woman Prime Minister. We did what public servants do so well, we rolled up our sleeves and went on to serve in our new departments.

These events had a lasting impact on the public service and on me. Many came to realize that the way things are done matters as much as what is being done. People in Machinery of Government worked on this reorganization for a long time. People in Senior Personnel always have views about who could fill what DM position at any given time. Ultimately, it is the responsibility of the Clerk to ensure that organizational changes are well managed and do not leave ministers exposed. As Campbell noted, with this reorganization, "in many cases, the ministers were trying to get a handle on new issues and responsibilities" when she needed policy proposals for the coming election.[3]

I had the highest respect for Glen Shortliffe. He was a pragmatic and resolute leader. We agreed to disagree on the need for a shuffle on this scale and on the way such a massive reorganization was handled. A year later, Shortliffe asked me, "Did you forgive me for moving you so soon?" My answer was "no" … and we went for a drink. Over the years, I have made my fair share of decisions; some did not unfold as expected and some were mistaken. While serving as Clerk, people do the best they can, and the passage of time will reveal the difference between good and not so good decisions.

The reorganization of 1993 reinforced my view that reorganizations should be avoided whenever possible. Reorganizations are sometimes done for good reasons, but more often for dubious ones. Bad reasons include restructuring to make a symbolic gesture rather than to address the issues. A reorganization may be used as a pretext to remove people instead of having frank discussions with them. It may be done to internalize trade-offs between two or more domains of public policies, such as trade-offs between environmental protection and energy development. The reality is that *governments cannot reorganize their way out of this dilemma. Working across multiple boundaries is a defining characteristic of serving in the twenty-first century.* The challenge is to learn to connect knowledge, know-how, and capabilities across multiple systems.[4]

Even with the best intentions, reorganizations are costly, and there are generally better ways of achieving the desired outcomes.[5] Some are of the view that, since the 1993 reorganization remained in place after the election of Prime Minister Chrétien, this implicitly demonstrates its quality. I beg to differ. As Clerk, I briefed PM Chrétien on the impact of the 1993 reorganization. My view was that if anything significant was to be achieved during the first term of his government, departments needed to be left alone. There was a need to restore a degree of stability. It was preferable to work with what was there rather than to introduce more changes. I was grateful that he supported this view. It would take more than five years to bring departmental legislation in line with the 1993 reorganization.

A Master Class: Transport Canada

Huguette Labelle was sent to CIDA, and I replaced her at the Department of Transport. Following the announcement, I asked Huguette to call a meeting so that I could meet the management team and introduce myself to Minister Jean Corbeil.

The scene is still vivid in my mind. Two emotional Deputy Ministers met the management team with Minister Corbeil present. With my arm around Huguette's shoulders, I told the management team that what they were witnessing was that Deputy Ministers get deeply attached to their team and the department they lead. The shuffle announcement was effective immediately but, on that day, I was unable to be their Deputy Minister. My priority was to say goodbye to the employees of CIDA who had trusted me and who were feeling hard done by at the moment. Huguette also needed time to say her goodbye. Come the following Monday, 28 June, I would be back and ready to serve as their Deputy Minister.

I was a member of the Committee of Senior Officials (COSO). Chaired by the Clerk, COSO is the highest human resources committee in the public service. As a senior deputy minister, I had a voice in deputy minister human resource management discussions. I promised myself that I would do what I could to ensure that, in the future, there would be at least a few days between the date of a shuffle announcement and the appointment taking effect. I kept my word.

I had the highest respect for the *Department of Transport*. This was the department I had joined twenty years earlier and where I discovered the public service of Canada. Twenty years later, I was coming back as Deputy Minister. This assignment was one of my most important master classes as a senior public servant and, unbeknownst to me, the last one I would get before becoming Clerk.

In previous positions, I had witnessed the cumulative impact of expenditure reductions through the 1980 and early 1990s. Nowhere were the debilitating effects of successive cuts over so many years more tangible than in the Department of Transport. The department was the owner, operator, legislator, and enforcement agency responsible for all transportation modes. It was over-extended and did not have the resources or capacity to fulfil its mission. The insider view was that MOT was overseeing an expanding "rust belt." There were thousands of kilometres of rail in excess of needs and no money to maintain the rail segments Canada most needed. MOT was responsible for all airports, yet did not have the resources to modernize any of them. Coast Guard vessels needed retrofitting, harbours were in decay, etc.

The department had a good knowledge of the problems and possible solutions. Because of the work of Moya Greene and Louis Ranger, respectively ADM and Director General Policy Branch, the department had years of solid research, forecasts, and trends analysis. Furthermore, it had regularly shared the findings with the industry, which essentially had similar views. The department had done its homework.

The challenge was to find a way to stop the bleeding and put forward a different approach. More cuts were not the way. The key question was not what to cut but *what to preserve* for the future. This came down to making choices. Repositioning the Department of Transport was not a managerial challenge; it was about reconceptualizing the role of the department in the future. It was a political challenge, involving making choices about the role of government in society. When the current reality is unsustainable, and the costs are unaffordable, invention is the less risky course of action.[6]

The department engaged in a process of reinvention. As I familiarized myself with the research work the department had done over the years, weekly meetings were scheduled to share the findings with Minister Corbeil. Public servants presented the results of their work. They were being heard. My primary focus was on how the key elements might all fit together in a meaningful synthesis. What was the overall narrative? How would the sum of the proposed changes amount to a meaningful and affordable role for the Department of Transport in the future?

The exercise began under Minister Jean Corbeil, a Progressive Conservative, and continued with Minister Doug Young once the Liberal government of Prime Minister Chrétien came to office after the election. They both played a key role in shaping the overall reform agenda. They provided invaluable insights about the political acceptability of such ambitious reforms.

The size and the scope of the reform agenda was enough to scare even the bravest minister. However, ideas have a way to move around. Windows of opportunities belong to those who have ideas to put forward. A window of opportunity would soon open up that would influence the course of events from 1995 to the end of the first mandate of Prime Minister Chrétien. MOT provided the inspiration for the design of the Program Review Exercise that would lead to the elimination of the deficit a few years later.

The Pearson Airport Case

The year 1993 was formative for other reasons as well. PM Campbell wanted the privatization of the Pearson Airport to go ahead even if the federal election campaign was underway. Opposition leader Jean Chrétien, for his part, had indicated strong opposition to the project and had pledged that the transfer of Pearson would be cancelled should he become Prime Minister.

The Clerk instructed the Department of Transport to finalize the transfer of Pearson Airport in spite of the election campaign underway. MOT was not opposed to the transfer of Pearson – in fact, the idea originated from the department. But, there was a problem: the Clerk's instructions conflicted with the constitutional convention that should guide the conduct of officials during an election campaign. In short, the *caretaker convention* is that, out of respect for democracy, the proper conduct for public officials during an election is to refrain from taking actions that would limit the discretion of a future government. At the same time, it is understood that the governing party retains the right to govern – particularly when it comes to routine business or in response to emergencies – in all circumstances, including during an election. The principle at the heart of the convention is to act with restraint.[7] A decision to depart from the caretaker convention is a serious matter; my opinion was that this decision belonged to the Prime Minister.

There was no doubt that finalizing the transfer would limit the discretion of a future government. The transfer was halfway done; half a dozen key documents had not yet been signed. The transfer was being done under the authority of the Minister of Transport; it is his signature and the signature of MOT officials that would appear on the transfer documents. I instructed MOT officials not to go any further until I had discussed the matter with the Minister and the Clerk.

The issue involved several dimensions: the Prime Minister's prerogative, ministerial accountability, officials' responsibility for the exercise of delegated authority, and loyalty to the government in office. For some, the concept of ministerial authority is arcane, but in fact it is at the heart of the Canadian system of responsible government. Ministers are constitutionally responsible for government actions. Ministerial responsibility is individual as opposed to institutional. It is the person of the Minister who is responsible. Ministerial responsibility can be shared with no one, not even the Prime Minister.

Minister Corbeil was supportive of the project but concerned about finalizing the transfer during an election. The department had obtained the necessary Cabinet decisions. From an administrative perspective, I could assure the Minister that things were in order. The issue came down to one question: who should decide to depart from the caretaker convention in a matter that would tie the hands of a future government over the long term?

My view was that the decision to derogate from a constitutional convention in this case was a serious matter. I thus requested and received written confirmation that the PM had been briefed about the convention and the implications for a future government. The Prime Minister remained of the view that the transfer of the Pearson Airport should go ahead.

As Deputy Minister of MOT, I was responsible for ensuring that the department would not take actions that would unduly constrain a future government. I was also responsible for loyally implementing the decision of the current government. PM Campbell had been briefed and decided on the balance between precaution and the government prerogative to govern. The Prime Minister had spoken. The Minister was satisfied that, in the circumstances, the devolution of the Pearson Airport could go ahead.

It is important for Deputy Ministers to have a solid understanding of the extent of their authority and that of their Minister, the Prime Minister, Cabinet, and each branch of government. Amid a crisis, there is no time to start learning about constitutional conventions or to think about when a matter needs to be escalated to a higher level.

It is important for senior public sector leaders to think in institutional terms. This helps to depersonalize discussions and focus on the essential: the public trust in public institutions now and in the future. Thinking in institutional terms helped me to navigate through many challenging circumstances over the years. Looking ahead, I worried that there had been progressively more confusion in the public service between the authority of Ministers and the Prime Minister. Sometimes, the confusion is deliberate; it increases the influence of people who do not have to carry the heavy burden of ministerial responsibility. I would have occasion to think more about these questions in the years ahead.

On 3 November 1993, Jean Chrétien formed the thirty-fifth government. Shortly thereafter, he appointed Robert Nixon to review the agreement on the devolution of the Pearson Airport. On Nixon's recommendation, the government asked the Department of Transport to rescind the transfer. On 4 May 1995, after years of debate around the decision to transfer the Pearson Airport, the Senate announced the appointment of a special committee "to examine and report upon all matters concerning the policies and negotiations leading up to, and including, the agreements respecting the redevelopment and operation of Terminals 1 and 2 at Lester B. Pearson International Airport and the circumstances relating to the cancellation thereof."[8] It was clear that I would be a prime witness (or prime suspect) because of my role as Deputy Minister of Transport before and after the cancellation of the Pearson agreement. Fortunately, the department had been rigorous, consistent, and principled in serving both the outgoing and incoming governments.

This is a good case study for a professional non-partisan public service. Officials are accountable to their ministers. In this case, it meant that I was answerable on behalf of Minister Corbeil in the Conservative government of PM Campbell and answerable on behalf of Minister Young under the government of PM Chrétien. The life of a Deputy Minister is never boring … It was about to become even more exciting.

When Policy and Politics Converge

The Honourable Douglas Young was sworn in as Minister of Transport on 4 November 1993. He would serve as the twenty-first Minister of Transport till 1996. The department had done excellent research work and had a story to tell.[9] Mr. Young was a dynamic and courageous minister. He was not afraid of bold ideas.

The department started briefing Minister Young about his portfolio, the situation prevailing in the transport industries, and the work initiated under his predecessor. Minister Young does not scare easily. He took on board the findings and challenged the department to be more ambitious. The Minister could foresee that the government would soon need bold ideas.

The Chrétien government released its first budget on 22 February 1994. In the words of Paul Martin, the 1994 Budget "was not a success."[10] Suddenly, the environment was favourable to new and ambitious ideas. Minister Young's soundings of some key Ministers convinced him that it was possible to build support for an ambitious transformation of Transport Canada. A window of opportunity was opening.

The approach was unheard of. The department was proposing to position its role around safety and intermodal connectivity. To fulfil its mission, the department did not need to be the owner, operator, and legislator of all transportation modes. Some activities were inherited from a prior time and reflected the economic landscape of the 1950s. Canada had changed, and as a result some programs could be abandoned with pride because they had served their purpose. In some cases, others in society were better positioned to take on some responsibilities and achieve better results.

A political champion, Doug Young, was taking charge of an ambitious project to reposition the role of the Department of Transport to serve Canada and Canadians in the future. *Policy work and political leadership were converging*. Courageous policy decisions and skilful implementation over a number of years could yield significant savings and better serve Canada. Governing and serving are a process of invention;[11] this was an exciting time.

***

Early in 1994, I was invited to meet PM Chrétien at 24 Sussex. The Pearson Airport was on my mind; however, the topic was entirely different. I had no prior personal relationship with Prime Minister Chrétien. At the request of PM Mulroney, I had briefed Mr. Chrétien as leader of the opposition on two occasions during the Charlottetown negotiations; that was all.

Prime Minister Chrétien had decided to make changes at the senior level of the public service. The choice of a Clerk is a delicate decision. In the aftermath of the 1993 reorganization, I thought the Prime Minister was wise to seek input from inside and outside the public service. I took the question of who could serve as Clerk very seriously. I mentioned the names of some of the most experienced Deputy Ministers and did my best to outline why their appointment would be well received. I did not take seriously the PM's question of "What about you?" My answer was simply that he could do much better, that there were more qualified people around. In truth, I never aspired to be Clerk; I prefer to run a department.

The public service, at the time, was not in a good place. Years of cuts had eroded the fabric of the institution, the ability to provide quality services and to sustain core functions. Years of downsizing and staffing freezes meant that the public service had been deprived of an inflow of new skills and that people had not gained the diversity of experience normally acquired through lateral and upward mobility. The question on my mind, as I left 24 Sussex, was: If asked, would I be willing to lead the public service through what I knew would be a challenging period? If not, could I assume that the public service would be in better hands?

PART 3

The Clerk

6 And So ... I Became Clerk

I became the first woman Clerk of the Privy Council and Secretary to the Cabinet for Canada on 28 March 1994.

Being the first is to be the one taking the last step in a long sequence of courageous actions taken by others. That said, I understand the importance of being the first and the responsibility that comes with it to ensure that it will become normal thereafter.

It was a bold decision on the part of Prime Minister Chrétien to appoint someone like me. He was appointing a woman, someone a generation younger than most Deputy Ministers, a French-speaking Canadian from the small Ottawa Valley town of Papineauville. I had served as Secretary to Cabinet for Federal-Provincial Relations under the government of Prime Minister Mulroney. My appointment was in the best tradition of a professional non-partisan public service. I served two Prime Ministers of different political stripes with the same ardour and commitment; I am proud of this. I believe that the Clerk should be and be seen to be non-partisan in all circumstances.

By the time I became Clerk, I was an experienced Deputy Minister. I had served in several departments in challenging circumstances. I had served at the centre of government, in line departments, in headquarters, and in the regions. I knew the public service of Canada and what it could accomplish. I knew the people of the public service of Canada and their deep sense of duty to serve Canadians. I also knew the pain and frustration that had accumulated for years below the surface.

My appointment triggered an unusual reaction. It is usual to receive good wishes and congratulations from colleagues and leaders across a broad spectrum of activities in Canada. I was grateful that Premiers took the time to wish me well. The constitutional negotiations of 1991–2 had given me the opportunity to get to know them. I was touched by the generosity of the RH Brian Mulroney and the friendship of Paul Tellier. I was especially touched

Chère Jocelyne,

Je tiens à vous féliciter sincèrement pour votre nomination récente comme Greffier du conseil privé et Secrétaire du conseil des Ministres.

Vous comprendrez qu'il me sera parfois difficile d'applaudir aux nominations que le Premier Ministre sera appelé à faire! Votre accession à ce poste me comble d'aise. Je ne connais personne dans la Fonction Publique Canadienne mieux qualifiée que vous pour occuper de si importantes responsabilités dans l'administration de notre pays.

Je conserve un excellent souvenir de vous, suite à notre longue et féconde collaboration.

Veuillez agréer, chère Jocelyne, l'expression de mes meilleures salutations.

Brian Mulroney

Figure 6. Letter from the Right Hon. Brian Mulroney, 8 April 1994 – congratulations for becoming Clerk.

by Gordon Robertson's letter. After all these years, I have kept some of the letters. They are among the documents being transferred to Library and Archives Canada.

But something else was happening. Flowers and little notes flowed in from junior staff and senior officials from across the public service and across the country. People were expressing hope for a better future, aspirations for a more inclusive approach to the management of the public service, and a willingness to help bring about change. Above all, they were expressing the hope that *we would see the end of never-ending cuts and would leave to future public servants an institution in better shape than the one we had inherited.* This became the focus of my years as Clerk. I would soon discover that all this goodwill and more would be needed to see the public service through an unprecedented period of change.

I have never been enamoured of the description of the job as "Deputy Minister of the Prime Minister." Prime Ministers are not ministers unless they assign to themselves the responsibility of a department (this is generally not advisable). The Clerk of the Privy Council Office is not a Deputy Minister acting on behalf of the delegated authority of the Prime Minister. Most of the functions of the Privy Council Office do not have equivalents in departments. The part of the role of the Clerk that is similar to a Deputy Head is in fact quite small. The expression is used as a shortcut to avoid getting into details, but details matter and so does the view of the incumbent.

The job is a combination of functions that have evolved over time. The Clerk of the Privy Council and Secretary to Cabinet are two complementary but different roles. More recently, in 1992, the Public Service Reform Act added the responsibility of Head of the Public Service to the mix.

Three factors shape the role of the Clerk and Secretary to Cabinet: the views of the incumbent about the role, the Prime Minister in office, and the circumstances.

The Incumbent

My views about the role of the Clerk were shaped by what came before, personal experience, and personality. They may not reflect the way the role is understood today or will be exercised in the future. Institutions are not immutable. However, an understanding of the way I thought of the role at the time is relevant to how I exercised my responsibilities.

At its origin, the PCO was a clerical office. Decisions needed to be recorded. Orders in Council had to be put into effect. In the post-war period, PCO took on its modern configuration and the functions progressively expanded.[1] The Privy Council Office covers a wide range of functions related to the Prime Minister's overall responsibilities. Then and now, it is possible to trace the role of various units in PCO to some aspects of the role of the PM. Machinery of government supports the PM in creating departments and agencies, ensuring the internal coherence of mandates, and keeping up to date the enabling legislations giving effect to departmental mandates. Senior personnel vets, screens, and prepares Orders in Council appointments. It provides advice on the most senior appointments. A foreign and defence policy unit supports the Prime Minister in representing Canada abroad, in bilateral and multilateral relations. A security and intelligence unit has progressively taken a more expansive role. A legal unit, separate and distinct from the Department of Justice, provides legal and constitutional advice. An intergovernmental affairs unit supports the Prime Minister on constitutional matters and in federal, provincial, territorial, and First Nations relations. A communication unit ensures that the government speaks with one voice on major priorities. One also finds a number of administrative services, from office space to archives, information technologies, and switchboard, as well as temporary units for special projects.

The most important responsibility of the Clerk is to pursue any issues requiring the attention of the Prime Minister or critical to the coordination of government. During my mandate, these matters were discussed during a daily briefing session.

Other functions related to the Prime Minister as an elected official in his or her riding and as leader of the governing political party were handled by the Prime Minister's Office (PMO). PMO "exempt staff" are *exempt* from the responsibility to be non-partisan and the controls and constraints imposed on the professional non-partisan public servants. They are partisan and aligned to a political party. They enjoy the confidence of the PM they serve.

February 25, 1994.

Dear Jocelyn,

I am prepared to predict right now that you will be one of the best Secretaries to the Cabinet we have had. I have spent enough time in the job to know what kind of a person it requires, and I have seen enough people in it to know what kind of a person should not be there. Unless I am very wrong, you are exactly right for the role.

It is extremely important for the Prime Minister, for the Cabinet and for the Public Service to have someone in that critical position with good judgment, not interested in power or influence for himself or herself, and dedicated to preserving the highest traditions of government in the public interest. I am confident enough of my own assessment of people to be sure you fill the bill in every respect.

I send you my very best wishes for your success.

Please do not reply – you have too much to do.

Yours sincerely,

Gordon.

Figure 7. Letter from former Clerk Gordon Robertson, 25 February 1994 – congratulations for becoming Clerk.

The theory, and by and large the practice at the time I was Clerk, was that the Prime Minister's Office does not have a distinct legal personality from the Prime Minister (see chapter 3). It frequently makes requests, but it cannot instruct departments or make decisions on behalf of the Prime Minister. It has no authority over the machinery of government or the use of public funds. Its role is of another order of magnitude. It is concerned with the vital importance of politics in a liberal democratic society: this is about getting in power, using power to advance a political agenda while preserving public support, and staying in power. Politics is how people in a democratic society earn the right to use the levers of the state and to make decisions on society's behalf. *Politics is how peaceful societies resolve conflicts and conflicting views and move forward.* It is central to governance and the functioning of public organizations.

I disagree with those who describe the Prime Minister's Office as a central agency. This description has spread into Library of Parliament background research for parliamentarians,[2] and can also be found in academic literature and textbooks. Political staff in the Prime Minister's Office are powerful people and they exercise much influence, but they have no legal authority and therefore no normative power over ministers or the conduct of the public service. One of the duties of the Clerk is to ensure that the roles and responsibilities of PCO and PMO are understood and respected. At times, this is not an easy task.

The Secretary to Cabinet supports the Prime Minister as chair of a Cabinet system of government. It is in this capacity that the PCO calls on departments to advance policy work in support of government priorities and briefs the Prime Minister on emerging issues or matters of interest that will require decisions in due course. The PCO advises the Prime Minister on the design of the Cabinet system of government. It manages and supports a Cabinet system of collective decision making. The precise organization of a Cabinet system reflects the view of the Prime Minister in office. Some Prime Ministers prefer a larger or smaller number of ministers, or more or fewer Cabinet committees. There are no right or wrong ways; the Cabinet system is designed to meet the needs and the preferences of the Prime Minister as chair of a Cabinet system of governance in the context prevailing at the time.

Three units generally support the Prime Minister as chair of the Cabinet system. *Operations* and *Legislation and House Planning* oversee, respectively, the work of Cabinet committees and the legislative agenda in collaboration with the House Leader. The *Priorities and Planning* unit supports Cabinet meetings chaired by the Prime Minister, including ministers' retreats. It is responsible for ensuring that the Prime Minister is on top of key decisions reflected in budgets, Speeches from the Throne, and other key government documents. The PCO focuses on the overall government agenda and helps ministers achieve timely decisions on government priorities over the course of the mandate.

The effective operation of a Cabinet system of responsible government depends on the Prime Minister as chair to forge consensus, on ministers invested with the fullness of their individual ministerial authority but mindful of their collective responsibility, and on non-partisan public servants to support the system. Canada's system of Cabinet government has served Canadians well. In our system, authority and hence responsibility are concentrated in the hands of ministers. This is the foundation of responsible government.

Ministerial responsibility is constitutional and individual while collective responsibility is conventional. Ministerial responsibility is personal in the sense that it is the person of the Minister, not the office, who is responsible.[3] Deputy Ministers have a special role to play in ensuring that their Ministers (and in particular newly appointed Ministers) understand the extent of their authority. This protects Ministers against the pressures that will inevitably be exerted on them from inside and outside government.

The collective responsibility of Ministers for Cabinet decisions helps maintain solidarity and ensures that the ministry retains the confidence of the House. Cabinet is the system used to ensure that the individual responsibility of Ministers is exercised in ways that serve the collective interest of the government. It is the prerogative of the Prime Minister to choose Ministers and invite them to join Cabinet. It is the leadership of the Prime Minister that creates a state of equilibrium where Ministers are encouraged to reach decisions they must defend collectively while respecting their individual responsibility and accountability.

A Cabinet system of government, working at its best, acts as a guardrail against an excessive centralization of power. One of the roles of the Secretary to Cabinet is to protect the authority of Ministers as the cornerstone of our system of government. A Cabinet system of government cannot be conducted through backroom deals. It is designed to ensure transparency and accountability for the exercise of power.

These ideas, among others, shaped my approach to the role of Clerk and Secretary to the Cabinet.

Democratic systems of government are vulnerable. Canada is no exception. A cursory look around the world reveals that democracies are often undone from within rather than by external forces. There are sadly many examples to learn from at this time. Once elected, some governments have used their legitimacy to curtail the power of the judiciary; others have amended their constitution to ensure that the governing leader or party remains in office indefinitely. Election laws may be manipulated. The power of money may stifle citizens' voices. Some illiberal states run elections to build their legitimacy but are democratic in name only.

My view is that in the case of Canada, the greatest vulnerability in our democratic system of responsible government and parliamentary system would be the erosion of ministerial authority as the cornerstone of the system. Ministerial authority can be eroded in subtle and not so subtle ways: usurping a Minister's responsibility by acting as a substitute for the Minister,[4] controlling staffing choices in Ministers' offices,[5] centralizing decisions in a few hands,[6] considering Ministers as subservient to a higher power, concealing information from Ministers,[7] speaking for instead of on behalf of the Prime Minister or Ministers, and more. Vigilance is needed even in the best circumstances.

A Cabinet system of government can always be improved; that is for sure. For instance, I am envious of countries that have been able to engage Cabinet in futures work looking beyond the electoral cycle. In Canada, the fiscal situation dominated the agenda during the thirty-fifth Parliament (1994–7) and as a result crowded out other possibilities. Cabinet retreats were a useful Canadian innovation. They were aimed at providing time away from the office to encourage Ministers to look ahead as a group. This innovation was emulated by several countries over the years, and many have since gone much further. By and large, the democratic parliamentary system of Cabinet government has served Canada well. *The challenge is to ensure that it will continue to do so in the future.*

The most important change to the role of the Clerk was introduced in 1992 as a result of an amendment to what were then sections 40 and 47 of the Public Service Employment Act to provide for the statutory appointment of the Clerk of the Privy Council and Secretary to the Cabinet as *Head of the Public Service.* The responsibility comes with the requirement to submit a report on "the state of the public service" each year to the Prime Minister, who then tables the report before each House.[8] Since 1992, the Clerk has had to balance three roles: Clerk of the Privy Council, Secretary to Cabinet, and Head of the Public Service. This is a difficult balancing act that entails some risks.

The role of Head was first exercised by Paul Tellier, who spearheaded its 1992 introduction and wrote the first annual report prior to its being legally mandated, and then formally by Glen Shortliffe from 1992 through March 1994. I was the first to exercise the role of Head of the Public Service for an extended period of time (1994–9). I believe that no one foresaw how much work the role of Head would entail and how much energy would be needed to lead the public service through an accelerating period of change. The dilemma is that in no circumstances should the role of Head of the Public Service affect the capacity of the incumbent to serve as Clerk and Secretary to Cabinet, and yet the stewardship of the public service requires a considerable commitment of time.

I think it is time to take stock of the experience to date. The state of the public service is a serious matter and so is the role of the Head of the Public Service.

The Prime Minister

The person who occupies the office of Prime Minister of Canada shapes the exercise of power in the Canadian parliamentary system of Cabinet government. I have served under eight Prime Ministers, worked closely with five of them (Mulroney, Campbell, Chrétien, Martin, and [albeit not as PM] Clark), and served directly as Secretary to Cabinet for two Prime Ministers, Brian Mulroney and Jean Chrétien. The Prime Minister is the most influential factor in shaping how the Clerk will fulfil its role.

People do not become Prime Minister by accident, and they come to occupy the office through different paths. Some had many years of experience in government before becoming Prime Minister, and others much less. Some have grown through the ranks of their political party; others are latecomers or changed party affiliation along the way. That said, they display some common characteristics. First, they like power. They like politics and the process of getting in power. They enjoy the exercise of power. They are not overwhelmed by the responsibility of the office. They prefer to stay in power as long as circumstances permit. They trust themselves more than anyone else with the exercise of power.

Second, they have different ideas about what is good for the country, but they display a profound commitment to serving Canada and Canadians. Put simply, the Prime Ministers Canadians have chosen were deserving of serving as Prime Minister for Canada. Some are more partisan than others, some are more pragmatic and others more ideological, but all the PMs I had the honour to serve and see in action had an unquestionable commitment to serving Canada. Canadians have shown wisdom in choosing the Prime Minister the country needed at various times in Canadian history.

Third, one way or the other, the office will change them. The exercise of power changes people and their way of thinking. The longer they are in office, the more vulnerable they become to being hostage to a small coterie of people and losing touch with an ever-changing political landscape.[9]

Prime Minister Chrétien was the Prime Minister Canadians chose to lead the country in the mid-1990s. He brought to the office thirty years of experience as a politician and seventeen years as Minister. He had served in a wide range of Cabinet posts, including (among many others) Minister of Indian Affairs and Northern Development, President of the Treasury Board, Minister of Finance, and Minister of Justice and Attorney General. He was comfortable in the job. Becoming Prime Minister was the achievement of a whole life dedicated to politics. He was at peace with himself and had nothing to prove. His most profound motivation was "to provide Canadians with a good government" and "to be remembered as a competent Prime Minister." These often stated views were the yardsticks giving the measure of his success.

He understood that the country had lived through a number of existential crises and profound changes. He aspired to bring some calm. People had had enough with political, social, and economic re-engineering. They wanted some peace in their life. As he said, "Crises and confrontations were to be avoided or downplayed rather than manufactured or blown out of proportion. I had no interest in creating any more problems than we already faced simply to set myself up as the messiah who was going to solve them."[10]

He was generous with Kim Campbell, the outgoing Prime Minister, as well as with his opponents during the Liberal leadership campaign. He surrounded himself with competent people. Jean Pelletier was one of the best Chiefs of Staff I have seen in action and had the pleasure to work with.

Prime Minister Chrétien operated with a streamlined Cabinet system without a two-tier structure. Matters were going from a Cabinet committee to full Cabinet. He made sure that the incentives encouraged decisions at the Cabinet committee level, leaving time for more important matters to be discussed in full Cabinet. Drawing from his personal experience, he wanted Ministers to be Ministers and gave instructions to his office accordingly. This modus operandi started to change during his third term in office. The exercise of power changes people in office as well as those behind the throne. During his last few years in office, some in the PMO became emboldened to circumvent the Privy Council Office, Deputy Ministers and even Ministers in some circumstances, thus creating risks for the Prime Minister and some confusion about whether they were representing their personal views or the Prime Minister's agenda. He referred to this in his memoir.[11]

The Prime Minister wanted to bring a sense of calm in the country and in government. For my part, I wanted to bring some calm in the public service. Early in our working relationship, we discussed the need to avoid structural changes. The PM shared my view that reorganizations are disruptive. There was too much to do to waste time re-engineering departments. As well, he supported extending the tenure of Deputy Ministers in their departments. During the first mandate, I avoided recommending moving Deputy Heads who had not completed at least two full years in their departments. As a result, after five years the average tenure had significantly increased.

Each Prime Minister has a different modus operandi. There is not one way to be prime minister, but as many ways as there have been incumbents. Some actively work the phone inside and outside government at all times of the day. Some prefer face to face interactions. Some like group sessions for brainstorming, and some are more reflective and need time alone to think through the issues and the avenues open to them. Prime Minister Chrétien was disciplined. He read the documents PCO sent him. He stayed on top of issues and provided clear guidance when he was ready to decide.

The daily work with Prime Minister Chrétien started with a briefing session with me and Chief of Staff Jean Pelletier. No one else attended the daily briefing sessions. These sessions might be short (thirty minutes) or longer (an hour or more) depending on needs and circumstances. I structured my briefings along three timelines: decisions or guidance needed that day, issues moving ahead that would require Cabinet decisions in the near future, and issues requiring a high level of advance work to ensure progress over the coming months, the year, or the mandate. This helped ensure that the agenda for Cabinet meetings reflected the PM's needs. It also helped ensure that the urgent would not displace more important matters.

Jean Pelletier did not interfere with PCO briefings. PCO notes always reached the Prime Minister. I respected and did not intervene in discussions of a more political nature between Jean Pelletier and the Prime Minister. Politics is not separate from public administration – in fact, public administration is enabled by politics. Things run smoothly and mistakes are avoided when people understand and are respectful of each other's role. As Robertson famously said, "The Prime Minister's Office is partisan, politically oriented, yet operationally sensitive. The Privy Council Office is non-partisan, operationally oriented yet politically sensitive."[12]

Figure 8. Photograph of the first day of work as Clerk of the Privy Council, 28 March 1994, alongside and signed by the Right Hon. Jean Chrétien.

A key role of the Prime Minister is to set an agenda for governing the country. This requires a keen political judgment to reconcile aspirations for a better future and the actions needed in the here and now.

A governing agenda is different from a political platform. Both play important but distinct roles. Too much rigidity in interpreting and implementing a political platform stifles the capacity to adapt to changing circumstances and to govern effectively. A political platform is crafted by a political party in a more or less inclusive way. It is an instrument for shaping and building a public consensus around the most important ideas that a political party will present to the population in order to be elected. It shapes party politics, contributes to public education and enrolment, encourages civic engagement, and more.[13] Politics is how peaceful societies resolve conflicting ideas.[14]

Once in office, the government must shape a *governing agenda for all Canadians*. One of the most important responsibilities of the Prime Minister is to rally people elected under a political banner and a political platform that may contain hundreds of ideas to coalesce around a few overarching ideas that will dominate the governing agenda over the mandate. This is a delicate operation that plays a key role in ensuring the success of the government in office. A political platform is directional and speaks to what a party stands for. A governing agenda is about the choices needed in the here and now to fulfil aspirations for a better future. The challenge for government is to be true to the philosophy of a political platform without being hostage to the details or the timing of specific initiatives.[15]

The Liberal platform, "Creating Opportunity," provided a good example of the difference between a platform and a governing agenda. The "red book" was a very detailed document. In 112 pages, it covered the whole spectrum of Liberal ideas at the time about economics, investing in people, innovation, sustainable development, health, parliamentary reform, Aboriginal people, and foreign policies. The preoccupation with deficit and debt is found under "Track Two."[16] The proposed approach was to reduce the deficit through spending cuts: "expenditure reductions will be achieved by cancelling unnecessary programs, streamlining processes, and eliminating duplication."[17] The "Liberal government would seek to reduce the federal deficit to 3 percent of gross domestic product by the end of its third year in office."[18]

Once a government is in office, the transition to shaping a governing agenda begins.[19] The Speech from the Throne on 18 January 1994 did not signal an overarching set of priorities. More or less, everything mentioned in the "red book" was on the table. This was also the case for the first budget tabled on 22 February. It announced multiple policy "reviews": a new strategy for innovation, a new strategy for small business, a review to build a responsible social security system, a review of Canada's defence policy,[20] and a departmental spending review.[21] A strategic governing agenda had not yet taken shape.

This would change in the aftermath of the 1994 Budget. Before the end of 1995, the Prime Minister would set his government on a clear path. *Regaining Canada's fiscal sovereignty* would come to dominate the government agenda until the end of its first term in office. This phase would be followed by re-investments along the philosophical lines of the Liberal platform. A governing agenda and a governing strategy were emerging.

The Circumstances

In March 1994, as I stepped into the job as Clerk, the public service was in difficulty and the executive cadre was frail. By then, the public service had been "reviewed" and studied to death by internal and external task forces. The announcement of half a dozen new "reviews" as well as the usual cuts, staffing freezes, and salary cuts was not warmly received, to say the least.

Each reform effort was piling up on top of the preceding ones without consideration for how the pieces might fit together. The cumulative effect was debilitating. "Between 1984 and 1993, the [government of Canada] made a total of *22 budget cuts*, each more difficult than the previous and each more demoralising for the Public Service."[22] There were years of salary freeze, staffing freeze, and salary rollback. The elimination of performance pay that had been funded by a reduction of employees' salary was adding insult to injury. The 1993 reorganization led to further cuts and a delayering exercise to further reduce the number of executives. This accentuated the "tenuousness of the executive group" as nine Deputy Minister and fifty-three ADM positions were cut, as well as a number of positions in policy branches.[23]

Would anyone be surprised that, in the circumstances, morale was low in the public service of Canada? What was especially dispiriting was that in spite of all the effort, there was no end in sight.

For a short while, it was possible to hope that the cuts would end. In 1987–8, the government of Canada achieved a small operating surplus; for the first time in twelve years, it did not borrow to cover its operating costs. The budgetary deficit had been reduced from 8.3 per cent of GDP in 1984–5 to 5.2 per cent.[24] But as a recession took hold in 1991–2, much of the progress that was painfully achieved over many years was wiped out, leading to yet more cuts and more stringent measures.

The reality was that from 1978 onward, the deficit had become chronic. That meant that public debt charges, rather than the cost of the public service, were the most crucial factor in the growth of the deficit.[25] No amount of cuts in the public service would solve this problem. It was a myth or a cynical lie to pretend that "efficiency gains" and "productivity improvements" in the public service could eliminate a fiscal deficit of the scale Canada was facing at the time. The Canadian experience and that of other countries told us otherwise. The public service could not bear the burden of achieving a healthy fiscal balance alone.

If governing is a process of invention to generate solutions to the problems that cannot be solved without government interventions … then this was a most propitious time for invention. The status quo was unsustainable and unaffordable. The times called for a different way of thinking, a different approach to problem solving, and a different approach to decision making.

The question was, would Canada be up to the challenge?

7 Regaining Canada's Fiscal Sovereignty

I have previously mentioned that the first budget of the Chrétien government in February 1994 was not well received. The debt had reached 67 per cent of GDP. Servicing the debt consumed 35 per cent of revenues. The deficit was 5.3 per cent of GDP, 3 percentage points lower than when Prime Minister Mulroney took office in 1984 but much higher than other developed countries at the time.

Canadians' concern for the deficit was at an all-time high and was even outpacing concern for job creation. The government proposed to set a deficit target of 3 per cent of GDP. This would be achieved by relying on the same approach that had been used for the last fifteen years: a mix of expenditure reduction and an extension of salary freezes and of pay increments within grade. This time around, Canada's fiscal measures were losing credibility with the financial market. The country now had the second highest debt-to-GDP ratio among the G7 countries, after Italy.

The budget did not go over well with public servants either. It was more of the same: more cuts, no external recruitment, no upward or lateral mobility, and a constant erosion of the quality of public services. Nobody wanted to eliminate the deficit more than the people of the public service of Canada, and no one was more convinced that across-the-board cuts were not the way to go. They had been tried repeatedly and had failed repeatedly. Insanity is to do things the same way repeatedly and expect a different result. There had been twenty-two unsuccessful expenditure reduction exercises. There was no reason to believe that one more round of cuts would yield anything but more pain. Multiple "policy reviews" had been announced in the 1994 budget; this would generate a flurry of activities, but the view of senior public servants was that it was unlikely to bring the country out of its predicament. It was too slow, too little, too late.

A Different Way

The time had come for a different approach. Marcel Massé was the President of the Privy Council and the Minister responsible for Public Service Renewal. He had previously served as Deputy Minister and briefly as Clerk, and, like me, he had managed his fair share of expenditure reduction exercises. We were both convinced that across-the-board-cuts were not the approach to take.

The time had come to make decisions: what programs and services were needed going forward? What programs and services should end? These are political decisions that go to the heart of the role of government in society. From there, it would be possible to re-engineer systems, reduce overhead, or streamline organizations. Form should follow purpose, not the reverse. We had been on the opposite path for years; a major turnaround was needed.

The challenge was not to figure out what to cut, but *what to preserve for the future*. It was preferable to abandon some programs and missions entirely rather than further weaken the capacity of the public service in every domain of activity. Better to do less but do it well than to pursue the never-ending agony through a thousand cuts the public service had been subjected to.

Another consideration was that it is possible to terminate programs with pride. There is no pride in attrition and salary freezes. There are many legitimate reasons to end public programs and services. For instance, they may have fulfilled their intended purpose, society may have grown beyond the initial needs, the problems may have been solved, or some agents in society may be better positioned to take on the responsibility. Government needs to adapt; this cannot be achieved by announcing new programs and services without freeing itself of prior responsibilities. An approach focused on the role of government in the future could provide departments with an opportunity for renewal.

From a managerial perspective, ending programs is preferable to attrition. When a program ends, all employees irrespective of levels or of their individual performance are "affected employees" and become entitled to special assistance measures. Since the approach is targeted, it is possible to work with affected employees, leaving others to go about their work in the normal way. There is no stigma associated with the decision to end a program, no reverse order of merit, and no blame for poor performance.

The public service had learned from experience that attrition is one of the worst ways to reduce spending. It is unpredictable. It leaves holes in mission-critical areas with limited possibilities for course corrections. Staffing freezes deprive public organizations of the skills they need to renew themselves and to keep pace with innovative technologies and practices. Salary freezes create resentment and inversions of salary scales between groups. *The public service had learned from experience what did not work and why.* The public service needed to propose a better way.[1]

I briefed Marcel Massé about my experience at Transport Canada and explained how an approach based on the role of the department in the future had generated ambitious results. We worked together for a few weeks to design an approach that would engage every department in repositioning the role of the government of Canada within the overall fiscal parameters set by the Prime Minister. The approach drew heavily from our knowledge of the public service and our experience as senior public servants. By the time we briefed the Prime Minister, the concept of a *Program Review* had taken shape.

Ministers and Deputy Ministers would be given a free hand and a list of questions to guide their reviews.[2] They would not be given targets for as long as possible. Across-the-board cuts would be explicitly discouraged. It was not about doing more with less. It was about making choices for the future. The half-dozen policy reviews announced in 1994 would be rolled back into the Program Review exercise or sidelined. A consolidated and integrated approach was needed.

Three committees would review and vet departmental proposals. The system was designed to protect those who would bring forward ambitious ideas. First, a Deputy Ministers' Committee that I chaired would provide professional oversight and a challenge function. Second, a Ministerial Committee chaired by Marcel Massé would bring political oversight and encourage ministers to be ambitious. Third, Cabinet retreats chaired by the Prime Minister would consolidate the results, ensure cabinet solidarity, and make sure of the overall balance and fairness of the effort across sectors and regions.

A publication entitled *Program Review: The Government of Canada's Experience Eliminating the Deficit*, published in 2009, has documented the approach and tracked the fiscal results in detail. There is no need to expand further on this here. Briefly, the deficit was eliminated in three years, and program spending was reduced from 16.8 per cent of GDP in 1993 to 12.1 per cent of GDP in 1999.[3] The government of Canada recorded unprecedented surpluses for twelve years that allowed significant investments in health, education, child poverty alleviation, and more.

The Prime Minister readily embraced the approach. He immediately understood that there was nothing to lose by trying it. If successful, it would yield better results than what could be achieved through general cuts, and the measures would enjoy a higher degree of support by ministers and departments. If it failed, there would be time to revert to the traditional approach of cuts across the board. The Prime Minister improved the proposed approach by appointing ministers who had expressed serious reservations to serve on the ministerial committee. This was wise. His argument was that unless the process convinced the most reluctant ministers, there would be little chance to convince caucus members and Canadians.[4]

The approach was unprecedented. If it worked, the approach was transformative rather than incremental. It was turning a closed budget process into a collective effort to reposition the role of the government of Canada in society for the future. Program Review was opening the possibility to do less but to do it better rather than the perennial call for doing more with less. Not everyone was convinced. The Department of Finance was reluctant. They had little confidence that this approach could work, and indeed, there was no guarantee that it would. Through the whole process, they stood ready to roll out "target cuts" to departments in the traditional fashion.

There are reasons why Departments of Finance, in Canada and elsewhere, tend to rely on target cuts. One reason is that they have a good knowledge of the overall fiscal situation but limited knowledge of programs. In the Canadian context, Treasury Board Secretariat (TBS), which has the responsibility for main and supplementary estimates, has a more detailed knowledge of government programs than the Department of Finance. As a management board, it also has a better knowledge of the challenges departments are facing in practice. During the exercise, we found that the Treasury Board Secretariat had better data about program costs. Despite the discrepancies, it was decided to use Finance numbers to avoid unnecessary tensions.[5]

Central agencies do not have the granularity of information needed to identify programs and services misaligned with a changing Canadian landscape. This knowledge rests with departments. As a result, the tendency has been to give departments target cuts, leaving them to figure out what to do. Setting a broad direction, like reducing the deficit to 3 per cent of GDP in three years, is helpful because it conveys a sense of the magnitude of the effort needed. On the other hand, giving departments a target – be it 3, 5, or 15 per cent – prevents them from coming forward with ambitious ideas. *Target cuts limit the space of possibility for reinvention and constrain the range of options open to departments.* For instance, no Deputy Minister could justify, to their employees, union representatives, or users of their services, going beyond what is asked of them even if it is possible and even desirable. Taking an example I know well, the Deputy Minister of Transport could not put forward a proposal that would re-engineer the department from twenty thousand employees to five thousand by releasing thousands of kilometres of rail surplus to need, commercializing air traffic control by putting airlines and unions in charge, renting airports through long-term leases, and transferring the Coast Guard to another department if the Department of Transport had been asked to cut spending by 15 per cent. The pressure to keep existing programs and services by doing more with less would be unbearable.

There are good reasons why ministers find it difficult to close a program, shut down a military base, or decommission a harbour even when it is demonstrated that the costs far exceed the benefits for society. Behind every program and service, behind every word in every law, there are beneficiaries that will fight to preserve existing benefits. Public goods and services cannot be managed like private goods, where market value is a driver of change. In a public sector setting, there is a need to find ways to *make what is desirable feasible in the court of public opinion.* What cannot be done by a department individually may become feasible as part of a government-wide effort.

Program Review was creating the conditions for departments to shed responsibilities in order to adapt to a changing fiscal, economic, social, and political landscape. A government-wide approach engaging the collective responsibility of ministers was shifting the focus from specific cuts to the overall balance and fairness of an effort aimed at serving the needs of Canadians in the future. Program Review was creating the conditions to shut down programs with dignity, not because they were underperforming or were wanting but because they had fulfilled their public purpose.

In May 1994, there was no assurance that this approach would work, but there was nothing to lose. Marcel Massé had to convince his colleagues to come forward with ambitious proposals. I had to convince Deputy Ministers and public servants that this was an opportunity to put an end to death by a thousand cuts. The Minister of Finance had to manage the politics surrounding this effort by preparing the ground so that the proposals would be well received by the financial market. He needed to bring caucus on board and to encourage ministers to do more through countless one-on-one meetings. He opened the budget process and engaged parliamentarians like never before. The Prime Minister had to maintain ministerial solidarity, ensure that no one would be exempted, and make sure that there would be no end run.

I delivered my first speech as Clerk to the public service on 11 May 1994, at the annual conference of the Association of Professional Executives of the Public Service of Canada (APEX), two months after my appointment on 28 March. I invited public sector leaders to be part of a collective effort to align the role of government in society and the fiscal capacity of Canadians, and to work collectively in "preparing for the future and leaving the institution better than we found it."[6]

A few days later, on 18 May, Program Review was officially launched. The President of the Privy Council and Chair of the Cabinet Committee on Program Review wrote to his colleagues to outline the approach and the guiding principles. The same day, I called a meeting of Deputy Ministers to discuss what was expected of them. Departments had three months to develop their plans and submit them to the Program Review Secretariat by 31 August 1994. Until the end of 1994, I met with departments as often as I could and answered Deputy Ministers' calls to speak to their employees. The speeches we have collected from this period were aimed at encouraging departments to seize the opportunity for making tough choices, rethinking the role of their departments in contemporary terms, and avoiding across-the-board cuts. On 22–3 June, a Deputy Ministers' retreat was used to ensure that departments were ready to present their proposals to the Steering Committee of Deputy Ministers for review.[7]

The Privy Council Office, Finance, Treasury Board, and Public Service Commission were the first to be invited to appear in front of the DM committee I chaired. This was deliberate. As Chair, I signalled that the committee was expecting central agencies to set an example. I indicated that the committee would not review a proposal representing less than a 15 per cent reduction of their total budget. This was not a target, but a floor. Central agencies tend to exempt themselves from the demands they put on departments, arguing that they are "a special case." It could not be so this time around. PCO, FIN, TBS, and PSC rose to the challenge. The Office of the Auditor General protested. They argued that they should be exempted, to no avail. Public servants were waiting to see if they should take the Program Review exercise seriously; a clear signal had been sent.

The Program Review Secretariat, headed by Suzanne Hurtubise, played a key role in coordinating the work across departments and ensuring a seamless transition between the DM committee, the ministerial committee, and Cabinet. It was decided that the assessment notes and the recommendation of the DM committee about the departmental proposals would be circulated to members of the Cabinet Committee, not just the Chair. The process needed to be open and transparent from the start. The Deputy Secretary, Mrs. Hurtubise, would present the findings of the DM committee to ministers at the next Ministerial Committee meeting. This was a challenging role for an official. However, it allowed ministers to distance themselves from their departmental proposals and to signal if improvements were possible in light of the comments from their colleagues. A skilful Chair, Marcel Massé, helped ensure that officials would not become the targets of ministers' frustration.

Marcel Massé and I knew from the start that, one day, some ministers would try to be exempted and appeal to the Prime Minister. We also knew that if they were successful, it would put the whole effort in jeopardy. That day came. The DM committee had reviewed a particular department proposal. The assessment note was that the proposal was not sufficiently ambitious, and that more work was needed before sending it to the Ministerial Committee. The Minister brought the matter to full Cabinet. It was a defining moment. The Prime Minister listened to the arguments of the Minister and concluded, "If the task is too difficult for you, let me know. I will get it done for you." Case closed. Both Chrétien and Martin have talked about this moment in their memoirs.[8]

The ministerial retreat in October 1994 provided ministers, for the first time, with a full update on the scale of the efforts under way.[9] It was ambitious. I used the opportunity of a speech at the Public Policy Forum to reiterate the importance of avoiding across-the-board cuts.[10] A speech at the ADM forum on

30 November signalled that Program Review was now entering a new phase, shifting from a review of departmental proposals to a government-wide assessment of the overall balance of the reform agenda.[11] This was a delicate operation and an important moment. In order to deserve public support, the proposed measures had to pass a fairness test. They needed to be and to be seen to be fair by sectors, regions, income levels, etc.

Closing in on the end of 1994, it was increasingly difficult to resist the pressure to give departmental fiscal targets. Marcel Massé and I had held the line as long as we could. At least, by then, it was possible to put out targets aligned with what departments were able to achieve. As the deadline to finalize the budget approached, the pressure to do more was unrelenting. The peso crisis in December 1994 triggered more nervousness.[12] Late in the game, the Department of Human Resources Development was asked to do more than initially envisaged and more than they were able to handle. Given more time, I believe that the department would have been able to bring forward reforms that would have withstood public scrutiny. Mistakes were made that had to be corrected, and some measures were later reversed.

The Prime Minister provided constant support to the Minister of Finance and the Minister responsible for Program Review. He was instrumental in preventing serious mistakes that could have undermined public support, most notably by preventing premature changes to the Old Age Security (OAS) program and by resisting pressure from his own office to overturn some decisions. This was mentioned by Chrétien and Martin in their memoirs.[13]

In Praise of a Cabinet System of Government

I believe that some of the lessons of Program Review remain relevant today. It showed the power of engaging Cabinet as a whole in shaping an ambitious agenda, the importance of building on the knowledge that resides in departments, and the importance of bringing political leaders and professional leaders together in a joint effort for collective problem solving.

Program Review was designed as a collective decision-making process. This starts with questions, rather than targets and answers. It requires letting go of some degree of control, trusting that a collective effort may generate better results than anyone could achieve on their own.

It was hard for ministers, hard for officials, and challenging for people at the centre of the process. Through it all, the relationship between the Deputy Minister of Finance, the Secretary to the Treasury Board, and the Clerk was exemplary. I could not have been part of a better team. There could be differences of views between David Dodge (FIN), Robert Giroux (TBS), and me (PCO), but the shared goal was never in doubt. To this day, I have only praise and admiration for my colleagues. We earned our salt!

Successful public policies require the public service to play a key role at every stage even though its role is less visible to the public. *A successful public policy is one that, once implemented, achieves the desired policy outcomes while minimizing the disruptions, unintended consequences, and costs for society.*[14] Policy ideas, public policy decisions, and policy implementation are not separate from each other. They are part of a process of invention that converts ideas into a reality that citizens experience collectively as members of society.[15]

Implementation is the most critical phase of a policy-making process. It reveals the true value of policy choices that were made.[16] A public policy may fail for many reasons. It may be a bad idea to start with. It may not adequately account for the context where a solution is supposed to take root. It may exceed the institutional capacity to make it happen. By all accounts, Program Review was successful. It achieved the desired outcome, regaining the fiscal sovereignty of Canada. The government of Canada recorded surpluses for the following twelve years; Canada had the capacity to invest in the future of its choice.

In Praise of Public Servants

The fact that Program Review was achieved peacefully is an achievement that deserves to be celebrated. Just a few years prior, in September 1991, Canada had experienced its largest federal public service strike in history, owing to a round of salary freezes. This time, public servants remained supportive while forty-five thousand employees were directly affected and everybody else was indirectly affected. *This did not happen by accident.*

The Secretary to the Treasury Board, both Robert Giroux and later Peter Harder, maintained open channels of communication with the unions the whole time. I sought and obtained Cabinet approval for extraordinary measures to assist affected employees. The Early Retirement Incentive Program and the Early Departure Incentive were unprecedented measures at the time. The unions helped with the redeployment of affected employees who aspired to pursue their careers in the public service. Deputy Ministers created units dedicated to assisting employees. The Public Service Commission played a key role in supporting those employees most directly affected.

Collective successes deserve to be celebrated as collective achievements, and the contributions of all deserve to be recognized. On 27 February 1995 the Minister of Finance tabled a budget that outlined the "largest set of actions in any Canadian budget since demobilization after the Second World War."[17] Ministers had reasons to be proud of this achievement. It would not have been possible without the staying power of the Prime Minister, the resolve of the Minister of Finance, the steady hand of the Minister responsible for Program Review, and the courage of ministers across all departments.

It would also not have been possible without the contribution of the public service and the ideas put forward by public servants. However, for the public service, it was far from over. Federal public sector employment went from 231,000 in 1994 to 186,000 in 1999 when transfers to other employers are included. The heavy lifting for the public service and for public service leaders was just beginning. There was a need to manage downsizing *and* to preserve the capacity of the public service to fulfil its mission in the future. To downsize on an unprecedented scale *and* prevent the erosion of critical functions, including the public policy capacity that is the trademark of a professional non-partisan public service. To eliminate programs and services *and* improve services to Canadians using modern technologies wherever possible. To generate hope for a better future *and* restore pride in a profession like no others. To rejuvenate the public service *and* repair the damage done by years of cuts, staffing freezes, and salary stagnation.

The goal of reducing the deficit to 3 per cent of GDP never meant much for public servants. The public service wanted nothing less than to get the deficit eliminated once and for all. By the end of 1995, it was possible to believe that it would be done if the government stayed the course and resisted the temptation to spend the dividend prematurely. By the end of 1996, the government announced that a balanced budget was in sight. By the end of 1997, it was a reality.

The public service initiatives launched in 1995, 1996, and 1997 were designed to see the public service through a disruptive period. They were launched for defensive and proactive reasons. Defensive, to prevent the risk of damaging the core functions of a professional non-partisan public service. Proactive, by taking actions to build the capacity of the public service to fulfil its mission in the future. This is the story behind initiatives such as the Policy Research Initiative, Citizens First, and La Relève.

The challenge in early 1995 for the public service was to stay the course. Time was the enemy of such a vast and comprehensive package of reforms. But staying the course would not be so easy. Canada was about to face another existential crisis.

8 The 1995 Referendum

National unity has been a central concern for the management of the Canadian federation since its inception and it will continue to be so in the future. National unity results from multiple tangible and intangible factors. It contributes to a sense of togetherness, belonging, and solidarity. It engenders optimism for the future and a sense of common purpose. A focus on the future and a sense of shared destiny among fellow citizens help to transcend differences and encourage cooperation. Some countries went to war over unity and identity issues including ethnicity, religion, political beliefs, or social status. Canadians debate about the best way forward, but over the years they have overwhelmingly managed to shape a course peacefully, democratically, and legally. While there have been exceptions, their rarity and the shock with which they have been received only underscore Canadians' dedication to resolving these differences through peaceful, democratic processes.

Canada has worked hard to reconcile conflicting ideas about the future and conflicting views about individual and collective rights, but as a country, Canada has managed to set a path that blends a concern for democracy, solidarity, and prosperity. Canadians enjoy a high standard of living and the peaceful enjoyment of life, a rare achievement at the global scale. There is much to praise about Canada's past achievements and Canadians' commitment to peace, order, and good government.

Unity – *the collective capacity and the collective will of citizens to build and share a better future together* – is an ambitious and elusive goal. It is never fully achieved and is forever in the making. As the context and the forces at play are constantly changing, so are the actions needed to ensure cohesion and the capacity to surmount collective challenges. There are important lessons to learn from each chapter of Canadian history so that the past may inspire a better future. In 1995, a challenging chain of events tested the will of Canada and Canadians to address issues through legal and constitutional means.

The Context

As early as 1993, another unity crisis was looming. The federal election of 1993 nearly obliterated the Progressive Conservative party. The Bloc Québécois became the official opposition with fifty-four seats in the House of Commons, representing 49 per cent of the popular vote in Quebec.[1] The Bloc had successfully channelled disaffected Quebec voters. The Reform Party took fifty-two seats, most of them west of Manitoba. It had successfully channelled voters who could not recognize themselves in the Conservative or Liberal parties. Regional alienation was on the rise again.

Canadians wanted "change" after nine years under the Conservative government of Prime Minister Mulroney. Aspiration for change is a powerful driver, but it is often directionless. It may be a reaction to recent events rather than an expression of hope for a different future. As such, it may be channelled in very different and even contradictory directions.

When Prime Minister Chrétien was elected in 1993, he was a thirty-year veteran of the House. He commanded a sizeable majority and faced a divided opposition. He sensed that Canadians were suffering from constitutional fatigue. The country was fractured; the economy was in bad shape and Canadians were increasingly anxious about it. He wanted to focus on providing Canadians with a good government, addressing the challenges of a weak economy, rising unemployment, and a mounting debt crisis.

There were serious concerns at the time that addressing the deteriorating fiscal situation would exacerbate federal-provincial tensions. The fear was that it might erode the social safety net Canada had built over the years by reducing spending for programs such as pension, health, education, and social services. However, the efforts aimed at repositioning the role of the government in a fiscally responsible way did not plant the seeds of disunity some expected. In fact, they contributed to reducing federal-provincial overlap and duplication and helped ensure that social programs would be sustainable in the future. By the end of 1995, Canada was quickly regaining the capacity to invest in the future, and Canadians would soon reap the benefits of a balanced budget.

This is a lesson worth remembering. Future governments of Canada would be well advised to maintain a healthy financial situation to resist the centrifugal forces that characterize the Canadian federation. In retrospect, it was fortunate that most of the difficult decisions around Program Review were made in the early part of 1995. Without them, Canada would have been more vulnerable, and the Canadian dollar would have experienced more volatility in the context of a looming national unity crisis.

In 1991–2, Paul Tellier, the then Clerk, asked me to serve as Associate and then Secretary to Cabinet for federal-provincial relations to take on some of the load for the constitutional negotiations that would ultimately lead to the

Charlottetown Accord. In 1994, I took a similar approach. Ronald Bilodeau was appointed Deputy Minister for Intergovernmental Affairs on 9 May 1994, reporting to Minister Marcel Massé, who was cumulating the responsibilities for Intergovernmental Affairs, Privy Council Office, and Public Service Renewal. With a dedicated Minister and Deputy Minister, Intergovernmental Affairs operated with a high degree of autonomy while enjoying the support of the Privy Council Office. Ronald Bilodeau was a seasoned Deputy Minister. He enjoyed the confidence of the Prime Minister, and he helped ensure a close collaboration with Jean Pelletier, the PM's Chief of Staff. These arrangements allowed me to stay focused on ensuring the successful implementation of Program Review decisions and the support of the public service to bring about the desired policy outcomes without delay or slippage.

The government of Canada remained focused on economic recovery and balancing the budget from the time of the election in November 1993 till well into the summer of 1995.[2] Meanwhile, the Parti Québécois (PQ), under the leadership of Jacques Parizeau, was consolidating its position. Many factors contributed to the return of the Parti Québécois to power in Quebec in 1994, among them the failure of Meech Lake, the failure of the Charlottetown Accord, and the rise of the Bloc Québécois at the federal level.

In retrospect, I think it is fair to say that, on balance, constitutional negotiations have generated favourable conditions for the rise of the sovereigntist movement in Quebec. On 26 September 1994, the Parti Québécois became the government of Quebec and Jacques Parizeau the Premier. There was now a sovereigntist party in Ottawa as official opposition and a sovereigntist party governing Quebec. The conditions were in place for national unity issues to get centre stage once more.

The 1994 PQ platform opened by promising a referendum,[3] and Mr. Parizeau spoke of holding one in 1995.[4] That said, the campaign focused on "Gouverner autrement." Jean François Lisée noted that the election was not "un vote pour la souveraineté."[5] On 6 December 1994, the government of Premier Jacques Parizeau tabled a draft Bill 1 on *Quebec sovereignty:* La *Loi sur la souveraineté du Québec.* The draft bill announced that the people of Quebec would soon be invited to participate in a referendum on sovereignty at a date to be determined.

Ronald Bilodeau expanded the activities of his team in view of an upcoming referendum. This included monitoring and tracking political declarations and media coverage, as well as serving as liaison between the Minister of Intergovernmental Affairs, Quebec Ministers, and Jean Pelletier. Two Assistant Deputy Ministers, Howard Balloch and Marc Lafrenière, were added to his team.

The pre-referendum campaign began immediately in Quebec. Starting in February 1995, fifteen regional commissions criss-crossed the province inviting people to participate in improving Bill 1. As long as the date of the referendum was not set, the government of Premier Parizeau was free to use government resources to prepare the way for a successful referendum. These efforts included a communication campaign to build support for sovereignty. Per Quebec's treasury board, the regional commissions spent well over budget.[6] This was not illegal, though questionable. Daniel Johnson, the leader of the Liberal party in the Quebec legislative assembly, challenged the approach repeatedly in the legislative assembly, calling the commissions an "effort de propagande du gouvernement."[7] The government of Canada eventually used a similar approach by using federal organizations to promote Canada, thus circumventing the spirit but not the letter of the Quebec referendum legislation. Both sides blamed each other for taking similar actions. The *not illegal but questionable actions* included funding by the PQ government for sixteen reports by the National Institute of Scientific Research (INRS) on diverse aspects of a proposed treaty to be presented to the government of Canada in the event of a successful referendum. Funding provided by the government of Canada to the Conseil de l'Unité nationale or Option Canada gave rise to similar questions.

Both sides used similar campaigning approaches, including frequent opinion surveys and polling; advertising through brochures, posters, billboards, and television; and rallies and events. Campaigning activities may play an important role in raising public awareness, but they are sometimes credited with a power they do not have. Personally, I think that the advertising activities leading up to the referendum of 1995 played a marginal role; the important decisions were of a different nature.

The Protagonists

Under the Quebec referendum legislation, the two main protagonists were the leaders of the Yes and No coalitions. In the context of the 1995 referendum, the leader of the coalition in favour of the Canadian federation was Daniel Johnson, the leader of the Liberal party in the Quebec legislative assembly.

There is an element of unreality to this situation. According to this view, all other voices must be silenced and rolled under the authority of the leader of the opposition in the Québec legislative assembly. The one point about which Daniel Johnson and Jacques Parizeau agreed was that the matter of Quebec's future was for Quebecers alone.

The government of Canada did not question this view in the context of the 1980 referendum, and it remained unchallenged in the period leading up to the 1995 referendum. Preston Manning and Stephen Harper gave voice to this concern in the House of Commons; Manning would later say in his memoir that "it was not just the future of Quebec that was being decided by the Quebec referendum but the future of all of Canada, and Canadians in the rest of Canada wanted a say."[8] Their voices were not heard.

In reality, the two main protagonists were the Premier of Quebec as leader for Quebec independence and the Prime Minister of Canada. Only the Prime Minister of Canada can speak for Canada under the existing constitutional order. A Prime Minister may voluntarily decide to operate under the Quebec referendum legislation, but this in no way diminishes his or her responsibility to defend Canada's constitutional order in all circumstances. This question of whether the Prime Minister of Canada should feel constrained by provincial legislation deserves more attention than it has received to date. Personally, I do not think that the responsibility of the Prime Minister of Canada can be restrained by provincial legislation on matters that affect the existence of Canada or that a Prime Minister of Canada could be absolved of the responsibilities of the office by a provincial edict. Years later, the Supreme Court would shed some light on the role of the government of Canada in the context of a referendum on sovereignty, although this specific question has not been addressed, nor was this the purpose of the reference to the Supreme Court. Sooner or later the question will need to be addressed. The potential for another referendum in Quebec or in other provinces remains only too real.

For years, public opinion surveys in Quebec had projected the same picture. The support for sovereignty did not rally a majority of Quebecers. Faced with a choice between sovereignty and the Canadian federation as it was known, a majority of the people of Quebec favoured Canada. At the same time, for years, surveys had revealed a desire for change and recognition. The only two options likely to rally majority support at the time were sovereignty with an economic association with Canada or a renewed federalism.

In the course of the 1995 referendum campaign, the two main protagonists were about to undertake significant course corrections to broaden support for their options.

The Course Correction of Premier Jacques Parizeau

The Premier had a clear objective: the sovereignty of Quebec as a distinct country from Canada. He committed his life to this mission. There was no ambiguity about his position and his actions were consistent with this goal. Sovereignty-association was not the goal he was pursuing. He was not the man of the "beau risque." He was not interested in constitutional negotiations or the renewal of the Canadian federation. His agenda was sovereignty. An association with Canada was not a pre-condition or a necessary condition for Quebec independence.

The Premier made some key decisions to increase the appeal of the sovereignty option he was defending. First, he gave space to the idea of association without changing the nature of the referendum question on sovereignty. In the context of the regional commission report, on 19 April, the Premier signalled for the first time that the door was not closed to making a partnership offer to the government of Canada. “You are asking us to clearly indicate that Quebec accession to sovereignty does not exclude forms of political union that would be mutually advantageous to Quebec and Canada,”[9] he said, adding that “such propositions for common institutions must obtain the agreement of our Canadian partners” but that “it should not stop us from extending a hand in good faith and in a constructive way.”[10] The Premier made sure that a signal for openness would not change the nature of the referendum question: a yes was a vote for the sovereignty of Quebec as a separate country.

The Premier expanded the coalition for sovereignty with the Bloc Québécois (BQ), then the official opposition in the House of Commons, and l’Action Démocratique du Québec (ADQ) in the Quebec legislative assembly. The coalition worked out a tripartite agreement ratified on 12 June, included as an annex to Bill 1. Several elements were reflected in the preamble of the final version of the bill on Quebec sovereignty without affecting the key elements.

The Premier appointed Lucien Bouchard as chief negotiator on 7 October. This, according to several observers, *“changed everything.”*[11] Lucien Bouchard’s view was that a successful referendum would generate the inevitable conditions for a partnership agreement with the rest of Canada. An independent Quebec could keep the Canadian currency, preserve the pre-existing borders, join NAFTA, and achieve international recognition. Canada would have no choice but to agree. Lucien Bouchard gave credibility to the idea that some form of partnership was inevitable.

By the terms of the accord between the three leaders, “negotiations will not exceed one year, unless the National Assembly decides otherwise,” and “if the negotiations prove to be fruitless, the National Assembly will be empowered to declare the sovereignty of Québec without further delay.”[12] As Robert Wright would later summarize the situation, *“Quebec would become sovereign within a year of a Yes victory, with or without a new deal with Canada.”* Premier Parizeau had all the levers and the final say. The course correction he initiated was successful.[13]

On 18 October, the *Toronto Star/La Presse* published a survey showing the Yes and No sides virtually equal. Prime Minister Chrétien recalls in his memoir that the “No side was in freefall.”[14] Nothing had changed materially, but perceptions had changed, and therefore everything had changed.

The Course Correction of Prime Minister Jean Chrétien

Jean Chrétien is an ardent defender of Canada. He is proud of the achievements of generations of Canadians in building, against all odds, a country worthy of respect and a source of inspiration for many around the world. He dedicated his life to building a better Canada by addressing problems Canadians were facing in every department where he was called upon to serve, and now as Prime Minister.

Canada had demonstrated its capacity to evolve and adapt to changing circumstances to serve the interest of Canadians. Canada deserved to be defended on merit. Prime Minister Chrétien would not make promises he could not keep. He would not promise another round of constitutional negotiations. For him, Canada can grow, prosper, and adapt within the existing constitutional order. His option is Canada and Canada includes Quebec. He was confident that faced with a clear question, Quebecers would choose Canada.

On 6 September the final version of Bill 1 on Quebec sovereignty was tabled in the legislative assembly.[15] The referendum writs were released on 1 October; the date for the referendum had finally been set. The vote would take place on 30 October 1995.

Prime Minister Chrétien could not expect to grow a coalition across the floor in the House of Commons. In fact, he was challenged daily by the leader of the Reform party and the leader of the Bloc Québécois, the latter insisting that the Prime Minister confirm the exclusive right of Quebecers to decide the future of Canada, the former trying to force the PM to clarify the rules of engagement if the Yes side won. Preston Manning earned high praise from Lucien Bouchard for taking a hard line. Politics decidedly makes strange bedfellows. Chrétien's most important ally in the House of Commons was Jean Charest, leader of the Progressive Conservative Party, who also played an active role in the referendum campaign.

Prime Minister Chrétien's course correction took place on two fronts: first, by signalling openness to change, and second, by putting markers down around the concept of secession in the event of a unilateral declaration of independence. On 24 October, the Prime Minister delivered his most important speech in Verdun. He extolled the virtue of Canada. He reaffirmed his support for the recognition of Quebec as a distinct society, as he had done before in the context of the Charlottetown Accord. He affirmed that "any changes in constitutional jurisdiction for Quebec will only be made with the consent of Quebecers."[16] This breathed some life into the concept of renewed federalism.

An important but delicate part of the course correction was to set markers around the concept of secession. The Prime Minister began putting down markers as early as 19 December 1994. When the draft Bill 1 was tabled in the Quebec legislative assembly, the Prime Minister declared that Bill 1 was illegal and non-constitutional. This was the most important marker.

In the background, some voices had raised questions about the legality of a unilateral declaration of independence (UDI). The Quebec Superior Court justice Robert Lesage made the point that a UDI is "manifestly contrary to the Constitution of Canada" and "patently unlawful."[17] Patrick Monahan for months had warned Canadians about the risks and consequences of a UDI.[18] The issue did not get much public attention.

The Prime Minister would progressively put down a few more markers:

- No automatic recognition of the referendum results. The situation would be assessed in light of the results – as he said on 20 September, "we are not about to divide Canada following a judicial recount to see whether there is one vote more on one side or the other."[19]
- The clarity of the will of the people. "The Prime Minister of Canada cannot agree to independence from Canada as a result of a simple majority vote plus one on an ambiguous question."[20]
- The responsibility of the Prime Minister to defend Canada's constitutional order. "Who could [the Quebec] negotiator-in-chief talk to following a YES vote?"[21] The Prime Minister of Canada has no mandate to negotiate the secession of Quebec – "Who has a mandate to speak on behalf of the so-called rest of Canada? […] there is nothing to suggest that they would be willing to give the federal government free rein to establish the terms and conditions for breaking up the country."[22]

The Results

The results were a razor-thin majority for Canada: 50.58 per cent No, 49.42 per cent Yes, a margin of 1.16 per cent. Canadians owe fifty-five thousand people for having avoided an unprecedented crisis with unpredictable consequences. To quote Chantal Hébert, "If anything is true in politics, it is that watershed events take on a life of their own and control over them quickly moves beyond the grasp of those who set them in motion."[23] The chain of events set in motion by Premier Jacques Parizeau was stopped by fifty-five thousand Quebecers who chose Canada.

No one knows, but one can imagine the situation if the numbers had been the other way around. A razor-thin result would be put in doubt; requests for recounts and allegations of fraud would flare up. It took four years to get to the bottom of the high reject rate in some ridings. One can also imagine the challenge of reconciling conflicting rights. The rights of the Inuit, Cree, and Montagnais, who had voted by more than 90 per cent to stay in Canada; the rights of people in densely populated areas of Quebec, who had voted in majority to remain Canadians. One can imagine the economic volatility, the political uncertainty, and the risks of social unrest. Secession is not an easy journey.

The least that can be done is to learn from the 1995 referendum. One lesson is that Canada was ill-prepared for the chain of events that might have unfolded from a successful Yes vote. Another observation is that avoiding talking about the tough questions concerning the separation of a province for fear that it might inflame the situation had served no one's interest – not the people of Quebec, other Canadians, the provinces, or the government of Canada. A safer course for all concerned is to think through the consequences, the impact, the parameters, and the rules of engagement if ever a province of Canada wishes to leave the Canadian federation.

The 1995 referendum was radically different from the 1980 referendum. The latter was seeking a mandate to negotiate; the former was seeking support to legitimize a unilateral declaration of independence. Outside a limited circle of experts, the concept of a unilateral declaration of independence (UDI) was not well understood by Canadians, including Quebecers.

While Intergovernmental Affairs focused on supporting the Prime Minister during the referendum campaign, I held one-on-one meetings with a limited number of Deputy Ministers to ensure readiness whatever the outcome might be. The Prime Minister never asked the public service to undertake contingency work, and I did not ask permission for doing what a professional public service should be expected to do. This meant reaching out to a handful of Deputy Ministers to ensure that their departments would be able to act at a moment's notice. I had a number of meetings with the Deputy Minister of Finance, the last one on the night of the referendum. The Department of Finance needed to reassure financial markets and prevent currency speculation should it be required. Minister Martin acknowledges this preparatory work in his memoir.[24] The Department of Foreign Affairs and International Trade needed to be in a state of readiness to respond to the Prime Minister's request should he wish to relay a message to the international community. Close coordination between the department and Canada's ambassadors to the US and France, Raymond Chrétien and Benoît Bouchard respectively, was particularly important. The issue of public safety was sensitive. Some level of readiness was needed to respond to the needs of civil authorities in case of civil unrest, while the government of Quebec might be engaged in a process rejecting the authority of Canadian laws. The contributions of Justice Minister Allan Rock, Deputy Minister of Justice George Thompson, former Deputy Minister of Justice John Tait, and Associate Deputy Minister of Justice Mary Dawson were invaluable.

A reasonable observer would have expected a professional public service to ensure an appropriate level of readiness for any eventuality. Prime Minister Chrétien said, "They were routine precautions for any government"; the Prime Minister had the right to expect that the public service would be able to serve.[25]

The Post-Referendum Period

From the time of the election in November 1993 to the end of 1995, Prime Minister Chrétien was for all intents and purposes his own federal-provincial relations minister and his own advisor. His experience was uncontested. He had paid a high price on the altar of national unity over the course of his political career.

The Minister for Intergovernmental Affairs was saddled with the added responsibilities for Program Review and public service renewal. Quebec ministers were meeting regularly during the referendum campaign but had limited roles. The post-mortem after the 1995 referendum left no doubt that a full-time minister for intergovernmental affairs was needed.

Stéphane Dion was appointed President of the Queen's Privy Council for Canada and Minister of Intergovernmental Affairs in *January 1996.* In February, the Speech from the Throne (SFT) announced the orientations of the government of Canada for the second half of the thirty-fifth Parliament. This was the first statement of the priorities of Prime Minister Chrétien's government since 18 January 1994. The government reported that steps had been taken to ensure that the economic and fiscal situation of the country was sound and that fiscal targets would be met. The time had come for the government of Canada to invest in Canada's social security (health, transfer to provinces, Canada pension fund, etc.), environmental security, personal security, and international security. Two pages of the SFT were prepared in close collaboration with Minister Dion. They were dedicated to building a "Modern and United Country." The speech reiterated a number of actions and commitments, some already acted upon, others to come.

An important message was that as long as the prospect of another referendum exists, "the Government will exercise its responsibility to ensure that the debate is conducted with all the facts on the table, that the rules of the process are fair, that the consequences are clear, and that Canadians, no matter where they live, will have their say in the future of their country."[26] This foreshadowed the work that Minister Dion would lead until the end of the thirty-fifth Parliament and well into the second mandate.

Some changes were made to support Minister Dion in this effort. Ronald Bilodeau was appointed Deputy Clerk on 6 August 1996, and George Anderson was appointed Deputy Minister for Intergovernmental Affairs. Minister Dion and Anderson made a powerful team. Both are cerebral, rigorous, and methodical thinkers. Over the next few years, Dion played a key role in raising public awareness about the implications of secession, educating Canadians about the risks of a unilateral declaration of independence and the need to set rules of engagement to protect citizens' rights. His efforts would lead to a reference to the Supreme Court on 30 September 1996, and three years later, the tabling of the Clarity Act on 13 December 1999.

Several commentators spoke about the Lucien Bouchard effect in the context of the 1995 referendum campaign. This effect was significant and measurable, but it may not have been lasting. The Dion effect was to educate Canadians by publicly discussing issues no one had dared to tackle before. His public letters are of seminal and historical importance. His legacy will be long lasting.

Canadian Exceptionalism

Is Canada better prepared should a similar chain of events occur in the future? My view is that the answer to the question is yes and no.

Canada may once again face events similar to those of 1995 in the foreseeable future. A scenario where the Bloc Québécois forms the official opposition in the House of Commons and the Parti Québécois is elected in Quebec is not inconceivable. Much of the attention to date has focused on the province of Quebec, but the Canadian federation is changing. The next national unity challenge may be quite different.

In some ways, the government of Canada is better prepared as a result of the reference to the Supreme Court and the Clarity Act. It is now understood that provinces do not have a right to secede unilaterally and that the House of Commons must determine if the referendum question on secession is clear and if the results reveal a clear intention by a clear majority of the population. It is also understood that for a province to secede, there would have to be constitutional negotiation and a constitutional amendment.

That said, I do not think that Canadians appreciate the exceptional nature of Canada's position on secession or the significant impact that the secession of a province would have for all Canadians. International law protects a country's sovereignty and territorial integrity. Many countries have declared that they are "indivisible" (France) or that their union is "indestructible" (USA). Some consider separatist movements illegal. Some require prior permission from the government for a constituent party to hold a referendum (United Kingdom). This is intended to limit how many times citizens are forced to live through periods of existential insecurity.

A quick review of international practices makes clear the extent of Canada's exceptionalism. Canada recognizes that a province may leave the Canadian federation and that a province is "entitled to consult its population by referendum on any issue and is entitled to formulate the wording of its referendum question."[27] Furthermore, this entails an obligation to negotiate if the question and the results are free of ambiguity. This is a rare stance for countries to take, especially as broadly as Canada does.

Unlike in other countries, nothing is preventing subjecting Canadians repeatedly to referendums until the proponent's desired result is achieved, and nothing protects Canadians against serial referendums on secession. Canadians are exposed to the danger of direct democracy on an existential question.

In the recent past, a province signalled its willingness to act illegally and unconstitutionally by using a unilateral declaration of independence. Some provinces have used or have signalled their intention to use the notwithstanding clause of the Charter, thus suspending citizens' rights and their recourse to the judicial system. This is the case in Quebec regarding religious symbols and the use of official languages,[28] in Saskatchewan regarding its Parents' Bill of Rights,[29] and in Ontario regarding restrictions on teachers' right to strike.[30] The Saskatchewan government has refused to collect and hand over federal taxes,[31] and Alberta has passed legislation to shield the province from federal initiatives in general.[32]

What can be done to reverse these trends and strengthen national unity? Provincial governments have recently signalled an interest in modernizing equalization. Could they work together to propose an approach that would be fairer for all Canadians and respectful of Canada's fiscal capacity? Could they come together to propose an approach to modernizing health care within Canada's existing level of financial resources, since Canada already spends more than most developed countries? How can governments make a success of the long chain of interrelated actions needed in immigration, from the border to the integration of immigrants in the Canadian labour force? The opportunities are many.

The goal is to reap the benefits of federalism. The idea of federalism is to reconcile diversity and collective solidarity; to benefit from operating at multiple scales from the global to the national and local scales; to benefit from proximity and the collective capacity to work across jurisdictions to achieve results of mutual interest. Canada has much untapped potential.

***

The end of the thirty-fifth Parliament was in sight. With a balanced budget and the national unity crisis subsiding, the government would soon be ready to face the electorate. The Head of the Public Service needed to dedicate more attention to the serious problems the public service of Canada was facing.

9 The Head of the Public Service

One should distinguish the roles of the Clerk of the Privy Council and the Head of the Public Service.[1] The Clerk has influence, though limited authority. The influence of the Clerk comes from a privileged access to the Prime Minister. Departments know that the voice of the Clerk will be heard on all important matters. The Clerk brings a professional, non-partisan, government-wide perspective on the issues of the day. It is this daily access to the Prime Minister that allows the Clerk to communicate to Deputy Ministers and the public service in an authoritative way the decisions, needs, and demands that emanate from the Prime Minister.

The other source of influence is that the Clerk plays a preponderant role in the appointment and deployment of Deputy Heads. The practice has been (when I was there and before) that the Clerk recommends to the Prime Minister the appointment of Deputy Ministers. Their appointment is made legal by an Order in Council by Cabinet. This signals that the incumbent enjoys the confidence of the Prime Minister and of the government of Canada. The practice has played a key role in building a team of senior leaders with the breadth and diversity of experience, skills, and competencies needed to shepherd the public service of Canada. It takes a team to shoulder the government's agenda. It takes a team to ensure that the public service is fit for the time and for the challenges ahead. The influence of the Clerk in recommending the appointment of Deputy Heads helps enable this. Clerks do not work alone in managing the deputy minister community. They are assisted by the Committee of Senior Officials (COSO), composed of senior Deputy Ministers who collectively ensure the stewardship of the senior public service. In other countries the Public Service Commission plays a key role.

A Clerk whose advice about the appointment of Deputy Heads is rejected, except in exceptional circumstances, would be well advised to have a serious conversation with the Prime Minister about the necessary conditions for serving as Clerk. The Clerk has limited legal authority but occupies a unique position that provides access to the levers necessary to fulfil its mission.

The situation of the *Head of the Public Service* is different. The Head of the Public Service has no legal authority and few levers to bring about change in a very crowded space. Several agencies have a legal role that impacts the performance of the public service. *The Treasury Board* is a statutory Cabinet committee created pursuant to the Financial Administration Act. It has many responsibilities. It is the *management board* responsible for general administrative policies, and a *budget office* responsible for financial management, including estimates and the review of annual expenditure plans. It is the *employer*, responsible for labour negotiations and human resources management practices in most but not all cases. In broad terms, Treasury Board Secretariat, the central agency supporting the work of the Treasury Board, sets the regulatory regimes and norms governing the public service of Canada. It has a primary concern for management, compliance, performance, probity, and accountability. Its responsibilities were significantly expanded in human resources management as a result of 2003's Bill C-25, the Public Service Modernization Act.[2] The Treasury Board was mandated to report annually to Parliament on human resources management. This requirement was revoked in 2012.

The mandate of the *Public Service Commission* is more difficult to encapsulate, since so many changes have been introduced since I served as Clerk.[3] At the time, the PSC had the responsibility for appointments to and within the public service of Canada, to uphold the merit principle and protect appointments and promotions against political influence. Today, most of the PSC's responsibilities have been delegated to deputy heads. The merit principle has been redefined as meeting "the essential requirements" of the work to be performed as defined by the deputy head without the need for competition or consideration of any other qualified candidates.[4] In 2015–16, the PSC delegated to deputy heads much of the responsibility for monitoring the performance of their own organizations, thus further reducing its role to periodic audit and the review of complaints.[5] The importance of the PSC's annual report to Parliament has progressively declined – the 2022–3 report is about a third as long as that of 2014–15. It provides sparse details on the state of the public service.

The Public Service Commission of Canada plays a much-reduced role compared to other countries using the Westminster system. In Australia, the PSC plays a major role in deputy head appointments[6] and, starting in 2023, has been in charge of public-sector-wide bargaining.[7] In New Zealand, the PSC is the statutory employer of the public service. It is responsible for "ensuring that [the public service] works as one system to deliver better services and better outcomes for the public," and for the appointment of chief executives.[8] Since 2003, Canada has been following a divergent path from other Westminster countries.

A wide range of other agencies also play a key role in shaping the *management ecosystem* of the public service of Canada. They include but are not limited to the *Auditor General, the Canadian Human Rights Commission, the Commissioner of Lobbying, the Commissioner of Official Languages, the Conflict of Interest and Ethics Commissioner, the Federal Public Sector Labour Relations and Employment Board, the Information Commissioner, the National Security and Intelligence Review Agency, the Privacy Commissioner, the Procurement Ombud, the Public Sector Integrity Commissioner, the Public Servants Disclosure Protection Tribunal* ... and others! These amount to an ever-expanding compliance system.

Each agency adds to the overall burden of administrative controls. Each periodically reports to Parliament. These reports focus on areas of respective responsibility, thus providing a fragmented and, as a result, a distorted view of the state of the public service.

As things currently stand, the Clerk, as Head of the Public Service, is the only person as an institution with the responsibility of reporting to Parliament on "the state of the Public Service."[9] Implicitly, the assumption is that the Head of the Public Service will "do something" about it. This may not be a realistic assumption.

Not surprisingly, Heads of the Public Service have reduced the scale of what is asked of them to a more manageable level. Successive Heads of the Public Service have used their annual reports to signal their priorities and provide a summary of the year in progress. An annual report is informative of the views of the Head of the Public Service, but none of these reports, mine included, fulfilled the promise of reporting on "the state of the public service."

In my opinion, there are currently no instruments that would allow the Parliament of Canada, the Prime Minister of Canada, and the senior public service to have an informed view of the state of the public service of Canada. After thirty-some years, it may be timely to take a sober look at the *stewardship of the public service of Canada*, and to clarify what is expected of the Head of the Public Service and others in this context.

The stewardship of the public service is the central issue. It cannot be discharged by the Clerk alone. This entails a shared responsibility for Parliament, government, the Prime Minister, Ministers, Deputy Ministers, and the centre of government. Some countries have given serious thought to the question and have defined responsibilities more clearly. Canada has given the matter insufficient attention.

The stewardship of the public service deserves attention. It goes to the heart of the readiness of the public service of Canada to fulfil its mission and includes talents, core capabilities, critical data and knowledge, technological readiness, the safety of public service systems, public infrastructures, and more. A comprehensive report on the state of the public service would help to detect risks, analyse trends, and reveal the need for investments and course corrections. It would enable Parliament to form a view on the overall *fitness of the public administration arm* that every government depends on. The system is not currently designed to fulfil this role.

Context Is Not Destiny

In the mid-1990s, the public service was in a precarious situation. Years of spending cuts had eroded the fabric of the institution. Many public sector managers lacked the diversity of experience that upward or lateral mobility normally provides. For years, the public service had been unable to replenish its ranks and to renew its skill mix through external recruitment. Executives and Deputy Ministers were more or less of the same age; a serious succession planning problem was looming. These factors and others shaped the Canadian context at the time I was there.

Other factors, beyond Canadian borders, were also at play. Globalization was transforming economic and geopolitical landscapes. New technologies were reshaping the economic, social, and political spheres. A changing demographic profile, including an aging population and increased heterogeneity, was transforming citizens' expectations of government and generating new pressures for government actions. The world over, governments were grappling to adapt to a fast-changing landscape resulting from a more global economy and a hyperconnected world.[10]

The challenge for the Head of the Public Service and the Deputy Minister community was to figure out how to turn necessity into an opportunity. How to downsize at a rapid pace without harming the core functions of service to Canadians and policy advice to elected officials? How, in the midst of rapid downsizing, to modernize the service delivery capacity and improve the policy capacity of the public service of Canada? How to build the institutional capacity to adapt to fast-changing needs and yet unknown circumstances?

These questions and the quest for answers would underpin the public service reform agenda during the period of 1994–2000 when I served as Head of the Public Service and even beyond.

An Integrated Strategic Planning Cycle

The most difficult phase of Program Review was ensuring the successful implementation of hundreds of decisions. Implementation is the key to a successful government agenda. It makes or breaks public policy choices.[11] This is when public policy ideas become a reality that citizens experience collectively. For this, we needed to find a way to bring ministers and officials together to ensure cohesion across government during the critical period of three to five years that was needed to implement the Program Review decisions.

The opportunity presented itself to introduce an *Integrated Strategic Planning Cycle.* The idea was not new. Ministerial retreats had been used previously to build ministerial solidarity around major initiatives such as the Canada-USA free trade negotiations or the Canada round of constitutional negotiation. This time around, the idea was more ambitious: It was to put in place an annual cycle of strategic ministerial retreats that would run over several years. Ministers would meet in January to discuss the budget, in June to look ahead, and in October to review progress on the overall government agenda. This system was put in place in 1994–5. It helped government to stay the course during the implementation of the Program Review decisions until the election of 1997.

I progressively added other events prior to and after ministerial retreats. Deputy Minister retreats were scheduled to prepare ministerial meetings and ensure follow-up. This helped to ensure a public-service-wide focus on the government agenda. It also contributed to coherence and collaboration across departments. Deputy Heads were better equipped to guide the work of their departments. A year later, I added Assistant Deputy Minister retreats to this annual cycle. ADM retreats were initiated by Paul Tellier in 1986. Tying them to ministerial retreats gave them a new purpose. It was rewarding for senior officials to see their work being presented to ministers and to reach Cabinet, the most important decision-making table in the country.

An integrated planning cycle had a number of benefits.[12] One was that it generated a growing awareness of the need to work across departmental boundaries. In a public sector setting, the incentives to think along vertical and hierarchical lines are very strong. Historically, it was possible for departments to work relatively independently from each other in their respective areas of responsibility. However, by the mid-1990s, an increasing number of public policy challenges exceeded the capacity of any single organization working alone. They required pooling knowledge across multiple agencies to generate viable solutions. Issues like poverty, homelessness, and climate change do not fit within the boundaries of any single organization – they require working across boundaries both inside government and with others in society. New networks and new relationships were needed to rise above the boundaries of traditional public agencies and departments.[13]

The End of a Downward Spiral

Working as one team may be nice, and feeling that ministers value your work may be rewarding, but it rings hollow if public servants are not getting decent pay for their contribution to society. If the public service of Canada was to successfully manage an ambitious turnaround, it was urgent to bring back some peace in the workplace. There was a need to end salary freezes, reinstate labour negotiations, and address the most urgent compensation issues. Without progress on this front, the call to action to build a better public service would be hollow at best, if not hypocritical. The government agenda and the public service agenda were intertwined; success on one front would impact success on the other.

All through my period as Clerk and Head of the Public Service, I enjoyed a supportive and productive relationship with the Treasury Board Secretariat (TBS). Peter Harder became Secretary to the Treasury Board in November 1995, and Marcel Massé, after serving as Chair of the Cabinet Committee on Program Review and Public Service Renewal, became President of the Treasury Board in January 1996. A close collaboration between us and with the Prime Minister contributed to ensuring a relationship of trust between government, senior public sector leaders, and public servants. The Treasury Board is an important institution in the ecosystem of central agencies, without parallel in some countries. The triangular relationship between PCO, primarily focused on the policy agenda, the Treasury Board Secretariat, primarily focused on management issues, and Finance, primarily focused on the fiscal health of the country, has served Canada well at critical times.

After years of wage and salary controls, the government announced in 1996 the end of salary freezes and a return to collective bargaining.[14] Quick progress ensued. By February 1998, six collective agreements had been completed and ratified, twenty negotiations were under way, and eight more were at various stages of third-party assistance.[15] Progress at last.

Management and executive compensation was a more challenging issue. The public service needed to stop the inversion of salary scales between professional groups and management. The government needed public support to move forward with the compensation adjustments needed for managers and executives. The solution was the creation of an *Advisory Committee on Senior Level Retention and Compensation* in 1997. This was a key step. The first report of the Commission was tabled less than a year later. It echoed the diagnostic I had presented to Parliament in February 1997 when I argued that the public service was facing "a quiet crisis."[16] In the words of the Commission, the public service had reached "a watershed" moment.[17] There were inversion problems – managers at the EX1 level had subordinates who were paid more than they were. This problem was compounded by the fact that unionized subordinates received overtime whereas managers did not. There were compression problems between management levels when people at a higher level were paid at the same level or less than people at a lower level (e.g., 25 per cent of EX2 were paid at the same level as EX1). Performance pay was discredited. It was implemented in only seven of the seventeen prior years – it was seen as an easy cut. The Commission found that the most serious inequities were at the most senior levels and among Deputy Heads where the total compensation was significantly lower than in the broader public sector when compared to municipalities, universities, hospitals, and not-for-profit organizations.

In February 1998, the government of Canada accepted all the recommendations. The support of the Prime Minister was critical. Performance pay was reinstated and significant pay increases, ranging from 4 per cent for EX1 to 9 per cent for EX4 and 17 per cent for DM2, were introduced to address the inequities created by compression and inversion at the most senior levels.[18] The impact of the early decisions to put an end to salary freezes and stop the downward spiral was significant. People who were planning to leave because they were feeling undervalued and underpaid had reasons to reconsider their decision. Staying for a few more years would have a significant impact on their pension based on the compensation earned during the last five years. The data shows that the demographic crisis was delayed; this gave us some breathing room to prepare the next generation.

The work of the Commission ensured continued progress and depoliticization of compensation discussions for the next fifteen years. This meets my definition of a good idea: one that works in practice and achieves the desired outcome within the parameters set at the start while minimizing unintended consequences. Ideas, even clever ideas, have unintended consequences that need to be corrected. In this case, the compensation adjustment left the impression that the public service renewal agenda was primarily aimed at executives, even though labour negotiations had been reinstated first. This perception needed to be corrected.

In the end, no idea is fit for all times, and new ones must come to the fore. The last report of the Advisory Committee on Senior Level Retention and Compensation was tabled in 2015. Today, the public service is better paid than before, but once again inversion problems have emerged. Senior public service leaders will need to find new ways to address these issues to ensure that the public service is able to attract and retain its fair share of the best talent the country has to offer.

The Power of Weak Signals

My Archive Project gave me the opportunity to reconnect with colleagues and to go down memory lane with some of them. The anecdotes people remember after so many years are interesting. They reveal the importance of small gestures that take on a disproportionate symbolic importance. They become part of the legends of the public service.

The capacity to lead an organization through an ambitious process of change does not depend solely on the power of the brain (although it helps), but on people's reading of the spirit of a leader, revealed through everyday actions. Some call this to walk the talk, but I think it is more complex than that. People read the real motives of their leaders, and their reading influences their willingness to follow the lead of people in authority.

One anecdote kept coming back as I was meeting people and gathering my papers for Library and Archives Canada. At the end of 1995, in the midst of the most significant cuts in the history of the public service and a few months after the turmoil generated by the 1995 referendum, I brought back Holiday Season celebrations. I did not think much of this at the time, but the event took on symbolic value. PCO was managing a 15 per cent cut of its budget. For an organization with no program, no external service, and no grants and contributions, expenditure reduction means only one thing: cutting jobs. The Prime Minister shared my view that public servants who were managing downsizing at great cost to themselves deserved to be celebrated. So, we used the main corridor of the Parliament building and dressed up the space with round tables, white tablecloths, tableware, flowers, and musicians for a fancy sit-down dinner. And yes, we used taxpayers' money, employees contributed, and managers paid for the wine. PCO employees dressed up for the event. The Prime Minister came over to shake hands and made a speech. There was music and dancing, and pictures were taken. The signal went well beyond those present at the PCO party on Parliament Hill. The message was that it was OK to celebrate. This story is not important in the overall scheme of things and yet it is a reminder that the spirit that animates people in senior positions is revealed in the smallest gestures.

Gratitude and respect are priceless. On an entirely different scale, I think that Canadians trusted Prime Minister Chrétien to do the right thing to eliminate the deficit, not because they read the fine print of the budget bill, but because they believed that he cared about the well-being of Canadians. The "Vive le Canada" at the end of all his speeches is not a cliché, but the anchor of his actions in political life. *The character and motives of the carrier are as important as the message*. On a much smaller scale, I think public servants believed I was committed to the well-being of the public service; that helped immeasurably in gaining their support.

Nothing great comes out of pettiness or by treating public servants poorly. Nothing meaningful is achieved by changing the name of DM breakfast to DM meeting to avoid offering coffee or by not living up to normal hospitality standards for international dignitaries coming to Canada. Pettiness does not display a concern for the use of taxpayers' money. Hopefully, Canada will soon snap out of this mindset; I'm heartened to hear that the coffee has returned.

Over the years, I have encouraged organizations to celebrate success because this unleashes energy and generates an impetus for doing better. With the support of the Prime Minister and of Governor General Roméo LeBlanc, the *Outstanding Achievement Award* was revived in 1998. It had been cancelled after some criticism about the expenses involved. I also launched the *Head of the Public Service Award* in December 1998. Celebrating success does not mean being blind to the many failings and weaknesses of the public service. Recognizing success raises the expectations and aspirations for doing better. It creates a culture where recognizing weaknesses is part of the learning process, helping people to make progress and adapt to changing circumstances.[19] My word of advice to managers has been: "Celebrate your many achievements without arrogance, acknowledge difficulties without complacency, and take on with confidence the exciting task of inventing solutions that would not exist without you."[20]

In the mid-1990s, the public service of Canada needed to make progress in recognizing success without complacency and weaknesses without fear of blame.[21] Blame and finger pointing are symptoms of a culture drifting away from the capacity to learn, adapt, and course correct. This is guaranteed to lead to more failures.

The Power of Ideas

Behind the public sector reform agenda in the second half of the 1990s lay a set of ideas about public administration, the role of the state, the public sector, and public servants in society. These ideas have guided my actions and decisions as Clerk, Secretary to Cabinet, and Head of the Public Service. Later, they would influence the international research work I would launch after leaving the public service.

In short, it is my deep conviction that a well-performing society requires a well-performing public sector, a well-performing private sector, and a well-performing civic society. None of that happens by accident and no institution is fit for all times. Public institutions reveal ideas about the exercise of power in society and what it means to be a citizen of a country. These ideas are not immutable. Periodically, there are changes in the world and society that bring about a realignment of fundamental ideas about governance, the role of government, and the role of the public service. It was the case in the mid-1990s, and it is the case today.[22]

I hold a high opinion of the role of the state and the role of government in society. The role of government, public organizations, and public servants is to invent solutions to the problems that stem from living in society that cannot be solved without some use of the levers of the state and to generate results that we enjoy collectively. Every action, decision, or government intervention is designed to influence behaviours and to bring about change in society, build a better future, and improve human conditions. *Public innovation is the core mission of government and of public servants.* Public servants contribute to the task of building states with the authority and legitimacy to get things done and the capacity to evolve with the changing world we live in.[23] Public institutions and public servants exclusively exist to serve a public purpose. At the most fundamental level, this is what makes them most valuable for society and what gives meaning to their decisions and actions.[24]

Public administration is my area of expertise and my domain of practice. Public administration transforms politics into results that we experience as citizens. Politics and public administration are not two solitudes. They are part of a dynamic governing system. The world over, governments depend on their public apparatus to make things happen and give shape to ideas about the public good and the collective interest.

As Alasdair Roberts said, "the broad aim of public administration is the construction and renovation of public institutions to fit the needs of the moment."[25] It is the individual and collective responsibility of every public servant to ensure that public institutions and the public service are fit for the challenges ahead. *Institutional capacity-building is the duty of each and every public servant.*

Would I have framed these ideas exactly that way in 1994? Maybe not, but I can trace these ideas back to every job I held over the years. They were consistently reflected in the speeches I delivered as Clerk, as President of the Canada School of Public Service, and later as an international public servant.

Deputy Minister Task Forces

Leading the public service of Canada through an unprecedented process of change in the second half of the 1990s was not a linear process. It operated on multiple fronts. The early steps contributed to building trust and regaining credibility by giving the public service reasons to hope that things would get better. Much more needed to be done, though; it was time to shape a public service reform agenda to encourage a collective effort.

The efforts to bring the Deputy Minister community to coalesce around a shared public service agenda began with the First Deputy Minister strategic planning retreat on 22–3 June 1994. In a speech at the Public Policy Forum in October 1994, I summarized the work in progress as follows: "We need to modernize our service delivery, strengthen our policy capacity and build a vibrant institution capable of serving today and in the future."[26]

In 1995, I launched nine Deputy Minister Task Forces to explore various public service issues.[27] Their reports helped generate momentum about the most pressing issues at the time. They were composed of Deputy Ministers and Assistant Deputy Ministers, with a Deputy Minister designated as chair for each one. They had one year to explore an issue and bring back ideas. The topics were broad and the proposed solutions ambitious. The *Service Delivery task force* explored the design and delivery of government services from the citizens' point of view. It built on the work of Public Service 2000 and advocated for integrated service delivery built around the needs of users rather than the convenience of service agencies. Some provinces and other countries were already moving in this direction, with organizations such as Service Ontario, Service New Brunswick, and the Canada Business Service Centres.[28]

A task force on *the Future of the Public Service* looked ten years out using scenarios planning. It explored incremental changes, a renaissance scenario, and a market-based approach.[29] The task force on *Overhead Services* challenged the thinking about common services and shared services with a view to generating savings.[30] The task force on *Values and Ethics* is best known because it goes to the heart of the public service's mission as an institution.[31] The task force on *Managing Horizontal Policy Issues* explored how to work across boundaries to address cross-cutting issues such as global changes, climate change, security issues, poverty, and population migration.[32] Finally, the task force on *Strengthening Policy Capacity* provided a sober diagnostic of the need to improve data analysis and policy research across departments.[33]

Together, these task forces were the foundation of the public service reform agenda of the time.

10 A Public Service Reform Agenda

Setting a public service reform agenda is challenging. The public sector is a large ship to turn around. By June 1996, there were twenty-four departments, thirty-seven Crown corporations, twenty-six tribunals and quasi-judicial bodies, and forty-eight service agencies.[1] Their needs are many and only so much can be achieved in any period of time. Too many priorities disperse the collective capacity to bring about change. Too narrow a focus leaves many people disappointed that their issue is not getting attention. I erred on the side of ensuring continuity. I had just three core priorities for the whole period I served as Head of the Public Service. I focused on putting citizens first in service delivery, strengthening policy capacity, and, in an initiative called La Relève, putting people first in public service reforms. These three priority areas are reflected in every report I sent to Parliament from 1995 to 1999.

The story behind these three initiatives combines aspirations for a better future, modest progress, and much unfinished business. The tenure of a Clerk is short; my hope was to lay the basis from which others could do better in the future. The public service reform agenda of the mid-1990s had defensive and proactive dimensions. The defensive purpose was to prevent cuts from eroding the core capabilities of the public service. The proactive part was to use the opportunity of large-scale changes to explore new and better ways to serve and modernize it. Programs would be eliminated, but those that remained should operate better than before. Policy capacity could be strengthened to address complex issues. The public service, at the end of the day, should be better positioned than before. This was the hope and the driving force behind the public service reform agenda. Public servants are the stewards of the public service as an institution.

Citizens First

The capacity to deliver public services to citizens is the most fundamental responsibility of the public service.[2] High-quality public services, provided fairly, consistently, and competently without corruption, leakage, or discrimination, contribute to a well-performing economy and society. *Service delivery is the trademark of a well-performing public sector.* It builds a relationship of trust between citizens and government as well as between elected officials and the professional public service.[3]

The expectation was that by raising departments' awareness of the importance of service delivery, it would be possible to reduce the risk of collateral damages at a time when they were managing large-scale program cuts. Program Review was providing a window of opportunity to explore new ways of providing services.

This effort took many forms, including citizen-centricity in policy and program design, more integrated service delivery, the use of modern technologies to expand the range of options available to citizens to access government, and alternative service delivery (ASD). The task force chaired by Janet R. Smith on Service Delivery Models was highly influential in bringing a citizen perspective to service delivery modernization.[4] The task force argued that there are significant differences between service to clients and service to citizens. A citizen-centric perspective shifts the focus of attention from an agency-centric perspective to what a service may look like from the perspective of the people most directly affected.[5] This focus was reflected in my annual report to Parliament in 1995[6] and further developed in my later annual reports. As I summarized in a 1996 speech, "[Canadians] want services organized around their needs, not the convenience of those supplying the service [...] They demand an integrated approach to service delivery."[7]

Integrated Service Delivery

The idea of integrated service delivery, already in motion, was rapidly acted upon by several departments. The Canadian Food Inspection Agency (1997) consolidated services from the Departments of Agriculture, Health, Industry, and Fisheries and Oceans. From 1994 on, the Canada Business Service Centres network of single-window services for business expanded across the country. New organizational models, like the local airport authority model, gave a greater role to local communities in the management of airports. The commercialization of the air traffic controller system in 1996 brought together public, private, and labour interests. In 1998, Parks Canada was granted authority to retain revenue to accelerate park development. In 1999, Revenue Canada was transformed into the Canada Customs and Revenue Agency. It was given a management board in the hope that this would bring closer federal and provincial relations and a convergence of interests. It was also granted the authority to operate under the Canada Labour Code. The idea was to explore if different management models including more authority on labour negotiations and human resources management might yield better results and more creativity in organizing the work while respecting the principles of responsible government and ministerial accountability. Some initiatives were very successful; others did not live up to expectations.[8]

The main message to public servants was that this was a good time to bring forward creative ideas to better serve Canada and Canadians. The hope was that experimenting with a diversity of approaches would accelerate learning, monitoring progress would ensure early detection of problems, and course corrections would take place as the public service gained new insights and experience.

Over time, some departments went quite far in creating Alternative Service Delivery models. Some granted outside bodies discretionary authority over program design, planning, and delivery. This was the case, for example, with the *Canada Millennium Scholarship Foundation* and the *Canada Foundation for Innovation.* These new entities needed a new governance framework to prevent abuse and achieve results while preserving transparency and accountability. This did not happen fast enough. The learning was not keeping pace with the speed of experimentation. In 1999, years into the growth of alternative models, Auditor General L. Denis Desautels appropriately flagged the issue and was assured by Treasury Board that a revised framework would be in place in March 2000.[9] Earlier attention to the need for a governing framework for the new entities might have prevented some of the difficulties that foundations and other creative delivery models experienced later.

Several experiments over that period challenged the hypothesis that less control and more delegation ultimately led to better results. The reality is that a lot depends on the leadership and competence of the *management team*.

E-Government

The mid-1990s were the early days of an information technology revolution, soon to be followed by a digital revolution. The Treasury Board had launched an effort for IT-based government service renewal. Robert Giroux and Peter Harder would carry it on.

The 1997 Speech from the Throne was ambitious. "Canada is well-positioned to be a world leader in the global knowledge-based economy of the 21st century."[10] There were commitments to "make the information and knowledge infrastructure accessible to all Canadians by the year 2000, thereby making Canada the most connected nation in the world."[11] These goals, though ambitious, were within reach. Canada was doing better than most other OECD countries at the time.

For instance, *SchoolNet*, led by the Department of Industry, aimed to connect all the schools and public libraries across the country to the Internet and develop the tools and services to achieve its potential. Industry Canada also ran the Community Access Program, establishing thousands of public Internet access points across the country, each with computer and Internet support resources.[12] By 1995, these programs had earned praise from Microsoft founder Bill Gates.[13] In 1999, Industry Canada announced that SchoolNet had achieved its goal: Canada was the first country in the world where all schools and public libraries were connected to the Internet.[14]

In the inaugural United Nations index of e-government, Canada ranked sixth in the world. The report suggested that Canada "will be a case study on e-gov success for years to come."[15] Past success does not guarantee future successes, though; as of 2024, Canada ranks forty-seventh.[16] A question worth exploring is why, after such a good start, is Canada now lagging behind?

Today, the countries Canada could learn from are many; Denmark, Finland, Singapore, Estonia, Japan, and South Korea, to name a few.

The Citizen-Centred Service Network

A sustained effort to encourage a citizen-centred approach to service delivery required better data, common metrics, and measurement tools to monitor progress over time. In July 1997, at my request, the Canadian Centre for Management Development launched an action research effort that brought together federal, provincial, and municipal officials and academics to discuss the research work needed to improve service delivery. The *Citizen-Centred Service Network* (CCSN) was born.

The initial *Citizens First* survey was conducted in 1998. It identified five drivers of service satisfaction, timeliness requiring the most urgent attention. The survey provided public service managers with valuable information to make tangible progress. CCSN also developed a Common Measurements Tool (CMT). Since its release in December 1998, the measurement tool has continued to evolve and is used domestically and abroad. An institute for Citizen-Centred Services (ICCS) has since been created; it runs Citizens First surveys every two to three years. This effort continues to this day.[17]

By the end of 1999, progress had been made and there was reason to believe that it would continue. The challenge for the public service of Canada in 2000 and beyond was to keep pace with the speed of innovation, in particular in the areas of big data and artificial intelligence, and to stay ahead of the pack relative to other countries in providing services of the highest quality. Several countries have since outpaced the Canadian public service; there is a need to reverse that trend.

The Policy Research Initiative

A professional non-partisan public service is recognizable by a strong policy capacity. The public service must help government shape an ambitious governing agenda. It must be able to generate ideas to achieve government priorities in the most competent and effective way. It must translate broad policy direction into concrete and achievable actions leading to the desired public policy outcomes. It must anticipate emerging issues and opportunities, propose proactive interventions and preventative actions.

I hold strong views about the importance of the policy role of a professional non-partisan public service.[18] Years of experience in Canada and abroad have shaped my views about the importance of good policies for the overall performance of a country.

I think of the public service of Canada as the most expansive *knowledge platform* in the country. Each department is a depository of deep sectoral expertise. Departments are connected to, and they exchange information with, other organizations with similar interests across the country – at the federal, provincial, and municipal levels and in academia. They work and exchange knowledge with their colleagues in other countries and with international expert organizations. The challenge for public sector leaders is to harness the best available knowledge, wherever it may reside, to support government decision making in a timely way.[19] This challenge confronts every country as knowledge creation is expanding exponentially and as the velocity of change and the complexity of public policy issues are increasing.

This puts a premium on futures work, early detection, prevention, and course correction. This speaks to the need to build public organizations with the agility to adapt to a fast-changing landscape. These capabilities make a difference in the capacity of countries to prosper in unforeseen or unpredictable circumstances. Compared to other countries, the public service of Canada in the mid-1990s was not recognized for its capacity for futures work, foresight, or policy research work on complex issues that required a holistic approach to problem solving.

The inspirations behind the policy initiative were modest. First it was to preserve existing capabilities in spite of the cuts resulting from Program Review. Second, it was to build a public-service-wide policy community able to work together on cross-cutting issues. Third, it was to resist the pressure of urgent work displacing rigorous mid- to longer-term research work.

Building the policy capacity of the public service for the complex challenges ahead requires a different way of thinking, where the economic, social, environmental, and technological dimensions of public policy issues are not addressed separately but in a more comprehensive and holistic way. Complex issues are multidimensional, with multiple factors interacting dynamically. This is the case for issues like climate change, poverty alleviation, global population migration, and many others. Long chains of interacting factors are at play. Inventing solutions requires system thinking and its offshoots, an ecosystemic view of issues and the world. These skills did not characterize the public service policy community at the time, but we could give it a push.

A potent way to build policy capacity is to generate demand for high-quality policy work. Through this initiative as Clerk, I was generating demand and signalling a need for a longer-term focus to address challenges Canada would face in the future. My hope was that some progress could be achieved so that those coming after could bring the public service to a higher level.

The Early Steps

In December 1996, two key Deputy Minister Task Force reports were tabled. Mel Cappe's task force primarily focused on horizontal issues: how to build the policy capacity of the public service to address cross-cutting issues that require the active contribution of several departments and agencies.[20] Ivan Fellegi's task force on the public service policy-making and analysis capacity provided a compelling diagnostic.[21] A particular emphasis was placed on building a policy community across government and linking with the broader research community in academics and in provincial governments. This work led to the launch of the *Policy Research Initiative* (PRI) in July 1996.

I asked Alan Nymark (Associate Deputy Minister, Health Canada) and Jim Lahey (Assistant Deputy Minister, Labour, at Human Resources Development Canada) to take the lead. They were in charge of two of the most important policy branches in the government of Canada. Their organizations had best practices to share with the policy community. Their leadership was invaluable. The idea behind the PRI was to bring together the heads of the policy branches of departments and agencies to work together on cross-cutting issues. Alan and Jim, as co-chairs of the *Policy Research Committee* (PRC), reported directly to me to signal the support of the centre of government. They were free to identify issues of interest to the policy community. From the start, the co-chairs focused on cross-cutting long-term challenges.

Canada 2005 was born out of the work of the PRC. This was an effort to look ten years out at issues and pressure points likely to arise in Canadian society. A first draft report identified three areas for interdepartmental work, growth, human development, and social cohesion.[22] The list was later expanded to include a Knowledge-Based Economy project. A fifth topic on Global Challenges and Opportunities was added in February 1997.[23] Five interdepartmental networks were now hard at work.

By the summer of 1997, a *Policy Research Secretariat* (PRS) was set up to support the initiative. The title sounds grand but, in reality, the Secretariat operated on a shoestring. Laura Chapman was its first head. The Secretariat was lacking in money, but it was rich in talent. Departments seconded some of their best policy people to work with it. This was a vote of confidence by deputy heads. Looking back, it is fair to say that the Policy Research Initiative served as an incubator for future senior leaders by exposing them to a government-wide perspective. The rosters of its projects included future Deputy Ministers and future Clerks.

In November 1997, the Secretariat launched its first Policy Researchers Conference in Ottawa and a first-of-its-kind meeting of Canada's policy research think tanks to explore areas of mutual cooperation. This was an effort to align policy work in government and academia. Over the years, the PRI held many conferences, including a series of events in 1998 focused on regional issues in collaboration with regional policy research communities. That same year, the PRI launched a newsletter, *Horizons: Emerging Developments and Knowledge in Public Policy Research*, and in 1999, it established the *Canadian Policy Research Awards* to recognize people who had made major contributions to public policy issues as researchers, journalists, or graduate students. From 2000 to 2002, the PRI managed an online open access journal published by Les Presses de L'Université de Montréal, *Isuma: Canadian Journal of Policy Research*, bringing together papers from academics and Canadian public servants.[24]

The international community took notice of the Canadian initiative. The OECD worked collaboratively with the Secretariat on various projects. I proudly reported on progress in my annual reports to Parliament. Success is a collective achievement, and sustained success requires sustaining power.

Staying Power

The Policy Research Initiative continued after I stepped down as Clerk and after the departure of Laura Chapman, who had invested so much energy in this adventure. In July 2002, Jean-Pierre Voyer took the helm of the Secretariat to lead the PRI through its next chapter.[25] In 2008, Clerk Kevin Lynch asked the PRI to train public servants in long-term foresight in the context of Canada@150, and in 2010, Clerk Wayne Wouters emphasized the need for long-term policy capacity. PRI was renamed *Policy Horizons Canada* in 2010. Today, the work is more internally focused. The period of extensive outreach has ended.

There are many reasons old and new to ramp up efforts to improve the policy capacity of the public service. The first reason is the duty to advise government. *The public service is accountable for the advice it provides as well as for the advice it is unable or unprepared to provide.*

I am told that policy work has declined in recent years "due to a lack of demand." According to this view, ministers have shown little interest in seeking the advice of the public service. In my opinion, this is a self-defeating proposition. Policy work must be done on an ongoing basis irrespective of demands by elected officials at a given point in time. If policy research work begins when the government of the day asks for ideas, by definition, the public service would have nothing much to offer. Policy work takes time, and longitudinal data must be collected and analysed over multiple years to detect patterns and trends. This brings us back to the *stewardship role* of the public service I mentioned before. The public service must do what needs to be done to be able to advise government on the most significant issues of the time. A sustained demand for policy work should, first and foremost, come from the public service itself because it is central to its mission of serving government. From a strong base of research work, it is then possible to engage with confidence to support government priorities.

As mentioned, *Policy Horizons Canada* now carries the torch of the Policy Research Initiative on a very modest scale. It has been located with Employment and Social Development Canada (ESDC) since 2006. Its latest report as of this writing, *Disruptions on the Horizon*, recognizes that governments are confronted by multiple complex crises.[26] I have found no evidence that this work is reaching Cabinet and senior decision makers.

Futures work is key to building the *anticipative capacity* of government. Over the years I had the privilege of working with and learned from countries that have introduced innovative practices to improve their capacity to detect risks and opportunities and set an ambitious agenda. Canada could learn from their experience. I admire the Netherlands' long-term work and outreach, Singapore's scenario planning and risk-assessment methodology is second to none, Denmark's community-based approach to resilience is inspiring, and I am envious of Finland's idea of creating a parliamentary Committee for the Future.[27] A key element of success is ensuring that futures work *reaches decision makers* – the Prime Minister, Cabinet, and public sector leaders at the highest level – so that it shapes future-oriented government priorities. This will only grow more important as complex challenges like climate change intensify and similar new challenges emerge.

People First

The focus on institutional capacity-building dominated the public service reform agenda during my time as Head of the Public Service and later as President of the Canadian Centre for Management Development. The label of *La Relève* was used to describe this effort. The name never adequately captured the idea or grabbed people's imagination. I would have been better inspired to talk about the *stewardship of the public service* as an institution.

Paul Tellier's effort on Public Service 2000 focused on administrative barriers. He introduced the *Public Service Reform Act of 1992* giving departments more authority. This was in line with public sector reforms in most developed countries at the time. Public sector reforms meant streamlining administrative systems and procedures, introducing management techniques often inspired by the private sector, and introducing changes in the structure and machinery of government. Although necessary, there are limits to what can be achieved through administrative and legislative changes. Public organizations are people- and knowledge-based organizations. They are an ecosystem of interrelationships where people capabilities, public infrastructures, and technological platforms are used to generate results of value for society.

In the mid-1990s, I was of the view that the public service did not need more structural changes and that departments should learn to use their newly delegated authority before considering more legislative changes. Other factors required more urgent attention, including a culture of innovation, learning capacity, inventive capacity, adaptive capacity, resilience, modern technological platforms, shared data, shared knowledge, and the capacity to work across boundaries, to name a few.

A different mix of actions and a different concept of leadership were needed to steer the public service through a profound period of transformation. It called for *distributed leadership* where every public servant is individually and collectively responsible for acting within their sphere of influence to improve the public service. In my first speech as Clerk, I spoke of the stewardship responsibilities of public servants. "*Each of us, both individually and collectively, is responsible for the management of the Public Service of Canada [...] We are also responsible for preparing and leaving the institution better than we found it.*"[28]

Once the peak of the national unity crisis had passed and the key Program Review decisions had been made, my call to action to revitalize the public service became more explicit. I first used the expression *La Relève* inadvertently during a speech at an Assistant Deputy Minister Forum in June 1996.[29] It was customary for me to deliver speeches by alternating (without translation) between English and French. In my mind, the expression "la relève" was not a subject but an action, as in *prendre la relève,* the commitment of each generation of public servants for the future well-being of the public service. The expression "la relève" was now out there, so I stuck with it. The label may not have been the best, but the message was consistent in all my speeches.

> La Relève is a challenge. It is the challenge of building a modern and vibrant institution focused on people, and leaving for those who follow us a better institution than the one we inherited. La Relève is a commitment by each one of us to do everything in our power to ensure we have a modern and vibrant organization for the future. La Relève is the duty we have to those who come after us. We, the caretakers, and guardians of this institution, have a duty to leave an organization staffed with the most qualified and competent people.[30]

My second annual report to Parliament, 1997, dedicated a whole chapter to La Relève. My description of a "quiet crisis" attracted the attention of ministers and parliamentarians. I made it clear, however, that "the responsibility to act rests first with the Public Service. Public servants must take charge and do all in their power to remedy the situation. Their actions will provide the necessary credibility for them to ask elected officials and Canadians to join the effort."[31] This was in line with my thinking about the collective responsibility of public servants for the *stewardship* of the public service. Public servants, and in particular senior public servants, should go to the limit of their authority and ability to bring about changes before relying on the strengths of others. *Physician, heal thyself* may be a harsh medicine, but it is necessary. Viable solutions don't fall from the sky; they are homegrown.

The 1997 annual report to Parliament outlined a number of initiatives. Departments would prepare plans of action to build modern and vibrant public organizations. This was a first. The public service had operational plans, capital replacement plans, technology investment plans, office space plans, etc., on top of all the plans and reports they were sending to Parliament and central agencies. However, there had never been a requirement for departments to prepare a plan about people, the most important asset of the public service of Canada. There were no mandatory learning plans, development plans, or career development plans. What was supposedly our most important resource was the one the public service knew the least about. This may still be the case today.

A Call to Action

The preparation of departmental plans was a challenging idea. The public service had no prior experience and no model. Departments needed help and the Head of the Public Service needed assistance to coordinate departmental efforts. I turned to Peter Harrison, Associate Deputy Minister of Human Resources Development. He pulled together a small team of volunteers, including Richard Rochefort and others. This was the origin of the *La Relève Task Force*. I held regular meetings with them to ensure a close connection. I used the DM breakfast (a weekly meeting of Deputy Heads) to update the deputy community on progress. The task force coordinated the preparation of the plans from departments, central agencies, functional communities, and regional councils. Regional councils were especially creative. Before long, there was a healthy competition between departments to improve their plans by borrowing ideas from each other.

The Task Force did a huge amount of work, facilitating, animating, and disseminating creative ideas. In October 1997, they published a compendium entitled *La Relève: A Commitment to Action.* The documents outlined about 1,200 concrete actions spanning culture, values, innovation, pride and recognition, training, development, recruitment, and communications. Deliverables spanned several years.

The first page of the report is the one that attracted the most attention. There, the signatures of all Deputy Heads appeared prominently. This page had significant symbolic value. For the first time, there was a plan about the people of the public service and the actions needed to build "modern and vibrant organizations." Public servants could monitor progress. The Treasury Board Secretariat could identify actions needed to support departments, the Canadian Centre for Management Development could roll out training programs to meet demand, and the Privy Council Office could monitor progress in assessing the performance of Deputy Heads. In March 1998, the Task Force produced the *First Progress Report on La Relève: Overview*, accompanied by detailed departmental, professional community, and regional reports, celebrating progress and recognizing that more was to come.[32]

Corporate Initiatives

Departmental actions were necessary; this is where people experience their professional life as public servants. But there is more to a public service career than the position people hold in the department that uses their services and pays their salary. Public servants are members of the public service of Canada. Some initiatives can only be initiated on a public-service-wide scale.

Years of downsizing and staffing freezes had deprived public servants of the diversity of experience that upward and lateral mobility provides. Such experience was especially important for preparing future managers and executives. Growing through the ranks, I had the opportunity to run line and staff operations and to work in a regional office, headquarters, and central agencies. I gained experience in policy work and service delivery as well as in running large and small organizations. All of it contributed to my development as a manager. Not everyone aspires to that much diversity. But the public service of Canada should create the conditions for people to grow, develop, and acquire the diversity of experience that meets their career aspirations. This had not been the situation for many years, and it required attention.

At the time, there were two small corporate programs for management development: A *Management Training Program* (MTP) for professionals who aspired to become managers, and a *Career Development Program* (CAP) for managers who aspired to become executives and take on more responsibilities. In my second report to Parliament in February 1997, I announced two new corporate programs.[33] The idea was to create a continuum of training and development programs running from management trainee up to the Assistant Deputy Minister level.

The *Accelerated Executive Development Program* (AEXDP) was aimed at providing EX-1 to EX-3 executives with a diversity of experience to serve at a higher level. The program included a dedicated learning plan and work assignments. Candidates were encouraged to self-identify. Nominees were assessed by a panel of Deputy Ministers under the auspices of the Public Service Commission. In the case of MTP and CAP, the practice had been that nominees were being put forward by their home departments. In every department, there are people who aspire to gain new experience and serve at a higher level. For all kinds of reasons, they may not have had the opportunity to move ahead. Some may not be known to their senior managers because their functions did not give them much exposure. In other cases they were so important that their departments were reluctant to let them go. AEXDP was turning this upside down. Candidates could self-identify, and even if they were not successful, being interviewed by a panel of Deputy Heads gave them visibility. The new approach was a significant departure from past practices. It caused quite a stir. Departments were discovering that they had to compete to attract AEXDP graduates.

The *Pre-Qualified Program* (PQP) for Assistant Deputy Ministers was another step in creating an extended continuum in career development. Executives could apply to qualify at the ADM level. Once again, the interviews were conducted by panels of Deputy Heads with the support of the Public Service Commission. If candidates qualified, their names were put in a pool of pre-qualified people who could then be deployed to ADM positions. Deputy Heads with positions to fill could select a person from the pool without delay. This program also caused a cultural shock. Some candidates highly regarded by their departments did not qualify. Some people of exceptional talent at the EX-2 and EX-3 levels qualified despite being relatively unknown in the system. Panels made of three to five Deputy Heads were discovering the breadth of the hidden talent in the public service. Both programs were launched in January 1997.

There was immediately a strong demand: 460 people representing 15 per cent of the executive group applied for AEXDP and PQP during the first year. This was an exceptionally high take up; 56 candidates were enrolled in AEXDP, 20 candidates qualified for PQP. The number of qualified candidates exceeded the number of vacancies. As a result, while most qualified candidates were placed within a few months, some had to wait, thus creating frustration.[34]

From the perspective of the participants, aside from this limited frustration, these programs were opening up new avenues. From the point of view of the Head of the Public Service, they were addressing an urgent need to prepare future public service leaders. However, these programs were disrupting the dominance of departments over their employees.

Disruption and Disrupters

The La Relève Task Force was also a disruptor. On 4 June 1998, Prime Minister Chrétien announced the creation of the *Leadership Network* (LN). This was the approach used to provide some seed funding to the team supporting the La Relève initiative. The mandate was to "promote, develop, and support networks of leaders throughout the Public Service of Canada, and to assist them in the ongoing challenge of public service renewal."[35] The Leadership Network had no legislative or normative authority. The authority of the Treasury Board Secretariat as employer and the Public Service Commission for appointment and the safeguard of the merit principle was unchanged. The role of the Network was animation, facilitation, and networking across the public service. The Network launched a website, *leadership.gc.ca*, that garnered positive attention from out-of-government web guides. It also ran an online magazine called *A Day in the Life of the Public Service of Canada*, focused on profiling workers throughout the federal government.

The work of the Leadership Network was challenging at times. There were tensions with the Treasury Board Secretariat and the Public Service Commission in spite of supportive relationships at the highest level. I owe a debt of gratitude to the pioneers who served in the Leadership Network under the leadership of Peter Harrison – Richard Rochefort, Bob Chartier, Marilyn Hay, Margaret Amoroso, Danielle Labonte, Lisa Millar, and others. They were the real champions of La Relève. Bob Chartier best captured the initiative:

We went into La Releve believing leadership was singular to management.

We came out knowing leadership through practice was available to all.

We went into La Releve believing innovation was a program or maybe a committee.

We came out seeing innovation as part of our daily work.

We went into La Releve believing we needed outside consultants to make things work better.

We came out knowing that the real knowledge was in the system and in our own people.

We went into La Releve believing that consultation was the only route to our public.

We came out realizing that true workplace and civic engagement was the better key.

We went into La Releve believing that important things like values were just a workshop title.

We came out building core values into our own front line Team Charters.

We went into La Releve believing pride was a wish.

We came out with pride written on our faces.[36]

It is not easy to be a change agent. Eventually, the Leadership Network was re-integrated into the mainstream. It was transferred to the Treasury Board Secretariat in 2001 after I stepped down as Clerk, and elements of it melted into the rest of the human resource management apparatus over time.

The Leadership Network generated energy and enthusiasm when the public service needed it most. It created hope for a better future. It contributed in no small way to maintaining peace and preventing the kind of unrest other public services experienced while leading reforms on a much smaller scale. The Network had started something that did not end with its disappearance. Some of the ideas continued with the support of the Canadian Centre for Management Development, and the Leadership Network champions continued to nurture new ideas about management and leadership in their respective organizations.[37]

A Search for Balance

There are unresolved tensions in the public service of Canada between two desirable goals: building the capacity of individual departments and agencies and stewarding the public service of Canada as a whole. There has been insufficient discussion about the balance that would best serve the overall interest of the government of Canada and society.

Public organizations need flexibility to fulfil their mission and adapt to changing circumstances. This perspective led to a progressive transfer of authority to departments. The expectation was that this might increase adaptability and yield better public results without undermining the capacity of the public service as a whole to fulfil its mission. The evidence did not point in this direction at the end of the first quarter of the twenty-first century.

Over the years, several Secretaries to the Treasury Board, including Peter Harder, Wayne Wouters, and others, have made great efforts to delegate decisions to departments just to find out that the delegation went no further than the Deputy Minister's office – thus leading to no material difference for the vast majority of people in these departments. In other cases, abrogated central policies were replaced by departmental policies as stringent or even more demanding than before. I was unable to find compelling evidence that administrative delegation and staffing delegation from the Public Service Commission have led to better results, better service to Canadians, and a professional public service better fit for purpose.

The public service of Canada has had difficulty keeping up with technological changes or with the progress made by other countries, in spite of an exceptional period of growth that saw the size of the public service grow from 186,314 employees in 1999[38] to 367,772 in 2024.[39] Keeping in mind the rapid growth of the population, this translates to a ratio of about 9,000 public servants per million Canadians, up from a low of about 6,100 in 1999. *Growth did not translate into improved service delivery capacity and policy capacity.* Something else is at play that needs to be better understood.

Institutional capacity-building raises questions about what should be held in common to ensure that the public service of Canada can fulfil its mission: serving Canada and Canadians now and in the future. What common values and principles, what common practices, systems, platforms, competencies, and collective capabilities are needed to ensure that the public service of Canada is fit for purpose in a fast-changing environment? What balance between departmental flexibility and collective capabilities would best ensure that the public service of Canada is able to fulfil its mission?

Organizational weaknesses lead to service failures, mismanagement, or declining quality of service. Such weaknesses damage the reputation of the government of Canada, the public service as a whole, and the relationship of trust with citizens. However, *institutional weaknesses* are even more serious. They lead to an erosion of the capabilities, skills, and competencies of the public service and a weakening of the public infrastructure that Canada and Canadians depend on.

There are many avenues and different views about the desirable balance. Whatever path is chosen in the future, greater clarity is needed about the public service we aspire to build. This is necessary to reveal the trade-offs involved and the consequences that various choices entail.

Learning from the past may help the public service of Canada distinguish past decisions that helped build a stronger institution from those that eroded its capacity. Administrative delegation and growth of the public service were not the answer to its problems. In spite of these changes, a case can be made that the public service operates under a heavier burden of controls than before and is at increasing risk of politicization. A new balance must be found for the public service to chart its course with confidence to serve Canada and Canadians in the future.

11 Moving On: The Canadian Centre for Management Development

A Clerk transition is a delicate operation. People leaving the position of Clerk before me retired from the public service, often leaving to pursue other opportunities. I had watched Paul Tellier manage his transition. On 1 July 1992, the position of the Clerk was split. Glen Shortliffe became Clerk, Secretary to Cabinet, and Head of the Public Service. I became Secretary to Cabinet for Federal-Provincial Relations, reporting directly to the Prime Minister rather than through the Clerk, as was previously the case. Paul Tellier moved on to become President and CEO of the Canadian National Railway. Glen Shortliffe retired in March 1994, after which he turned to consultancy.

I was in a different situation from my predecessors. I was not yet fifty years old and I was not done with my interest in the public service of Canada. I wanted to leave the position of Clerk and continue to serve as a Deputy Head and a member of the Deputy Minister community. This was unusual, and to my knowledge had not been done before. Gordon Robertson stepped down as Clerk and served as Deputy Clerk when Michael Pitfield was appointed, but this arrangement was temporary and intended to appease concerns about the incoming Clerk's limited experience.

I reminded Prime Minister Chrétien that I had made a commitment to serve for five years and that we were now into the fourth year. The Prime Minister was not enamoured with the idea of making changes. We had worked together during the difficult years of the first mandate, and the reinvestments phase in the second mandate. His government was getting closer to the end of his second term in office, and things were going well – so why change?

The public service was in a better position than before, and I had diligently worked to ensure that there were people with the diversity of experience needed to serve as Clerk. Over the years, I had made sure to prepare people with experience in central agencies and line departments and to expose them to public service and government-wide issues. I offered the Prime Minister my assistance to help him reach a decision. Some potential candidates could be invited to brief him, discreet meetings could be arranged at 24 Sussex, etc.

The Prime Minister kindly inquired about why I wanted to leave and what I would do after. In truth, I was tired. I had not had any down time for years. I did not have my usual level of energy and I was not renewing my ideas fast enough for what lay ahead. We all have an image in our mind about how a job should be done and what it takes to live up to our own expectations. I had overcome the early doubts I held at the time of my appointment about not being the right person for the job. I felt that I had done a good job and that, after all, I had been the right person to lead the public service through this challenging period. I was proud of the way I fulfilled the role. I could leave happy about what was accomplished. At a personal level, I wanted to explore new ideas and get new experience. On the question of what I would like to do after, I assured the Prime Minister that he did not need to worry about this until he had found a successor.

The matter was set aside, and we went on working as usual. I raised the matter again a few months later. This time, there was an understanding that the selection of a successor needed to be taken seriously. Once the Prime Minister had chosen my successor, we returned to the question of what I would do after. I had given the matter serious thought and had considered several factors. First, I was not interested in retiring, running a large Crown corporation, or taking a Senate position. Second, I did not want to serve in a Deputy Head position where the insights I had gained by serving the Prime Minister could be used to advance the interests of a particular minister. With the exception of ambassadors and various international agencies, most senior positions in the public service of Canada report directly to a minister. Finally, I wanted to serve the public service and continue to support public service reforms.

My preference, if the Prime Minister agreed, was to become the next President of the Canadian Centre for Management Development (CCMD). I believed that the public service of Canada deserved a school of public administration of the kind that other developed countries enjoy. CCMD was reporting to the Prime Minister through the Clerk, and therefore I would be in a position to support the priorities of a new Clerk. The appointment was modest in the public service hierarchy and therefore could not possibly be threatening to a new Clerk. This assignment would give me time to think, read, teach, and undertake some research work of my own. I thought this was an elegant solution and a brilliant idea. To say that the Prime Minister was surprised is an understatement. He was worried about the perception: "People may think you are being pushed." This had never crossed my mind. He was the politician and as always, much better at anticipating public reaction. There had already been rumours that I might be pushed out.[1] The Prime Minister took care to prevent this perception. He celebrated my contribution as Clerk and showed me support in my new role. I was deeply touched by his generosity.

Figure 9. Sworn in as the Honourable Jocelyne Bourgon, 14 December 1998. From left to right: the Right Hon. Jean Chrétien, Prime Minister; the Hon. Jocelyne Bourgon; and His Excellency Roméo LeBlanc, Governor General. Photograph by Jean-Marc Carisse; used with permission.

On 14 December the Prime Minister announced my departure and the appointment of Mel Cappe taking effect on 18 January 1999.[2] I chaired my last Deputy Minister retreat with Mel Cappe by my side to signal a smooth transition. I put the finishing touch to the last Ministerial Cabinet retreat I would prepare as part of the annual cycle of Cabinet retreats initiated five years earlier. On the last day of the retreat, ministers were invited by Governor General Roméo LeBlanc for dinner at Rideau Hall. After giving instructions for the preparation of the record of Cabinet decisions, I went directly to Rideau Hall. When I arrived, the Prime Minister was already there. He asked me to keep company with Mrs. Aline Chrétien while he met the Governor General. I was happy to do so. Mrs. Chrétien had always been most welcoming in the private sessions I had with the Prime Minister at 24 Sussex and in more formal occasions.

Some time later, the Majordomo informed us that the Governor General was ready for us. Mrs. Chrétien and I walked together to the door of the ballroom. To my surprise, ministers were already seated, and at the front of the room the Governor General and the Prime Minister were waiting. Mrs. Chrétien whispered, "This is for you, this is all for you. Go ahead." I had to swallow hard as I walked down the aisle to be sworn in as the *Honourable Jocelyne Bourgon*.

Nothing had transpired in advance of the event. This was a most generous gesture on the part of the Prime Minister. The Governor General hosted an elegant dinner in my honour with all the ministers I had had the privilege to serve during the last five years.

Without being overly melodramatic, I must say that after all these years, I am still in awe that a young woman, a French-speaking Canadian born in Papineauville to a modest family, was appointed Clerk of the Privy Council for Canada in the mid-1990s well before any other G7 country. And yet, this is a story other women like Beverly McLaughlin, Kim Campbell, Jeanne Sauvé, and Flora McDonald could tell. This is a very Canadian story, one that Jean Chrétien, Brian Mulroney, and other prominent Canadians have experienced and contributed to writing.

Transiting Was Not So Easy After All

On 21 January 1999, I became the *President of the Canadian Centre for Management Development*. I had served seven years as Secretary to Cabinet: two years as Secretary to Cabinet for Federal-Provincial Relations under Prime Minister Brian Mulroney and five years as Clerk, Secretary to Cabinet, and Head of the Public Service under Prime Minister Chrétien. Seven years is a long time in these jobs. I am proud that I had the opportunity to serve under two Prime Ministers from different political parties and different political affiliations: an illustration of a professional, non-partisan public service in action. I was ready for a new adventure.

The next election was called on 22 October 2000. I had made the right call by leaving in time for Mel Cappe, the eighteenth Clerk of the Privy Council, to run a transition planning exercise, make some changes to the senior public service ranks, and get ready to welcome the thirty-seventh Parliament. The third mandate was tumultuous. Two Clerks would serve during the last mandate of Prime Minister Chrétien: Mel Cappe from January 1999 to May 2002 and Alex Himelfarb for the rest of Chrétien's mandate. Prime Minister Chrétien would step down on 12 December 2003 after entering politics forty years earlier and serving as Prime Minister for ten years.

In spite of careful planning, I mismanaged my transition in some ways. The announcement of my departure and of the appointment of my successor was kept under very close wraps. As a result, the outgoing President of CCMD was only informed of her new assignment a few days before the event. Janet Smith was appointed head of a task force on *A Truly Representative Public Service.* Jean Edmonds had published a well-known report on the "glass ceiling" ten years earlier, documenting the barriers to the upward mobility of women in the public sector. Progress had been made, but it was time to take stock of the progress to date and map out a new course. Janet Smith was eminently qualified to take on this task. To this day, I regret that she was informed at the last minute. The announcement of her appointment could have been better managed.

My main mistake, however, was to underestimate the difficulty for Deputy Ministers in adjusting to the co-existence of a Clerk and a former Clerk. For me, the matter was simple: there is only one Clerk. I hastened to say that Mel Cappe was always most generous and courteous with me. During his tenure, he never raised any concern about my role, and for my part I made sure that CCMD actively supported the Clerk's priorities. The problem was more subtle.

By temper and personal experience, I believe it is important to speak one's mind on issues while leaving no doubt about supporting decisions once they are made. This was the culture Paul Tellier inculcated during his years as Clerk and as I grew up as Deputy Minister. This is how I worked with colleagues – deputy ministers, ministers, and prime ministers. I continued to do the same now that I was a Deputy Head again. It took me a while to realize that it was not so simple. Deputies were decoding my every word from a different perspective – was the former Clerk overstepping her bounds when commenting on or challenging ideas under discussion? I first became aware of this during a DM breakfast meeting where Mel provided guidance to Deputy Heads on the precautionary principle during an election campaign. I was the Deputy Head with the most experience on this as a result of the Pearson Airport case during the 1993 electoral campaign.[3] I shared my experience, laid out the lessons learned, and stressed the need for prudence. Who was speaking in this instance? What voice were deputy ministers hearing? The voice of an experienced colleague, or a former Clerk adding her voice to the guidance provided by the current Clerk?

Mel Cappe and I were the first to live through the experience of managing the co-existence of a Clerk and a former Clerk over an extended period of time. I knew how difficult the job of the Clerk was; the last thing I wanted was to add to the difficulty. My best way to help was to build a school the public service would be proud of.

Serving in the Knowledge Age

The year began with an open house on 10 February 1999, when the Prime Minister outlined his expectation for CCMD. "The task ahead for all of us is to prepare Canada and Canadians for the knowledge-based economy and society of the new millennium. It also means that we need a public sector that is well prepared: prepared for its role in a digital society, prepared for its role in a global society, prepared for its role in a knowledge-based society."[4] This was consistent with the 1997 and 1999 Speeches from the Throne[5] that I helped prepare.

I was taken by the idea that an important transition was underway towards a knowledge-based economy and society, and by the implications this would have for democratic societies. From the late 1990s onward, many of the drivers of change that would shape society were known: globalization, the information and technological revolution, increasing complexity and velocity, changing global demography, and aging population in parts of the world … What was not known was how profoundly this would transform society and the governance of democratic society, and how different countries would adapt.[6]

As Clerk, I had encouraged the CCMD to explore the challenge of serving in the knowledge age. Driven by the leadership of Ralph Heintzman and Maurice Demers and starting just before I became Clerk, the Centre carried out a series of research projects bringing practitioners together with prominent academics – B. Guy Peters and Donald J. Savoie served as research leaders and editors. This work was jointly published by CCMD and a major university press, McGill-Queen's. The third volume focused on *Governance in the Twenty-First Century.*[7] It was a good start, but not sufficient to guide public sector leaders' decisions and actions.

The challenge for Canadian public sector leaders was to ensure that Canada would be among the countries that would successfully navigate through an accelerating period of change. This was no small task then, and it remains daunting today. The Canadian chapter was underway but not yet written.

Learning Organizations

In March 2000, the Clerk signalled in his first report to Parliament that learning was key to preparing the public service to serve Canada and Canadians for the knowledge age. I supported this view; serving in the knowledge age required learning and adapting at a much faster pace than before. The Clerk asked me to chair a Deputy Minister's Committee on Learning and Development to shape "an ambitious learning agenda." I was most happy to assist. With the assistance of the Leadership Network and Richard Rochefort in particular, a round of consultation was organized across the country over a four-month period. Meetings took place in eleven cities – thousands of civil servants participated in the events. The report of the Committee was entitled *A Public Service-Learning Organization: From Coast to Coast to Coast.*[8] It was presented by and endorsed by the Clerk on 13 July 2000.

This was an important milestone for the public service. To put it in perspective, it should be remembered that there was no training or development policy for the employees of the public service of Canada at that time. According to the Public Accounts of Canada, the public service was spending 0.97 per cent of its wage bill on training and development. By comparison, based on a Conference Board report, the average Canadian business was investing 1.7 per cent of its wage bill, while the financial sector was investing 2.7 per cent. The situation was even worse when one considered that the Canadian private sector was doing much less than their counterparts in the USA or Japan. The comparison between the Canadian public service and other developed countries was even worse. France was investing 3.8 per cent of its salary base in training, Ireland 3 per cent, and Singapore had guaranteed its employees one hundred hours of training per year.[9] In a speech to regional managers on 30 November 2000, I argued that there was "a growing gap between our aspirations and our actions. It is urgent that we close this gap. The credibility of managers depended on it."[10] The public service could not aspire to serve in the knowledge age if it was not prepared to invest in its human capital and to support the learning needs of public servants to keep up with the times.

The learning needed was not limited to the individual level; the public service needed smart organizations able to think through complex issues in new ways and to work across sectors and across boundaries. The task force fleshed out the concept of a learning organization – it was a relatively new concept in the public service at the time; Peter Senge's *The Fifth Discipline* had introduced the concept only in 1990. Several of my speeches in 2000 expanded on the idea and explored the concept in the Canadian context. The task force presented a detailed work program.[11] One of the recommendations was to put in place a learning policy for the public service.

The Treasury Board Secretariat took over, and two years later, on 1 May 2002, a *Policy for Continuous Learning in the Public Service of Canada* came into effect. This was a first in the public service of Canada. It included a commitment to learning plans for permanent employees, annual reporting, and a year over year increase of the training budget for the next three years. Institutional changes take time. This was a small step but one in the right direction.

Over the years, I continued to flesh out the concept of a learning organization in a public sector setting and to speak about the profound transformation needed to prepare public institutions for the challenges of serving and governing in the knowledge age. I began to explore with colleagues in other countries the challenge that a shift from serving in the industrial age to serving in the knowledge age entails. Government reforms, I argued, had barely begun.[12]

Talent Incubators

CCMD was running a suite of courses in support of various previously mentioned corporate leadership development programs, including the Management Trainee Program (MTP), the Career Development Program (CAP), the Accelerated Executive Development Program (AEXDP), and the Assistant Deputy

Minister Prequalification Process (ADMPQP). It was also hosting events of various kinds to encourage networking and shared learning across the management and executive community, up to and including Deputy Heads and Heads of agencies.

Much of the learning for managers takes place in action, not in the classroom. CCMD championed action learning and action research methodologies. In both cases, public managers are directly involved in exploring, debating, and pushing their thinking as practitioners by interacting with others within and beyond the public service, including research facilitators. In this context, research is not done for practitioners but by and with practitioners. The learning is not separate from practice; it is in the doing. This approach transforms the relationship between theory and practice into a dynamic approach that involves learning from practice, theorizing to capture the insights and potential broader applications, and bringing back ideas to practice, testing them and accelerating the learning. It brings together a diversity of perspectives and insights from multiple sources, including academia, other public organizations, and other countries. It is action oriented and driven towards problem solving. Action research projects at CCMD were one-year projects aimed at addressing real-life issues and making progress in practice. The projects brought together world-class experts and practitioners to generate cutting-edge ideas and practical results.

I am a strong believer in this approach, and I brought these ideas to the international work I would go on to lead in later years. CCMD action research projects contributed to disseminating new ideas and practices across the public service. They helped broaden the thinking of public sector leaders by exposing them to a diversity of perspectives as well as the global, national, and regional dimensions of public policy challenges that government was facing in practice. CCMD launched three action research projects per year between 2000 and 2004, covering subjects ranging from Risk Management, chaired by Ian Shugart, then ADM at Health Canada, to Official Languages in the Workplace, chaired by Michael Wernick, then ADM at Heritage Canada, and Canada-USA relations, chaired by Louis Ranger, then ADM at Transport Canada.

The membership of the action research projects sounds like the "who's who" of people who would take on positions of increasing responsibility in the coming years. This pattern is even more striking when one adds to the list the people who served in the task forces I launched as Clerk or before as Secretary to Cabinet for Federal-Provincial Relations. Looking back, beyond the immediate benefits of each project or report, they served a key purpose in the stewardship of the public service. Deputy Minister Task Forces, the La Relève Task Force, the Policy Research Initiative's research committees, the Citizen-Centred Service Network, the CCMD action research projects – all of these brought people together to work across boundaries and take on cross-cutting issues. They prepared future senior public servants by exposing them to a diversity of perspectives and training them to think across boundaries. Several members of these projects would become deputy ministers, such as Morris Rosenberg, Suzanne Hurtubise, Alan Nymark, Simon Kennedy, Mike Horgan, and many others. A whole generation of future Clerks – Mel Cappe, Janice Charette, Alex Himelfarb, Kevin Lynch, Ian Shugart, Michael Wernick, and Wayne Wouters – played parts in these projects. I have a gift for creating talent incubators.

I was not aware of this at the time, but it is an important insight: corporate projects can act as talent incubators by exposing managers to a diversity of perspectives and a government-wide perspective. Complex issues require a more holistic approach to problem solving because the economic, social, political, environmental, and technological dimensions are intertwined and interacting dynamically.

Bringing the Outside In

CCMD worked hard at building relationships beyond government and in particular with schools of public administration. On 29 November 1999, CCMD revitalized its *Fellows Program*. This was a multiyear program aimed at bringing outside experts – academic Fellows – into CCMD to teach and do research, and at bringing some senior public servants – Public Service Fellows – into the Centre to develop their skills and public service knowledge alike.[13] It was in line with the work done previously by the Policy Research Initiative. Meanwhile, the CCMD gave new life to its Annual University Seminar, extending an invitation to PhD students – the next generation of public administration scholars. The Annual University Seminar was already a flagship event at CCMD, bringing together senior public sector leaders and members of the Canadian academic community. The Seminar was held in conjunction with the Manion Lecture, another CCMD flagship event, given by a distinguished scholar or practitioner often from abroad. All this contributed to building a stronger relationship between academics and practitioners.

Learning from each other is an important step, but learning from other countries is essential to ensure that Canada remains at the leading edge. In April 2000, CCMD launched the *Partnership for International Cooperation*.[14] There was a growing demand abroad to learn from the Canadian experience in various domains, and an increasing need for Canada to learn from the innovative practices emerging abroad. Canada has a habit of focusing on USA and UK reforms even when the most innovative ideas and practices are taking shape in European countries, in Southeast Asia, and in other Commonwealth countries like Australia, Singapore, and New Zealand. CCMD actively engaged with international organizations to organize study tours, international projects, and partnership agreements. CCMD built partnerships with École nationale d'administration in France, ENAPE in Brazil, and the Australia and New Zealand School of Government, and with international organizations interested in governance such as the OECD, CAPAM (the Commonwealth Association for Public Administration and Management), and the United Nations.

The partnership between CCMD and the Singapore Civil Service was particularly significant. Singapore, a small and densely populated country, was in the process of creating its Civil Service College. Their aspiration was to bring a cultural change in the public service to encourage innovation and technological adaptation. Canada, a vast and sparsely populated country, wanted to prepare the public service for the knowledge age and was about to create the Canada School of Public Service. Both countries had common interests.

Public Service Modernization

In April 2001, the Prime Minister announced the formation of a Task Force on *Modernizing Human Resources Management in the Public Service,* headed by Ranald Quail.[15] The Fryer Committee report on labour relations in 2000, the Strong Committee report on senior level retention and compensation in the same year, and Auditor General reports in 2000 and 2001 all argued that human resources management was overly complicated, that streamlining was necessary, and that more devolution to Deputy Heads was the way to go. The Task Force went along with this view, recommending a streamlining of the role of the Public Service Commission and devolution to Deputy Heads. Mel Cappe, who had launched the effort, stepped down in May 2002 and the work continued under Alex Himelfarb, his successor.

Personally, I was not convinced that the proposed legislative reform was the answer to the challenges ahead. If the problems the reforms wanted to address were bureaucratic in nature, there were better ways. I was concerned that the proposed reform had not sufficiently considered *what the public service needed to preserve and what was needed for the future.*

Public organizations are human systems. Their behaviours are shaped by purpose, people, rules, norms, and many intangible factors. Laws are powerful but blunt instruments. They set boundaries within which actions are permissible, but they also create new rigidities and are known to cause unintended consequences. As the adage goes, "Every system is perfectly designed to get the results it gets."[16] If the human resources management system was bureaucratic, risk-averse, or slow to adapt, there were reasons for this. The key was to avoid fixating on the symptoms and to focus on the big picture. *What kind of public service do we aspire to build for the future?* What changes, big or small, could cause the human resources management system to behave differently and to generate more desirable results?

The staffing system and the human resource management system needed change. On that, there was a consensus. The Public Service Commission was at times conflicted between its roles as an agent of Parliament and as a service agency. It was indeed bureaucratic and risk-averse, but it had achieved good things. It had contributed to building a professional, meritorious, non-partisan public service. It had kept political patronage at bay and prevented the corrosive damage caused by corruption that other countries experienced. The public service had made some progress to adapt to the Official Languages Act and the Charter of Rights and Freedoms. It was responding to changes in the Canadian labour force and had been more hospitable than the private sector to people with a diversity of backgrounds. *Not everything was broken.*

On 21 March 2002, in a speech at a Conference of Public Service Commissioners from various countries, I argued that the PSC was a brilliant invention because it *reconciled the merit principle and the doctrine of ministerial accountability*. "The Commission can be viewed as a self-denying ordinance on the part of all members of Parliament, whereby they give up the right to intervene through patronage in recruitment and promotion decisions in favour of an agency reporting to them [the PSC] [...] Eighty years later, the Public Service of Canada can proudly claim to be one of the most professional public services in the world."[17]

Would the proposed decentralized system fare as well on the essentials – that is, in building a world-class professional public service? What needed to be done to reconcile the need for administrative flexibility and the overall interest of the public service? What measures were needed to mitigate the risks of new forms of patronage in which promotion depends on who you know in the public service rather than on competencies and prior achievements? Would this reform lead to a greater risk that elected officials would reclaim "their right to intervene"? Would the reform create an incentive for departments to operate as closed systems, thus limiting interdepartmental mobility, the competition for talent across government, or the diversity of experience needed to serve at the most senior levels? Overall, what was the balance needed between administrative flexibility and institutional capacity to prepare the public service of Canada for the challenges of serving in the knowledge age and keeping pace with the increasing complexity of the world we live in? There were too many unanswered questions around the proposed legislation for my taste.

Twenty years have passed, and it would be worthwhile to take a careful look at the results to date. Did the reform help ensure that departments have the skills and competencies needed to fulfil their mission? Did it ensure that the public service of Canada is one of the best in the world, recognized as a professional, merit based, non-partisan public service? *In short, is the public service of Canada better prepared for the challenges ahead as a result of this reform?*

Over the years, there has been a progressive but significant erosion of the merit principle in the public service of Canada. Today, merit means that a person meets the statement of qualifications for a position. There is no comparative requirement, no need for competition, no need to consider other candidates within the same department or beyond, and no opportunities for public servants to signal their interest in a vacant position. An appointment meets the merit requirement because a person is deemed to have met the basic qualifications.[18] Has this practice served the overall interests of the public service of Canada?

A comparative concept of merit looks at a candidate's qualification or suitability relative to others. This recognizes that merit is not an absolute notion, but a relative search for the best staffing decision with regard to the mission, the circumstances, and the existing talent in the team. A relative concept of merit has its weaknesses, but it prevented patronage and incentivized a dynamic internal market through competition for talent.

A well-performing public sector needs a strong centre of gravity. To me, this was and remains *serving Canada and Canadians*. On this, the public service should be uncompromising. This has a number of implications, including a commitment to excellence, abiding by public service values including incorruptibility, and getting the best talent the public service and the country have to offer in fulfilling its mission to serve. Today, a commitment to excellence is barely mentioned in the Public Service Employment Act. The increasing number of reported corruption cases is disturbing.

Bill C-25, the Public Service Modernization Act,[19] was introduced in the House of Commons on 6 February 2003. The portion of the Bill most directly relevant to me at that time was that the Canadian Centre for Management Development would become the *Canada School of Public Service*. The mandate of the School was expanded to all employees as well as managers and executives. The Board of CCMD and I had argued for a greater integration of the two in the 1996–2001 five-year review report, tabled in the House on 8 February 2002.[20] The internal discussions surrounding the creation of the Canada School were more challenging than I expected. There were conflicting views about its place and role. Should it continue to report to the Prime Minister through the Clerk, as before, or should it be an agent of the Treasury Board? Should it operate on cost recovery or be funded through appropriation? Should the Board of Governors be decisional or advisory? How much control should Treasury Board exercise over the school? I held strong views on all these questions. At the end of the day, I believed – and still believe – that the Canada School should reflect the views of the government of Canada and the Clerk of the day.

On 28 April 2003, as a witness to the Standing Committee on Government Operations, I explained and defended the reasons for creating the Canada School of Public Service. I was happy that I was not questioned on other aspects of Bill C-25. When asked if I would serve as its first President, my reply was that it was the right time for a change of leadership.[21] The Bill received royal assent on 7 November 2003, with the part forming the School coming into force on 1 April 2004.[22] By that time, I was the proud President Emeritus of the Canada School of Public Service I had helped to create and Canada's Ambassador to the OECD. I was ready for a new adventure.

PART 4

Working Abroad

12 The International Public Servant

The transition from Clerk to President of CCMD (now the Canada School of Public Service) gave me the opportunity to shift from twenty-five years of hands-on leadership of public organizations to an assignment providing more time to focus on the need to prepare the public service of Canada for the challenges ahead. Becoming Ambassador at the OECD in June 2003 was a second transition, this time from a Canadian to an international perspective. This change of scenery was most welcome.

My appointment as OECD Ambassador was not my first foray on the international scene. As Deputy Minister, Clerk, and President of CCMD, I played an active role there. This was important in a number of ways. I kept abreast of international developments relevant to Canada. I kept a watching brief of reforms introduced by other countries and, time permitting, I stayed in close contact with other Cabinet Secretaries or Heads of the Public Service. Over the years I developed a network of colleagues I respected. Later, I would build on this network to launch an international research network on *A New Synthesis of Public Administration*. Finally, I used international events and the opportunity to deliver keynote speeches to crystallize ideas by exposing them to an international audience of people knowledgeable about public governance. This practice has served me well over the years.

My international activities were not sequential. Several took place during the same period and overlapped with other responsibilities. I maintained a special relationship with the Commonwealth Association for Public Administration and Management (CAPAM) from its inception in 1994 to its dissolution in 2019. I served as board member for many years, and as President from 2002 to 2006. I served on the United Nations Committee of Experts in Public Administration (CEPA) from 2002 to 2009, including as Chair from 2006 to 2009, and on the board of the Institute for Government (IFG) in London, UK (2008–14). I was a board member of the Civil Service College in Singapore (1999–2003) and later a senior fellow (2008–present). To this day, I work regularly with

Figure 10. 2003 retreat of ambassadors to the OECD. Bourgon is in the front row, second from the right, in the white jacket. OECD Secretary General Donald Johnson is in the front row, fifth from the right.

colleagues in Singapore, France, Denmark, Finland, The Netherlands, and more recently some countries in the Gulf Region. Over the years, my experience as an international public servant blended with my experience as a Canadian public servant.

My international work ensured that my ideas were exposed to a diversity of contexts and that my research work was grounded in practice even once I was no longer involved in the day-to-day management of public organizations. Many of the ideas that emerged through my international work would later contribute to shaping *A New Synthesis of Public Administration*.

Delivering a keynote address for an international audience has been one of the ways I used to explore ideas. For me, it is not a writing or speaking exercise; it is a thinking process. It is an opportunity to synthesize my thinking and to capture the essential elements of a narrative that may span many years. It is also a way to expose emerging ideas to the light of day. This helps to reveal the weaknesses and the blind spots in one's reasoning. A speech is an invitation to others to enrich the conversation by contributing their ideas. This approach remains an important part of my practice. The learning is in the doing, in the sharing of ideas, and in exposing them to a diversity of practice – be it within a department, across the public service, or with an international audience.

As part of this project to transfer my personal archives to Library and Archives Canada, we have collected many major speeches, numerous PowerPoint presentations, and a considerable number of research papers. There are too many to give an account of the topics covered. This overview is therefore limited to sketching some of the ideas that would influence my leadership of an international research project on *A New Synthesis of Public Administration.*

An Ecosystem of International Relationships

As Clerk, I did not have much time to stay current with what other countries were doing. Nonetheless, I paid attention to the reforms in the United Kingdom and the United States of America. I was well aware of the difficulties experienced by the New Zealand and Australian governments in their attempts to bring rampant deficits under control. From the 1980s to the mid-1990s, the fiscal situation of several countries had deteriorated and urgent corrective actions were needed. The United Kingdom needed assistance from the International Monetary Fund in 1976, just years before the 1980s recession. New Zealand struggled with inflation and unemployment entering the decade; both Moody's and S&P downgraded the country's credit rating in the first half of the 1980s.

Two streams of ideas were shaping government response at the time. Proponents of a neo-liberal philosophy were of the view that less government was synonymous with better government and that leaving the lead to the private sector would generate a more prosperous economy and better results overall. The New Public Management, for its part, was proposing that government should be run in a businesslike fashion whenever possible. The two sets of ideas were different but their coming together had much influence in shaping government agendas in the mid-1980s and through the 1990s.

The government of Canada did not embrace the philosophy that less government was synonymous with good government or that tax cuts were the solution to every problem. In the mid-1980s the government of Canada opted for structural reforms with long-lasting effects. This included opening up the Canada-USA market and introducing a value added tax. In the mid-1990s, Canada's approach to balancing the budget rejected the New Public Management philosophy; not everything should be monetized or run like a business. Under Conservative and Liberal governments alike, the approach of the government of Canada was *to balance economic prosperity, solidarity, and fiscal responsibility*. In many ways, Canada's approach blended a European view of the role of the state in society with a North American view of a market economy.[1] Not everything can be left to market forces, and market forces should not be overly constrained. Canada was following a divergent course from the USA and the UK.

While Clerk, I was frequently invited to participate in international conferences to share Canada's experience with public sector reforms. I participated in only a few, because of time constraints, but used these events as an opportunity to speak about a *"Canadian Model of Reforms"* to bring together multiple strands of public sector reforms over several years. I first describe the concept in a speech on 25 August 1997, at the International Council for Canadian Studies.[2] I fleshed out the idea in the opening chapter of my third annual report to Parliament on the state of the Public Service.[3] I presented a fuller version of the idea on 22 April 1998, at a Commonwealth Conference in Public Administration,[4] and on 10 September 1998 in Singapore at a conference at the Civil Service College.[5]

In summary, the *Canadian Model* affirms the importance of the role of government for a well-performing economy and society. Government brings about change by building on the strength of the private, public, and civic sectors and in balancing public, private, and civic interests. It affirms the importance of citizens well beyond their role as consumers of services. It gives equal weight to service delivery and policy capacity in the public service. It requires strong political and professional leadership. It recognizes the importance of the role of public institutions, public organizations, and a professional non-partisan public service.

At a time when the New Public Management theory was dominant, Canada was presenting a distinct and original perspective that attracted the attention of countries that were uncomfortable with a reductionist view of the role of the state or with the push towards deregulation and privatization. This was the case for countries in continental Europe and some Southeast Asian countries, as well as some developing countries. In Canada, Peter Aucoin provided a useful analysis of the Canadian model.[6] The model and its results attracted the attention of international observers; the *Economist* ran a front-page story in 2003 highlighting Canada's fiscal turnaround: "a cautious case can be made that Canada is now rather cool."[7] At the end of the 1990s Canada *had a distinctive voice and an original approach to public sector reforms.*

From 1999 onward, as President of the Canadian Centre for Management Development (now the Canada School of Public Service) and later as Ambassador at the OECD, I became more preoccupied by the challenges faced by practitioners in the early days of the twenty-first century. The word "practitioner" is sometimes used with contempt. It is not in my case; I use it with the greatest respect. This term describes activities where practice is the essential driver of progress. It is the term I would use to describe professions like engineers, public servants, or professionals in applied sciences from cybernetics to aerospace or bioengineering. Practice is the means used to test the value of ideas, to gain experience and new insights that may then be used to theorize, generate new ideas, and move practice forward. I am a practitioner, and proud of it.

I was increasingly concerned about the growing gaps between ideas, systems, and practices inherited from the industrial age and the challenge of governing and serving in the twenty-first century. Public administration in the Western world had taken shape in the late nineteenth and early twentieth centuries. Public institutions in North Atlantic countries had taken form during a period characterized by an Industrial Revolution and a process of democratization. But that was then and this was the early days of the twenty-first century.

The world was witnessing the early stages of a technological and digital revolution. The impact would be as deep and as steep as the Industrial Revolution, but it would unfold at a much faster speed.[8] Practitioners, both elected and professional, were operating in unknown territory and without the benefit of a modern theory to guide their action. I believed that this was putting practitioners at risk, and I argued that *one cannot serve and govern in the twenty-first century with the ideas inherited from the nineteenth century and the practices of the twentieth century.* As I would sum it up in 2007, "We are asking public servants to serve with one foot in the future and one foot in the past. We are asking them to serve citizens in the 21st century with a model of the 19th century and to respond to citizens' expectations with the tools of a previous era. Are we really surprised that it does not entirely meet expectations?"[9]

I used international forums to voice concerns about the need to prepare government and society for the challenges ahead with progressively more emphasis. The reforms to date "have paid little attention to the impact of globalization and new information technologies on our concept of citizenship or on our system of representative democracy."[10] The technological and digital revolution that is transforming the market will transform as profoundly the role of government and the public sector.[11] We are witnessing "the most profound transformation since the Industrial Revolution. It is revolutionary in nature, not evolutionary. It is transforming the economic and social order, the market system, the role of the State and […] the public sector."[12]

In the early 2000s, some countries were taking actions to adapt to changing circumstances and have since reaped the benefits of their early efforts. They are better prepared to deal with increasing complexity, volatility, and a higher level of uncertainty. They have integrated modern technologies to service delivery and policy making. They have made early investment to adapt to a rapidly changing social-techno-ecological environment.

Looking back, I think that *Canada missed a turn in the early part of the twenty-first century*. At the time Canada had the fiscal capacity to invest in a future of its choice. Program Review, the last ambitious public service reform of the twentieth century, generated a budgetary surplus that lasted for twelve years. Twenty-five years later, the fiscal rent has been spent and Canada is once again facing a challenging fiscal situation. Some countries have made better use of the last twenty years and some have made better decisions. This is starting to show in Canada's overall comparative performance. No country is promised a prosperous future. Government decisions matter.

Over the years, I deliberately looked for opportunities to learn from public sector leaders in developed and developing countries. Working with international organizations like the Commonwealth, the United Nations, and the OECD enlarged my perspective.

I built an expanding network of practitioners starting close to home. The United States of America is in many ways a special case. There are avenues available to the USA that are not available to a country like Canada. The capacity for innovation of the USA is unparalleled. That said, their governance has been in a state of flux for many years. More recently, the USA has broken with some basic democratic principles like the peaceful transition of power. There are signs of illiberal changes. It will take time to discern the direction the country may take and how this may impact the rest of the world. For these and many other reasons, the USA could only be so much of a reference to prepare a country like Canada for the challenges ahead.

Nonetheless, I followed the work of the *National Partnership for Reinventing Government* that was launched in 1993 by President Bill Clinton and chaired by Vice President Al Gore.[13] I participated in some of the conferences, including one in Seattle in November 2000. The purpose was to identify "the trends that may shape the public reform agenda in the years to come, and to identify the issues that should be at the top of the research agenda if it is to guide public service reform."[14] As a speaker, I suggested that the trend that would most profoundly influence the government reform agenda would be a shift from the Industrial Age to the Knowledge Age. Twenty years of reforms had not prepared government for what lay ahead. "Modernizing government requires that we revisit the very foundation of government — and that means our concepts of citizenship, democracy, state, and public service."[15] Citizenship is a dynamic concept that sets the boundaries between the public and private spheres of life in society and the division of labour between the market, the state, and the community. What will it mean to be a citizen of a modern, democratic, post-industrial society in the twenty-first century in the midst of a technological and digital revolution? If democracy is understood as deliberative and participatory, what needs to be done to prevent a hardening of positions and a breakdown of a spirit of collaboration in a world of instant communication? What are the implications for the role of government, public institutions, and the public service?

My presentation surprised the chair, Vice-President Gore, and some of the USA participants. It did not fit well with the prevailing views in the USA administration. However, it resonated with some European delegates and in particular with delegates from the Netherlands. I had found kinship of spirit;

some public sector leaders shared my concerns. The Netherlands has been a source of inspiration for me and for others interested in governance. For centuries, they have mapped an original trajectory and have constantly adapted to a changing economic, geopolitical, and environmental landscape. Their academic work about the challenges of governing liberal democratic societies in a post-industrial era is second to none. Over the years, I maintained a relationship with Dutch colleagues. Years later, the Netherlands would be one of six countries I would invite to launch an international research network for exploring the new frontiers of public administration.

Continental Europe was a fertile ground to explore ideas about public administration. I paid attention to the work of the International Institute of Administrative Sciences (IIAS) and the International Association of Schools and Institutes of Administration (IASIA). They provided a broader perspective than I could find in North American literature. I spoke at a joint IASIA and IIAS conference in Athens in 2001 about *Public Service Leadership in the Knowledge Age.*[16] I argued that the signs of a shift from an industrial to a knowledge-based economy and society were all around us. This is when knowledge become the primary ingredient of what a country buys, makes, and sells; when the jobs created are knowledge-intensive and the ones disappearing are low-skill and repetitive; when companies buy more equipment to process information than to transform the physical world – then we know that this shift is well underway. I argued that the adjustment would be especially difficult for government because public organizations are governed by rules and because compliance has been rewarded more than innovation and public value creation. I expanded on this theme at the *Public Sector Leadership Forum* in 2001 co-hosted by Canada and Singapore,[17] and at the annual CAPAM (Commonwealth Association for Public Administration and Management) conference in Uganda the same year.[18]

By that time, the need to build the capacity of government and society to adapt to an accelerating pace of change resulting from the combined effects of globalization and a technological revolution was on every country's agenda – from the USA to the European Union, from China to India, from Singapore to Canada. Public servants were facing the dual challenge of advising government on the public policy mix that would best serve their country and, at the same time, preparing the public service for different ways of serving.[19] In the public service, the nature of work was changing from repetitive tasks to intangible services. As the assets of public organizations were becoming intellectual, the hierarchical management model was under stress. To address complex issues, public organizations needed to work across boundaries.[20] This was challenging the authority structure, transforming the role of the centre of government and the management of the political-professional interface. This is turn was blurring the lines of accountability.

A consensus was beginning to emerge that serving in the twenty-first century was different compared to prior times. It may not be more difficult in absolute terms than what prior generations experienced, but it is different. Serving in a post-industrial world, in the midst of a technological and digital revolution, in a world showing increasing signs of ecological and planetary stress had a number of unique characteristics compared to prior times.

There were early signs that democratic societies were finding it more challenging to adapt than authoritarian regimes. A more pointed question was *what needs to be done to ensure that democratic, liberal economies and societies would continue to outperform others in the fast-changing landscape of the twenty-first century?* The question is even more relevant today.

Europe and the USA played a crucial role in shaping the common norms and rules of twentieth-century governance. It took two world wars and tens of millions of deaths for the world to say "never again." The *Universal Declaration of Human Rights* – which recently celebrated its seventy-fifth anniversary – and the *Genocide Convention* rose from the ashes of these events. The *Human Rights Convention*, the *International Court of Justice*, the *United Nations*, the *World Bank*, and the *International Monetary Fund* gave the world a *common set* of norms and practices under which peace and prosperity flourished. Common principles reduced the risks of conflict; common rules constrained government behaviours. Globalization of trade and of the economic space encouraged interdependence and, when accompanied by conflict resolution mechanisms, reduced the risk of conflict.

Today, common rules and norms are challenged by authoritarian regimes and illiberal states even if they use some form of electoral system. They are also challenged by people who benefit from living in democratic societies, as principles promoting equality under the rule of law and human rights are being undermined by demands to entrench differences. The democratic net of intertwined principles is fraying, with unknown consequences. Serving and governing in the early part of the twenty-first century are more challenging than ever before.

In the mid-1990s and early 2000s, it was relatively easy to build a close relationship with European colleagues and to expand my network. The mood was optimistic and future-oriented. For European countries, building a better future meant building *Europe*. They had learned about the risks of exacerbated nationalism and had witnessed the danger of ethnic conflicts. The focus was on the expansion of Europe and building a prosperous future.

The world is not made of liberal democracies and developed countries alone. An ecosystem of international relations requires a deeper understanding of developing countries and an appreciation of the accelerating velocity of change in countries like China, India, and others that are reshaping the economic and geopolitical landscapes.

The Commonwealth

Working with the Commonwealth Secretariat and Commonwealth countries expanded my network beyond Europe and North America. Irony aside, I shared with Queen Elizabeth an interest in the Commonwealth. Some see it as anachronistic, a legacy of a colonial era and therefore a vision of the past. I saw the Commonwealth as a mix of countries well positioned to advance development and democracy in member states around the world.

The Commonwealth includes an unusual mix of countries at various levels of development, including some of the poorest countries, according to the United Nations Development Program index, and some of the wealthiest like Canada, Singapore, Australia, New Zealand, Great Britain, and two of the BRICS countries, South Africa and India. Commonwealth countries are present on every continent as well as the Caribbean and the Pacific islands. The Commonwealth is not as polarized as the United Nations, and member countries share some similarities in the design and functioning of their public institutions. My work with CAPAM allowed me to build enduring relationships with Singapore, Malaysia, Australia, New Zealand, and South Africa.

In 2003, I believed there was a window of opportunity for the Commonwealth to play a significant role as a geopolitical laboratory to explore how governance can help ensure that economic prosperity and solidarity progress in a mutually reinforcing way and ensure powerful links between governance, prosperity, democracy, and social progress. I was invited by the Commonwealth Secretariat to join a committee of experts to explore the interrelationships between democratic governance and pro-poor development. The committee was chaired by Manmohan Singh, former Minister of Finance in India. The committee reframed the conversation about development and pro-poor development. It defined development as "strengthening human capacities to lead long, healthy, creative and fulfilling lives."[21] A variation of this definition was later used by the United Nations Department of Economic and Social Affairs. Poverty was defined as deprivation of basic capability and development was described as the process of ensuring that the most basic capabilities are achieved by all.[22]

Poverty is the ultimate form of discrimination. Equality under the law means little to those who cannot support their basic needs for food, shelter, and security. Framing the conversation in terms of capabilities was an innovative move at the time. This is important to escape from the logic of blame and retribution. Poverty destroys one's soul and victimization destroys one's agency. The way one frames an issue has a direct impact on the solutions that will be found and the results that will be achieved. The importance of framing policy issues in broad and social terms would play an important role in the New Synthesis of Public Administration.[23]

Figure 11. Group photograph from the CAPAM High Level Seminar in New Delhi, 4–5 October 2005. CAPAM President Bourgon is in the front row, sixth from the left.

The committee of experts also broke from the logic of the Washington Consensus. Nowhere is the evidence of the damage done more visible than in Africa and parts of Asia. In the 1980s and 1990s, poverty alleviation was seen as a problem requiring technical solutions – reducing debts, improving conditions for foreign direct investments, opening markets, and deregulating. Financial flows in search of short-term gains created risks for developing economies, including overspending, rent capturing, and corporate bribery. The short-term costs of trade liberalization needed to be reduced to take full advantage of the benefits of trade while preventing negative impacts on food security or other local production.[24]

Governments needed to mitigate these risks to reap the benefits. Deregulation, privatization, and open market measures needed to be calibrated to ensure that economic development and social progress evolved in concert. This was true in developing countries as well as in the most developed countries. In every "first world" country, there are people living in "third world" conditions. Deprived individuals or vulnerable communities are not a faceless mass of people. Making progress means to see through their eyes, call their names, and hear their voices. We had not yet learned much about a circular economy, but the world would soon wake up to the reality of a circular world. Poverty walks and people left behind would sooner or later find ways to ensure their voices would be heard across Europe and the United States of America. Unbeknownst to many, the conditions were ripe for the rise of nationalism and favourable for the rise of authoritarian and illiberal states.

The United Nations

I worked closely with the United Nations over many years, first as member (2002–5) and then as chair (2006–9) of a Committee of Experts on Public Administration (CEPA), and later as an occasional advisor. CEPA studies and makes recommendations to improve governance and public administration. The committee is made up of twenty-four experts serving in their personal capacity. They bring geographic diversity to the deliberation of the committee as well as expertise from a broad range of academic disciplines. I served for two mandates of four years. The committee operates under the umbrella of the Department of Economic and Social Affairs (DESA), mandated to share ideas and practices among UN member countries about economic, social, and environmental development. It reports to the general assembly through the Economic and Social Council.

Serving on CEPA was an honour and an enriching experience. Looking at the membership between 2002–5 and 2006–9 brings back fond memories of animated discussions among an unusual mix of elected officials, professional public sector leaders, and members of academic institutions from around the world. Some members were well known to me because of my work at OECD or the Commonwealth. Some would later contribute to the New Synthesis project. Discussions with colleagues from countries and organizations where I had weaker links were invaluable. This was the case, among others, for Pan Suk Kim (South Korea), a former advisor to the PM who later became president of IIAS; Mikhail Dmitriev (Russia), who brought unprecedented expertise on leadership development in Russia; and Werner Jann (Germany), who introduced me to the remarkable public administration scholarship of the University of Potsdam.

All in all, we did good work on public sector innovation,[25] participatory governance and citizen engagement,[26] capacity building for development,[27] and the human factor in capacity building and development.[28]

In 2004, I was invited to deliver the opening keynote address at a conference co-hosted by the United Nations and the European University Institute in Florence, Italy. The topic of the conference was *Unlocking the Human Potential for Public Sector Performance*, but I decided to depart from the topic I was assigned. Before focusing on performance, were there not bigger questions to address?[29] The world had witnessed remarkable governance successes like the construction and expansion of the European Union, the peaceful transition from apartheid to equal rights for all citizens in South Africa,

Figure 12. UN Committee of Experts on Public Administration. Bourgon, chair of the committee, is in the front row, centre.

and a transition from a centrally planned economy to a market economy in Estonia, Hungary, and Poland. The world had also witnessed failures and setbacks like the HIV pandemics, the Asian financial crisis, and the devastating impact of failed states. For a time, it felt as if governments were losing faith in the role of the state and had unrealistic expectations of the market's ability to solve problems like poverty, rising inequality, drug trafficking, and social violence. Unleashing the potential of government should begin with a conversation about the role of the state in society. What kind of state do we aspire to build? What needs to be done to achieve prosperity and improve human conditions?

I argued that a lack of balance between markets and the state and a lack of clarity about the role of the state were responsible for the failures of a number of public policies and public sector reforms. For instance, the Asian financial crisis in 1997 was not caused by excessive regulation but by the absence of an adequate regulatory framework. Russia's post-Soviet difficulties were a compelling example of the need to build the state for the market economy to flourish rather than suffer rent capturing by the oligarchs. There never was any compelling evidence that cutting taxes lifts all boats. Korea, Thailand, Argentina, and Indonesia were advised to cut their taxes at the worst possible time in their economic cycle, which in turn magnified the crises they were experiencing. So, the first step is to "articulate in modern and compelling terms the importance of the role of the State" for a well-performing economy and society. This is the most important step.[30] The second step is to recognize that governing *is a search for balance* between the private, public, and civic spheres of life in society. It is ultimately the responsibility of government to define where this balance may lie in the context and circumstances prevailing at the time.

The theme of *governing as a search for balance* resonated with the participants. This idea would play a central role in the New Synthesis Project. CEPA explored some of the barriers to a balanced approach to reconcile prosperity, solidarity, and sustainability.

My work at the UN was converging with the lessons I had learned working with Commonwealth countries and with the work I had done with the International Institute of Administrative Sciences. A notable example was the first IIAS Conference in Sub-Saharan Africa. The conference took place in Yaoundé, Cameroon. It brought together three hundred participants from forty-nine countries. As rapporteur general, I was assisted by four academic scholars of great standing from Cameroon, Saudi Arabia, Argentina, and the Netherlands. The theme of the conference was *Shared Governance*, a reminder of the shared responsibility of the public, private, and civic sectors to make progress and move society forward. "'Shared governance' implies the diffusion of power within society among multiple actors – including governments, civil society, business, academia – and acknowledges the responsibilities and interdependencies of these actors. It requires citizens' participation. It requires competence, transparency, and accountability at all levels."[31] What was remarkable during the conference was the recurring theme of the central role of the state to promote the public interest.[32] A second theme was that progress required a *state infused with purpose* so that economic growth is accompanied by social investments such as in health, education, and sustainable development.

A *state infused with purpose* is a powerful idea. When government lacks clarity of purpose, collaboration, convergence, and shared responsibilities are hard to achieve. Another theme running through the conference was that no one has all the tools to build a prosperous economy and society. Progress requires a collective effort. Power is a shared concept. It is vastly distributed between several actors within and outside government, across sectors and across and beyond the country.[33] A year later, IIAS published a special edition of its international journal to disseminate the key findings. I was honoured to write the Introduction.[34]

My work with Commonwealth countries, the IIAS, and the United Nations was converging. Some ideas were emerging over and over again. I began to see some common threads running through the practice of colleagues around the world. My assignment at the OECD gave me the opportunity to pull some of these threads together.

The OECD

My colleague Donald Campbell, then Deputy Minister of Foreign Affairs, had encouraged me to consider an international assignment after setting up the Canada School of Public Service. Ambassador positions with responsibility for bilateral relations involve a mix of foreign policy issues, trade, consular activities, security, and defence issues, and so on. I did not feel I was best qualified for these jobs. Multilateral organizations are different: they involve heavy public policy content and I knew a few things about policy making.

I will forever be grateful to Prime Minister Chrétien for the opportunity to serve as Canada's Ambassador at the OECD. This was a big change in my life at both professional and personal levels. My son had just finished his master's degree and was entering the workforce. My husband was retiring as CEO of SCO Health Service (now Bruyère Continuing Care) after over a decade at the helm of the organization. We prepared our house for rental, helped our son get organized, and moved to Paris. It was a good time to be there; the OECD was entering a new period of change.

The predecessor of the OECD, the Organization for European Economic Co-operation (1948), was born out of a shared commitment to cooperation. World leaders were determined to make sure the trade wars of the 1930s would not be repeated. They had first-hand experience of the consequences of choosing confrontation over cooperation and putting national interests above shared interests. These are lessons the world would be well advised to remember, as we are witnessing once more the return of protectionism and territorial conflicts. Once European reconstruction was completed, the experience of the OEEC was put to use in support of a broader purpose. The OECD was born to support the peaceful functioning of the world economy. It seeks common rules through consensual learning to ensure that the benefits of the global economy are more broadly distributed and reducing frictions through dialogue.

The story of the OECD is the story of how an international organization working by consensus managed to adapt and remain relevant in a changing world. It took ten years for the OECD to gain a North Atlantic perspective, and thirty years to build a broader international perspective. Japan joined in 1964, Australia and New Zealand in 1973, in the 1990s Mexico and Korea became members, and the OECD assisted East European countries in their transition to a market economy.[35]

The OECD is not the United Nations. Membership is selective and by invitation; members are "like-minded" in the sense that they share a commitment to a combination of democratic and market economy principles. It is an unusual organization. It provides no direct financial assistance and has no means to compel compliance. It works through peer review, peer learning, and self-regulation. Applied to the Canadian context, such an approach could be a source of inspiration for the management of a highly decentralized federation. Progress through shared learning should not be more difficult to achieve in a federation with ten provinces and three territories than among what was at the time thirty member states.

At the time I became ambassador, the OECD faced the inescapable reality that the weight of its members in the world economy was declining as China, India, Brazil, and Southeast Asian countries were rapidly growing; membership was not going to be the solution to ensuring the relevance of the organization in the future. New ideas and new approaches were needed.[36] As Ambassador and member of the OECD Council, my work focused on expanding the interactions between members and non-member countries. I served as chair of the OECD Committee on Cooperation with Non-Members, later renamed the External Relations Committee. A first step was to encourage the participation of non-members in substantive policy work. A key part of this was the approval by Council in 2005 of a policy framework on enhanced engagement with non-member countries that I had the honour to lead as chair.

The OECD played a key role in the accession to the European Union of countries like Estonia, Latvia, and Lithuania. They became members of the OECD in, respectively, 2010, 2016, and 2018. The OECD also deployed many efforts to build strategic relationships with Russia and China as well as Middle Eastern and North African countries. This work continued long after I left. However, there were early signs of what was to come.

For a time, there was an expectation that Russia would become progressively more democratic and more "like-minded." What began as a Western partnership with Russia ended not in Russia's liberal transformation, however, but in its return to one-man rule. The Russian system is one of personalized power, the antithesis of a state based on the rule of law. This period demonstrated the West's naivety, and the dangers of democratic countries' acquiescence at the expense of their own norms in the hope that this may bring about change. From 1999 onward, with the Second Chechen War, there were ample signals about the direction Russia was taking. A lesson to remember.

In the case of China, the situation was quite different. Their claim was and remains that modernization and progress are compatible with authoritarianism, that there is nothing inevitable about democracy and nothing universal about the liberal values of equality or human rights. China has rejected both a move towards democracy and the acceptance of human rights. It is a model of an illiberal regime committed to achieving economic growth while preserving authoritarian rule. It is demonstrating that it is possible to combine creating a large middle class and pulling people out of poverty with authoritarian rule.

One important lesson is that both Russia and China have learned to use the law to suppress opposition and to use cyberspace to shrink the civic space. They have skilfully and patiently worked to change the norms governing international organizations. They have had a remarkable level of success in reshaping international bodies founded to promote human rights and democracy into bodies favourable to regimes that do not endorse either.

The rise of illiberal states is an important trend. These countries claim legitimacy through elections but use the authority of the state to suppress democratic rights once in office. Some have introduced constitutional changes to stay in power – e.g., Orbán restricting opposition expenditures and entrenching party control of elections in Hungary, or Putin weakening term limits in Russia. In other cases there have been systematic actions to erode citizens' rights, human rights, and protections for minorities – e.g., Russia's crackdown on political dissent, especially in the wake of the 2022 escalation of the war on Ukraine; Turkey's extensive restrictions on the press and on social media; or China's persecution of its Uyghur minority.

There are many lessons for democratic countries to learn from events in the last fifty years. One is that the Western world has underestimated the power of authoritarian regimes like China, Russia, Iran, and Saudi Arabia. Second, it has underestimated the attractiveness of illiberal policies in democratic countries, in some European countries and the United States of America, to curtail immigration or limit human rights. In fairness, illiberal states have done relatively little to undermine liberal democracies; the latter's problems are largely self-inflicted. *The attractiveness of authoritarian regimes grows when the prestige of democracies declines.*

Serving as Ambassador at the OECD was an opportunity to learn from twenty-nine other countries. The OECD was a great platform to learn about the fast-changing geopolitical landscape of the world; much was happening that is now becoming more visible.

Breaking the Flow

Meanwhile, Canada was not so focused on the international scene – internal politics took centre stage. The "sponsorship scandal" was dominating in the news, Parliament, and public discussion.

In February 2004, four years after I had stepped down as Clerk, Prime Minister Martin launched a commission of inquiry, known as the Gomery Commission. Ten months later, 8 and 9 December, I flew from Paris and appeared as a witness before the Commission. I spent two days answering the questions the Commission put to me. The next day, I caught a plane and returned to work at the OECD.

The questions the Commission put to me centred on a sequence of memos I had sent to the then Prime Minister in 1996 and 1997. My view then was and remains that there was no "sponsorship program" at that time (a program would be created much later). A national unity reserve had been earmarked in the fiscal framework to address unforeseen spending related to national unity. Such reserves, as acknowledged by the Commission, were not new. At issue was how departments could access the reserve and how decisions were made to release funds. PCO was of the view that it was unwise for the Prime Minister to take the responsibility for allocating funds from the reserve, and this is the advice that I conveyed to the PM. In the end, the PM judged that, everything being considered, he preferred to retain the authority to allocate funds from the unity reserve.

What made the scandal significant was that a political party benefited from a corruption scheme and that government officials broke the law. This shattered the public perception that Canada was relatively immune from problems of corruption. Canadians always knew that mistakes were being made and that it is tempting at times for people to turn a blind eye. But the perception was that corruption on a significant scale was an issue for "other countries." Now there was evidence that there was no safe space and that Canada needed to guard against the risks of corruption. The "sponsorship scandal" shattered that view of the relative incorruptibility of the Canadian public sector leaders, both elected and professional – it was, in a way, the end of innocence. Was this a traumatic but isolated episode? Or, rather, was it a sign of a deeper and more widespread problem? Recent events give cause for concern.

13 A New Synthesis of Public Administration

In 2006, I was invited to give the *Braibant lecture*, the International Institute of Administrative Sciences' flagship lecture. This would prove to be a turning point in my work.

I gave many speeches over the years, but preparing a lecture is a different exercise. The text has a longer life span, and the audience is much broader. The Braibant lecture is held in high standing by the academic community, so I took it seriously and dedicated several weeks to preparing it. I freshened up on my reading on governance and with recent articles in public administration.

The Braibant lecture was an opportunity to bring together the many strands of what I had learned from practice, what I had learned from fellow practitioners in other countries, and insights I had gained by exposing my ideas to the scrutiny of colleagues and scholars in developed and developing countries. Much was known about some of the drivers of change. We knew there was a growing gap between the traditional model of public administration and the increasing complexity of issues and accelerating velocity of change governments were facing in practice. Some emerging ideas and some new practices were promising, but then what? There was a need to reconcile ideas of enduring value that had served governments well in the past and new ideas better suited for the times.

I decided to make the case for *"A New Synthesis of Public Administration."* This was a humongous claim with the very real possibility of being ridiculed. Honestly, I was fine with this. What is the point of having years of experience and years of reading and thinking about the challenges of governing and serving if it is not to venture where people at an earlier stage in their career would not dare to go? A scholar who would dare to propose the need for a unifying theoretical frame would immediately come under attack – some would argue that this is not possible, others would challenge the very idea of a meta-narrative … and as this debate would go on, the old narrative that everyone knew was discredited would remain in place and keep being used as a reference to judge practitioners' actions. A practitioner with a reasonable reputation was in better position to take that risky leap.

The Braibant Lecture

The old narrative of public administration in the Western world took shape at the end of the nineteenth and in the early twentieth centuries. It was – and remains – clear, simple ... and misleading. Government represents citizens' interests. Its decisions are deemed to serve the public interest. There is a strict separation between policy and implementation. Rule of law, due process, accountability, and compliance are the dominant values. Citizens' role is to vote, obey the law, and pay taxes. (Yes, I know that this is an over-simplification.) These ideas played a key role in shaping public administrations in a period characterized by an accelerating process of industrialization and democratization. These ideas were fit for that time.

I proposed that "... the test of a strong theory is not just its staying power. It is the trait of resilience that implies an ability to adapt to new and unforeseen circumstances."[1] There was a need for a theory that could integrate past strengths, current knowledge, and future challenges. There were limits to what can be achieved through the power of the law and the coercive power of the state. There were limits to what can be achieved by taxing and spending. Complex issues respect no boundaries. A broader perspective and a more dynamic approach to problem solving were needed to bring about viable solutions. I argued that "there is nothing so practical as a good theory" (quoting Kurt Lewin)[2] but nothing more dangerous than ideas that lag behind the times and yet remain the yardstick for making decisions and passing judgment.

Practitioners needed a frame of reference to guide their actions: "a theory that builds upon the strong foundation provided by the Classic model, incorporates the lessons of the last thirty years, and anticipates the imperatives of public service in the twenty-first century."[3] The nagging questions were: What would this mean in practice? What were the essential elements and how would they all fit together? And, assuming we agreed (which was far from obvious), how would we undertake such a huge amount of work? I did not have the answers, but I was inviting the academic community to engage with practitioners to theorize, test ideas, and synthesize them in a coherent set of dynamically interacting principles. I put forward four building blocks – citizenship, public interests, service to citizens, and public policy – to launch the conversation.

Citizenship was first understood as a legal construct: people as equal bearers of right under the law. As a legal concept, citizenship contributes to building a peaceful and governable society. The role of government is to make and enforce laws that set citizens' rights and responsibilities. But there is more to it. *Citizenship is an integrating concept*. As citizens, people must reconcile their multiple identities and roles in society as members of a larger community. Citizens must resolve the conflicts between their multiple identities and multiple interests as taxpayers, citizens under the law, parents, workers, and members of their chosen communities of interests with their interests as members of society. From this perspective, the role of government is *to make citizens* – that is, to build the capacity to think and act as citizens able to rise above individual preferences to make progress with others. The role of government is to build a *civic spirit to rise above differences to build and share a better future together*. The old and the new needed to be woven together in new ways to propel society forward.

In 2024, at the time of writing, I would still stand by that proposition. Today we see more clearly the risks of a polarized society encouraged by social media, the consequences of uncompromising positions, and the impact of an identity perspective that erodes the inclusiveness of a society built on a concept of citizens as equal bearers of rights. The challenge faced by government in 2024 is more intricate and polarized than in 2006 as the "I" of individual identity is replacing the "we "of our shared humanity.

Framing the concept of *public interests* was even more challenging. On this topic, one can find a theory for all seasons, including that there is no such thing. For some, the public interest is the aggregation of individual interests, and for others it is the result of an interplay of single interest groups. If we think of the public interest as distinct from single interest, *then the role of government is to ensure public interest dominates in public policy decisions.* Weaving the old and the new together, governments represent and promote the interest of citizens. They express the will of people to realize the public interest. In 2024, this is also more challenging than before, with political polarization driven by cultural polarization and by social media.

At the time, the growing gaps between conventional thinking and the emerging reality of practice were most visible in service delivery. Public policy making transforms ideas into a reality citizens experience collectively. *A policy decision that government does not have the capacity to implement is a bad decision, a bad policy, and ultimately bad governance.* The capacity to deliver is central to policy design and policy decision. Implementation is not an afterthought; it is a core policy function because it brings essential insights about public policy challenges. It facilitates course correction and adaptation. It provides intelligence about what works and what does not in the real world. The coming together of policy decisions and implementation brings together the world of ideas and reality.

The conventional view argued for a strict separation between policy decision and policy implementation, while in fact there was a need for dynamic interactions to improve the likelihood of success of government interventions. This means more interactions between professional and elected officials, more interactions across departments, more collaboration across sectors, and more collaboration across jurisdictions at the local, regional, national, and international levels. In 2024, I believe that this is as relevant as before. *Policy decisions separate from implementation considerations lead to announcements rather than achievements.* At best this leads to delayed implementation and the public frustration that comes with it; more frequently it leads to failures. In recent years, there have been a number of examples of policy breakdowns in Canada that illustrate the difference between announcing decisions and making them work in practice. In the Canadian context, this is due to a combination of factors, including the weakening of policy and delivery capacity, the weakening of government IT systems (especially but not exclusively legacy systems), the increasing influence of political staff, and so on.[4] In combination, these weaknesses lead to repeated systemic failures.

Public administrations that operate based on a concept of multiple separations reflect the ideas of the industrial age. This will be insufficient to invent solutions to the complex challenges that stem from living in the twenty-first century.

In the past as in the future, government must be able to set a course and to mobilize resources in support; this is not in question. However, setting a course requires more than making laws; it requires knowing when and knowing how to build on the strength of others to harness the collective capacity to bring about viable change. I argued that no one, not even government, has access to all the tools and capabilities needed to address the complex and intractable problems of our time. Dynamic system thinking and a collective approach to problem solving are needed to ensure early detection, anticipation, adaptation, and rapid course corrections. Practitioners are asked to invent solutions to the problems of the twenty-first century with an institutional model inherited from the twentieth century. This is putting them and the country they serve at risk.

Dr. Christopher Pollitt, a renowned public management scholar at University Leuven and editor of the *International Review of Administrative Sciences* for IIAS, was surprised when he listened to the lecture. His view was that I had taken a most unusual approach for a practitioner: "More common is the declaration of a five-step programme, or a civil service code, or a new model of customer-centred service or some other apparently concrete and practical set of actions […] Yet I fundamentally agree with Bourgon's line. It is indeed a theory (or possibly theories […]) that we need."[5] He published a special edition of the journal and he invited others to engage in a mini symposium on a *New Synthesis of Public Administration.* He contributed an article to encourage the discussion, where he made a comment that explained why I could get away with my ambitious gamble: "Jocelyne is well known nationally and internationally as an enormously experienced top public servant who has somehow managed to stay in close touch with the academic world."[6] In other words, people may not welcome the challenge, but I would at least get a hearing.

I am grateful for Christopher Pollitt's encouragement and for IIAS's efforts for launching a dialogue between scholars and practitioners. In spite of their efforts, the conversation died down. I had previously experienced a similar situation in Canada when I tried to encourage joint efforts between practitioners and scholars on the challenges of *Serving in the 21st Century*. Practitioners are busy people and scholars have their own areas of interest that may or may not coincide with the needs of the public sector at the time. This is a conundrum I had witnessed in Canada and in other countries as well. In other applied disciplines, academic research fuels practice, but this is not the case in public administration, where research generally lags behind practice.

An integrated intellectual frame of reference to help practitioners think their way through the complex issues they were facing was not in sight and not about to emerge. Donald Kettl said it best: "Public administration without a guiding theory is risky; administrative theory without connection to action is meaningless. That dilemma is the foundation of a genuine intellectual crisis in public administration."[7] What could a reasonable public servant do in these circumstances? My term as Ambassador was soon coming to an end, and I was about to return to Canada. I would give this some thought once I returned.

After four years at the OECD, returning to Canada in 2007 was both easy and challenging. Our house was waiting for us. My husband was the newly appointed CEO of the Children's Hospital of Eastern Ontario, a challenge he was eager to take on. Our son's personal and professional life had taken on new dimensions. Our daughter-in-law was enriching our life and it was wonderful to be closer to them and have them in our life.

Professionally, I was not sure what to do. For family reasons, another international assignment was not possible. Prime Minister Stephen Harper had not signalled that he was eager to see a former Clerk play too much of a visible role in the public service. I was President Emeritus of the Canada School I had helped to create and was happy to return to it. The Clerk, Kevin Lynch, and the President of the Canada School, Ruth Dantzer, were welcoming. The question, though, was what will the President Emeritus be doing?

I had thrown out a challenge for a new theoretical framework of public administration to bridge the growing gaps between theories inherited from a prior time and the reality of practice.[8] This call gained a reasonable amount of attention by the standards of journal articles and citations – but attention is not action. Exploring the new frontiers of public administration and generating an integrated narrative to guide practitioners could not be done by a single person. This work required iterative dialogue between practitioners and academics. The question became: Who was prepared to put some effort behind such an initiative? I did not think I was the right person to lead such an ambitious project, but I could give it a push by calling on colleagues I had met over the years and who shared similar concerns.

From Practice to Theory

Personal commitment gives credibility to a call for action. It is hard to convince others to enrol unless the proponents are personally prepared to put some serious effort behind the initiative. So, I started at home.

The Canada School of Public Service (CSPS) came on board first. This was an opportunity to modernize their leadership development curriculum. CSPS assigned one person to the project: Peter Milley, who had a PhD in adult learning. He became the first Head of Research for the New Synthesis Initiative. Next, Kevin Lynch, the Clerk of the Privy Council, signalled his support and opened doors for me at the University of Waterloo. The Centre for International Governance Innovation (CIGI) and the University of Waterloo became partners. Their involvement provided academic support and some research funds.

The Early Research Work

With a small team in place, the research work began. The first step was to identify authors who had discussed the fitness of public administration to serve in a context characterized by increasing complexity and uncertainties.[9] We discovered that many authors had written about the widening gaps between public administration theory and practice. That work did not go much beyond problem definition and as a result had not received much attention in government circles.

A key insight from this first literature review was that many of the newer ideas were coming from disciplines that were not traditionally associated with public administration. Political science, constitutional law, and public law have played a preponderant role in shaping the public administration doctrine inherited from the industrial age. To prepare government for the challenges ahead, insights were needed from disciplines as diverse as biology, ecology, cybernetics, complexity theory, dynamic adaptive system theory, and resilience, among others. Promising practices were also emerging in various countries, ranging from computer-assisted service delivery to citizen engagement in policy making and budgeting, foresight and futures work, collective intelligence, and collective learning. The research work in the early days deliberately paid attention to areas that had received less attention.

The second effort was to bring complexity theory to public administration. The results were published under the title "*Complexity Theories: What Are They and What Do They Tell Us about Public Administration in the 21st Century?*"[10] Today, it is understood that governments are facing an increasing number of complex issues. It is also understood that addressing complex issues requires a different approach compared to making difficult decisions or running complicated operations.[11] It *puts a premium on the capacity of government for early detection, prevention, and proactive interventions.* Twenty-five years ago, the concept and the implications for government were not so well understood. Complex issues are multidimensional – multiple factors interact dynamically. They have emergent characteristics and are not entirely predictable.

The third literature review focused on the concept of resilience. It was published under the title of "*Resilience: Key Concepts and Themes and Their Implications for Public Administration.*"[12] The concept came initially from ecology. It is the capacity of systems to absorb shocks and disturbances and to bounce back while continuing to undergo change and to evolve. It could also be found in psychology, the capacity of people to recover after being exposed to extreme stress and existential crises. However, this concept was nowhere to be found in the field of public administration. Between 2000 and 2009, the concept began to get more attention in government circles. Several authors began to explore the relevance of the concept in domains ranging from climate change to financial markets, from power grid failures to floods, fires, or community building.

The concept of resilience is important for government and some of the implications run contrary to conventional practices. Applied to society, the concept stresses the dynamic interrelationships between economic, social, and ecological systems. Building resilience points to the need for a portfolio of strategies rather than dependence on a single approach, even if the latter is more profitable or efficient. Recently, the COVID crisis has alerted the public and government officials to the importance of resilience. We have learned about the vulnerability of supply chains dependent on a single supplier. Building resilience means to counter the drive for efficiency in order to preserve a level of redundancy to absorb disturbances and respond to unforeseen circumstances. This was painfully obvious in hospitals during the COVID crisis, and in the frequent breakdowns experienced in the public health sector in recent years. We have learned about the risks faced by communities reliant on a single economic engine, the damage and vulnerability of monocultures in agriculture or forestry. *Resilience puts a premium on diversity and feedback mechanisms.* The work of C.S. Holling (2001)[13] on Panarchy and of Ann S. Masten and Jelena Obradović[14] on social resilience was especially influential on our team.

The next step was to explore the potential of new information and communication technologies. This work was published under the title of "*Collective Intelligence: What Is It and How Can It Be Tapped?*"[15] The field of Collective Intelligence (CI) had gained prominence in the early 2000s with the widespread adoption of modern communication technologies. Twenty-five years ago, there was much naivety in democratic countries about the potential of new technologies to expand "collective intelligence" and the democratic space. In fact, there are numerous examples of dumbing down collective knowledge. From the start, authoritarian regimes were concerned about the disruptive nature of information and communication technologies and, as a result, they took great efforts to control their reach. At the same time, they learned how to use these technologies to strengthen their hold on society. Democratic countries, for their part, struggled and are still struggling to reconcile how to reap the benefits of new powerful technologies with the need to regulate their use to prevent irreparable harm to individuals or the fabric of society. This part of the research work did not go very far. Nonetheless, it revealed some promising avenues for government to co-create and co-produce public results by working with users and recipients of services, as well as the potential for technology-enabled services that allowed citizens to get services on their terms rather than at the convenience of public service providers.

As the research progressed, a number of interrelated strands began to emerge. Conventional public administration was shaped by ideas of multiple separations: the public and private spheres of life, politics and administration, policy decision and implementation, the governor and the governed. The early research work was signalling the need for dynamic interactions to bring about viable solutions to the complex issues that stem from living in a modern society. This was a long stretch from a view of the public service operating in a predictable way under strict controls. And yet, there is a need to hold government to the highest standards of probity, integrity, incorruptibility, accountability, and transparency for the exercise of power in society. Not everything was changing or needed to change. The old and the new needed to come together; government needed to encourage stability and serve beyond the predictable.

A New Synthesis of public administration, if one was ever attempted, would need to square the circle and explain how the capacity to adapt and evolve must coexist with the need for stability, predictability, and compliance under the law. The team debated this for hours over many days and weeks. Four dynamically interacting functions began to emerge. There was a need for *compliance function* – government must set a course, mobilize resources in support, make laws, and enforce them. But this was only part of the story. A *performance function* is needed to convert ideas into a reality that citizens experience collectively. An *emergence function* encourages early detection, prevention, innovation, and course correction to propel society forward. A *resilience function* builds the collective capacity to adapt, absorb shocks and disturbances, and prosper both in predictable and in unforeseen and unpredictable circumstances.

The view of the team was that some practices were getting in the way of building a dynamic approach to public administration. One factor was the confusion between compliance and performance. This was the topic of the fifth and last literature review, bringing us into 2010: "*Disentangling Performance Management Systems from Control Mechanisms.*"[16] This paper was written fifteen years ago but, in a Canadian context, it sounds strangely prescient in light of recent failures and breakdowns in the federal, provincial, and municipal public service. It also sheds a different light on the increasing burden of administrative and political controls.

The paper argued that there has been a progressive blurring of the lines between the compliance function and the performance function in the public sector. *A compliance function* is needed to prevent risks of corruption, fraud, mismanagement, misappropriation, and abuse of power. It exists to "ensure that the rule of law prevails, that due process is followed, and that public servants are accountable for their use of their delegated authorities."[17] The mainstay of the compliance function is the audit system, supported by adequate departmental control mechanisms. A good compliance system is objective, evidence-based, non-negotiable, and enforceable. *A performance function* serves an entirely different purpose. Its role is to achieve results of increasing public value for society. The ultimate test of a good performance function is better policy decisions leading to better public results at a lower overall cost for society. It is about continuous learning to improve results.

The paper argued that over forty years, "there has been a progressive integration of audit, evaluation, budgeting, planning, control, performance measurement, and performance management systems."[18] There is a need to disentangle compliance and performance functions in government to reduce the risks of corruption and ease the pressure for ever more ex-ante controls every time a mistake is made. The integration of audit, evaluation, and consultation led to well-known scandals in accounting firms in the private sector.[19] The same risks exist in the public service. At the time of preparing these notes, the Canadian public service has recently suffered several scandals involving financial misconduct and/or conflicts of interest, particularly around procurement. The fundamental role of audit is the detection and prevention of corruption and mismanagement risks. Disentangling audit from all other management considerations, including value for money, may be worth considering to prevent further damage to the reputation of the public service of Canada. It may be time to refocus the audit function on the fundamentals.[20]

Finally, the research work was wrapped up with a literature review on *complex adaptive systems* (CAS).[21] Between 2003 and 2008 there was a flurry of work by scholars on CAS in relation to various topics: Bovaird on management,[22] Buckley on society,[23] Duit and Galaz on governance,[24] Homer-Dixon on the renewal of civilization,[25] and Mitleton-Kelly on organization.[26] The field of public administration was finally catching up with complexity theory and dynamic system theories. Suddenly, it did not feel so lonely to argue for a more dynamic approach to government and governance.

As the work progressed, we maintained the practice of exposing the work in progress as frequently as possible. A narrative of public administration began to take shape through speeches I delivered in 2008 and 2009,[27] in Malaysia,[28] Singapore,[29] Helsinki (Finland),[30] Salvador de Bahia (Brazil)[31] at the XIV International Congress of the Centro Latinoamericano de Administración para el Desarrollo, and in Stockholm (Sweden). The keynote addresses at the 2008 Public Administration conference, York (UK),[32] and at the Institute of Public Administration Australia (IPAA) in Sydney (Australia)[33] the same year best encapsulate the evolving storyline. Reforms to date had been shaped as if government operated in a predictable environment.

The challenge was to prepare government to serve in both predictable and unpredictable circumstances. The keynote address at the 2008 IPAA national conference in Sydney received particular attention.[34] I received the *IPAA's Sam Richardson Award*, recognizing the most influential paper published in the *Australian Journal of Public Administration* (*AJPA*) in a given year.[35] The early work was getting some attention.

The research team had reviewed the work of hundreds of scholars and thought leaders and thousands of articles. The literature reviews were bundled together and released in March 2010.[36] We had done our homework; we could now credibly invite colleagues to the table. The New Synthesis Initiative was about to be launched.

An International Research Network

There were now many voices arguing that, compared to prior times, there were significant differences to serving in a modern post-industrial world prone to cascading failures and on an increasingly fragile biosphere. The work needed to reconceptualize public administration could keep research faculties going for years to come, and indeed this work is still ongoing today. Meanwhile, public sector leaders do not have the luxury of time. They serve in real time, with imperfect knowledge and often at the limit of their comfort zone.

I was searching for a low-cost approach with quick turnarounds. This is how the idea of an international research network came about.[37] A small group of public sector leaders would engage in a two-year cycle of exploratory conversations about the challenges of serving in the twenty-first century. Over the first half of 2009, I invited public sector leaders from six countries in their personal capacity. This was done to ensure freedom of discussion. The representation included two countries from the Americas (Canada and Brazil), two European countries (the UK and the Netherlands), and one country each from Southeast Asia and the Pacific region (Singapore and Australia). These six countries had significant geographic, cultural, and historical differences, as well as different governing systems.[38] The network was called NS-6. They all accepted my invitation.

Figure 13. The launch of the first New Synthesis book, with representatives of most NS6 partner countries. Left to right: Wim Geerts (Netherlands), Piragibe dos Santos Tarragô (Brazil), Justin Brown (Australia), Jocelyne Bourgon, Guy McKenzie (Canada), Wayne Wouters (Canada), Andrew Pocock (United Kingdom).

The New Synthesis Project required a significant commitment on the part of the participants. Not only would it take two years, but country-partners were responsible for doing most of the work. They would contribute research work and develop case studies. Each would host one international event at their own cost, where the other five country-partners would be invited. They would participate in the conferences hosted by their colleagues. The country-partners were encouraged to ensure that their delegations included senior and young public sector leaders as well as scholars from a diversity of domains. There was no central funding, no endowment, and no academic grants to support an effort that would span two years. Participants needed to figure out how to cover their own costs, and I had to figure out how to cover the cost of my team. I stepped down from the public service of Canada in 2009, and launched Public Governance International (PGI) to support the New Synthesis initiative. PGI published much of the New Synthesis work over time, including on its website (pgionline.com).

The question at the heart of the work of the NS Network was: *What do we need to do to ensure that the capacity of government to invent solutions will keep pace with the increasing complexity of the world we live in?* The focus was deliberately future-oriented. There was no expectation of reaching a consensus or of generating a common document. Instead, the expectation was that participants would leave each event enriched by the conversation and the insights of others, and as a result, better able to ad-

Madame,

Comme vous avez quitté la fonction publique du Canada afin de relever de nouveaux défis, j'aimerais vous exprimer ma gratitude pour votre apport remarquable.

Tout au long de votre carrière, que vous avez menée avec vigueur pendant trente cinq ans, vous avez relevé de nombreux défis. Au fil de ces années, vous avez travaillé avec diligence et enthousiasme sur des questions touchant les Canadiennes et les Canadiens et vous vous êtes acquittée de vos responsabilités avec dévouement et compétence. J'aimerais souligner le professionnalisme dont vous avez fait preuve dans les divers postes que vous avez occupés, par exemple, à titre de présidente de l'Agence canadienne de développement international, de sous-ministre des Transports, de greffière du Bureau du Conseil privé et secrétaire du Cabinet, de présidente du Centre canadien de gestion et de conseillère spéciale auprès du ministre des Affaires étrangères, ainsi que d'ambassadrice et de représentante permanente du Canada auprès de l'Organisation de coopération et de développement économiques. En particulier, j'aimerais souligner vos réalisations à titre de greffière du Bureau du Conseil privé quant au renforcement de la capacité de recherche stratégique de la fonction publique et de la réforme de celle-ci dans le cadre de l'initiative La Relève. Votre engagement envers notre pays et ses gens est tout à fait remarquable, et démontre bien l'excellence qui caractérise la fonction publique.

Au nom de mes collègues du Cabinet et du gouvernement du Canada, je vous offre mes meilleurs vœux de bonheur et de succès dans tous vos projets futurs.

Je vous prie d'agréer, Madame, mes sincères salutations.

Figure 14. Letter from the Right Hon. Stephen Harper, on the occasion of Bourgon leaving the Public Service of Canada.

vise their country. This was a most unusual approach to research in public administration.

The first roundtable, 24–6 March 2010, was held in the Netherlands. It was hosted by Roel Bekker, then the Dutch Secretary-General.[39] The Dutch had volunteered to host the first roundtable and there were good reasons to start there. The Dutch are pragmatic innovators and explorers – of new lands in the past and new ideas in modern times. The Dutch academic community has an impressive track record in exploring the implications of complexity science for public policy. The host brought together experienced practitioners and leading thinkers to engage in an exploratory conversation about the themes of resilience and emergence.[40] At the end of each day, the group was challenged to identify guiding principles for practitioners.

Being the first, the Netherlands shaped the model that was later used and further refined for other roundtables. At the end of the event, two rapporteurs, one from the host country and one from my team, summarized the findings. A roundtable report was prepared by the host country in collaboration with my team and broadly circulated.[41] This practice proved to be invaluable. Over forty scholars and practitioners contributed to the first roundtable.[42] It generated a high level of excitement. A high bar had been set.

The second session, 4–5 May 2010, was in Canada. It focused on achieving results of high public value – and in particular, how government can shift from a focus on micro-results to system-wide and societal results to integrate factors such as economic prosperity, wellness, life satisfaction, and intergenerational fairness.[43] The Canada School of Public Service, the host of the event, brought forward two case studies that were highly regarded, one on Canada's homelessness strategy and the other on immigration settlement and labour mobility. Both issues required working across jurisdictional boundaries and in collaboration with multiple departments and agencies to bring about the desired outcomes.[44] As an aside, I would note that these two issues remain strikingly relevant today. Working across boundaries remains challenging in Canada.

The third, 13–14 July 2010, was in Brazil, and focused on state authority, collective power, and shared governance.[45] It examined how new developments such as citizen engagement, social capital, and co-production were transforming the role of government in society and the relationship with public servants. The hosts presented a historical overview of prior public reforms. This was particularly important for a country like Brazil that had a turbulent past. President Lula had been re-elected at the time and major reforms were underway.[46] The "Bolsa Familia" was a transformative initiative aimed at creating a social safety net to alleviate poverty by providing a preponderant role to the beneficiaries and their families. The Bolsa Familia became a source of inspiration for other Latin American countries. This was one of the most important case studies generated by the NS initiative.

At the end of the conference, two rapporteurs summarized the key findings to date. Unexpectedly, a vague consensus was starting to emerge … something dynamic and fluid "where government, citizens and multiple actors in society transform the environment in which they operate and are themselves transformed by the changes their actions provoke,"[47] where governing entails a collective effort and engages a shared responsibility between the public, private, and civic spheres of society. As we left Brazil, there was no expectation that the fragile consensus would last beyond this session. To everyone's surprise, ideas continued to coalesce during the following session.

The fourth roundtable took place on 21–2 September 2010, in Singapore. The focus was resolutely on preparing government for the future and the imperative of serving beyond the predictable.[48] How can governments improve their capacity to anticipate emerging trends, to initiate proactive interventions and improve the likelihood of more favourable outcomes for society? The conference was building on the well-known strength of the Singapore public service to scan the world over for ideas and to adapt them to their context. By the time we reached Singapore, the conversation had shifted from what is different about serving in the twenty-first century to how to prepare government for what lies ahead.[49]

The conference was hosted by the Civil Service College. They had invited colleagues from the Prime Minister's Office in Finland to participate in the event. The work of the Finnish government on foresight work and strategic planning was well known. They were ahead of many countries at the time. The United Kingdom had also made progress with a Foresight program looking at major trends fifty years out. Singapore's Risk Assessment and Horizon Scanning Program (RAHS) had been recently launched to complement their earlier work on scenario planning. Singapore had also created a Centre for Strategic Futures in 2009. The Netherlands had one of the most sophisticated outreach systems for early detection of emerging trends and weak signals. There was strong consensus that building the anticipative capacity of government was necessary to prepare government to serve beyond the predictable. Most, but not all, of the participating countries were already taking steps to make progress.

On the second day, half a day was dedicated to innovation and technology-enabled innovation and half a day to adaptive capacity. Preparing government for the future means anticipating and course correcting, but this is not enough. There is also a need to build the adaptive capacity of government and society to evolve and prosper in unforeseen circumstances. The conversation was influenced by the SARS outbreak of 2003 and the Victoria (Australia) bushfires of 2009. Looking back, these events are strikingly reminiscent of the COVID crisis from 2019 on and the devastating fires in Canada in 2023. Some countries learned from past events and made good use of the years between the SARS outbreak and the COVID crisis. Learning better and much faster is at the heart of preparing government for the future. By the end of the fourth session, the NS framework appeared in the summary of the session. Drawing from my notes as rapporteur, preparing government for the challenges of the twenty-first century required:

- *Institutional capacity* to set direction, make choices, ensure clarity of purpose, align resources in support of priorities, and make laws that encourage stability, predictability, and equality under the rule of law (a compliance function)
- *Organizational capacity* to get things done by working across boundaries, sectors, and timelines (a performance function)
- *Anticipative capacity* to detect emerging complex issues and course correct to bring about a more favourable outcome for society (an emergence function)
- *Innovative capacity* to bring about results that would not exist without the use of the levers of the state (also an emergence function)
- *Adaptive capacity* to build the capacity of government and the collective capacity of society to absorb shocks and disturbances, adapt, evolve, and prosper in unpredictable circumstances (a resilience function)[50]

There was no expectation that the emerging consensus would hold until the end. Two more sessions remained. The fifth event was different. The Australia–New Zealand School of Government (ANZSOG) was the host. It arranged a series of group discussions through Australia and New Zealand between 28 September and 14 October 2010.[51] ANZSOG is a unique multi-jurisdictional organization. The school is owned by national and state-level governments and has sixteen university and business school partners from across Australia and New Zealand. It draws the best from academics to support public sector leaders. It has a flagship Executive Master of Public Administration degree, a full master's degree, grounded in the needs of member governments. It publishes a peer-reviewed journal and conducts a wide range of research work.

By the time the NS network went to Australia, ideas had converged around the macro-level elements of a New Synthesis. ANZSOG was uniquely positioned to expose these ideas to a cross-section of practitioners at the national, sub-national, and local levels in Australia and New Zealand. ANZSOG was a most committed partner to the NS Initiative from its inception.

Finally, the participants met for their last session. It was hosted by the Institute for Government in London, UK, 16–18 November 2010.[52] The focus was on bringing everything together,[53] with particular attention to citizens. The second day focused on preparing future public sector leaders for the challenges ahead.

The conversation had taken us from The Hague to Ottawa, Rio de Janeiro, Singapore, Australia, New Zealand, and London. By the time of the meeting in London, enthusiasm was high, and no one wanted to down tools. Against all odds, an improbable consensus had emerged. It was not as refined as one might like, but it was better than what was on offer at the time. The view of the group was that a book was needed to capture and disseminate the findings to date.

Writing a book was not something I had envisaged. I had convened colleagues to a two-year effort, and they had lived up to their commitment. Hundreds of people had shared their ideas and insights. To share the burden, it was proposed that I would write the general chapters, and each country-partner would provide case studies and a chapter on the roundtable they hosted. NS was launched to extend a helpful hand to practitioners; capturing the key findings was one way to put the results of our work in their hands.

A core question had driven the NS exploratory process: "What capabilities, old and new, will government need to serve in the 21st century?"[54] By the end of 2010 the participants from six countries had a view about the capabilities most needed to help government keep pace with the increasing complexity of the world we live in, and they had gathered compelling examples in support. In 2011, McGill-Queen's University Press published *A New Synthesis of Public Administration: Serving in the Twenty-First Century*.

Years before, I had thrown out a challenge to close the gaps between a conventional and mechanistic view of public administration and the changing reality of practice. I had given the idea a push. The New Synthesis initiative had served its purpose and was coming to an end. *Or was it?*

From Theory to Practice: New Synthesis Laboratories

What goes around comes around. In 2009, I had reached out to colleagues to explore the new frontiers of public administration. Now, just a few years later, they were inviting me to be part of their journey in their countries. Some wanted to explore how NS insights might improve the likelihood of success of public interventions. Others wanted to integrate some of the NS ideas in their leadership development programs. This was an opportunity to return to the world of practice without leading large public organizations. Isn't life grand!

Singapore

The first opportunity came from Singapore. I have had an ongoing relationship with the Singapore public service since 1994 and they had been an active member of the NS initiative since its inception. I assiduously studied the reforms over the years that contributed to their remarkable success. I admired their capacity for pragmatic solutions. At times, I was a little envious of their capacity to stay the course over many years to bring a change process to fruition. The Singapore civil service is known for its capacity to scan the world in

Figure 15. Group photograph of the 2013 Master Class in Singapore.

search of good ideas, but unlike other countries, they are obsessed with operationalizing powerful ideas in practice.

The Singapore civil service wanted to introduce New Synthesis ideas to future public sector leaders. I am not a writer, but I had written a book. I am not a teacher, but I was eager to figure out how to bring NS ideas to the world of practice. The idea was to develop a *Master Class for Master Practitioners.* If this worked, it could be replicated elsewhere.

Senior public officials were selected from seventeen different organizations, from central agencies to line ministries to statutory boards. The Master Class would run over six one-day sessions every second week over a period of three months. This required a major time commitment by the participants. Flying back and forth between Singapore and Ottawa was not practical. So, my husband (who had retired for a second time) and I packed up and settled in Singapore for three months.

The design of the class required participants to work on a real case relevant to their home organization. Between sessions, they had time to digest the ideas, work with their peers and employees to apply the concepts and craft an approach to make headway. During the sessions, half the time was dedicated to introducing concepts and half the time to discussing the participants' live cases. Participants would share their ideas and benefit from the input of their colleagues. I would review the evolving narrative of all the live cases after each session and make suggestions.[55]

The NS framework was used as a map to explore possible avenues. A map does not provide answers, but it helps to frame probing questions and reveal the trade-offs that various choices entail. The exploration process was broken down into six phases. Each phase encouraged the participants to reframe the issue in light of the insights they had gained through discussion with their colleagues. The exploration process was dynamic and iterative.

- *The power of a broader mental map* – to position a challenge in the broader context of system-wide and societal results, shifting the focus of attention from agency results to what really matters – making a difference for citizens and society. This helps to reveal the multidimensional nature of complex issues.
- *The power of others* – to lever the contribution of others across government and across the public, private, and civic sectors. In every country, a limited group of people has the legal right to use the authority of the state to achieve results. The challenge is not for government to do more but to explore how government can use its authority to lever the contribution of others to bring about viable solutions to problems that exceed the capacity of government alone. This is a shift from a government-centric approach to a governance approach, one that entails a collective effort and shared responsibilities for results.
- *The power of citizens as public value creators* – engaging individuals, families, and communities as co-creators and co-producers of public value. One of the most fundamental roles of government is to transform people into citizens and build a citizenry willing and able to build a better future together. This requires a civic spirit conducive to collective actions and the collective capacity to address issues of concern to society. This is a shift from citizens as obedient under the law to co-producers of results of public value.
- *The stewardship role of government* – a search for balance to generate viable solutions and propel society forward bringing together economic, social, ecological, and technological perspectives. A shift from the efficiency of the parts to the effectiveness of the whole in generating a better future, improving human conditions, and preserving the life-sustaining capacity of the planet.
- *The power of a compelling narrative of change* – synthesizing and articulating a shared purpose and a compelling call for collective action. Serving a public purpose makes the public sector unique and most valuable for society.

An abundant literature is available on the NS Master Class that was run with the Singapore Civil Service College in 2013. A report of the key findings[56] and a self-help guide for practitioners[57] were prepared the same year. The Master Class worked well. The participants regrouped the following year to discuss in what ways the class had changed their practice.[58] Ten years later, in November 2024, they would meet again to discuss the staying power of some of the ideas and how their practice has evolved over time. By now, the participants in the Master Class have become senior public servants.

The Master Class project revealed that a dynamic approach to problem solving could be taught and that it made a difference in addressing complex issues. But could this be done faster? The following year, we returned to Singapore for three months to design a one-day program for managers and to facilitate a workshop on the centre of government. The one-day session did not do so well – it was too much, too fast. The workshop on the centre of government, on the other hand, inspired changes that were introduced in subsequent years.

Sarawak, Malaysia

In 2015, another NS laboratory took shape at the invitation of the State of Sarawak (Malaysia). Sarawak is located on the island of Borneo. It had a population of 2.6 million people composed of twenty-seven ethnic groups in twelve geographic administrative entities. The context and the subject matter could not have been more different from the project in Singapore. The question was, would the NS exploratory cycle have anything to offer to law enforcement officers?

The previous year, Sarawak State Secretary Tan Sri Datuk Amar Haji Mohamad Morshidi bin Abdul Ghani had introduced High Performance Teams (HPTs) to break down silos and encourage teamwork. Eleven law enforcement challenges were assigned to eleven HPTs. Their mandate was to come forward with a strategy that would be presented to the Chief Minister and Cabinet. The topics ranged from illegal logging to illegal sand extraction, border management, and water safety. The team had one year to develop their strategy. The last phase of the project would take place over three days in Kota Kinabalu, Sabah from 15–17 March 2015. Early on, the HPTs were introduced to NS concepts. My team prepared a research paper entitled *Rule of Law, Citizenship and Enforcement Strategies*[59] to ensure a common understanding of concepts, as well as a compendium of international examples based on existing case studies we had collected.[60] There was much back and forth during the year to explore ideas. When the time came to finalize the strategies, eleven teams were meeting at the same time, with me navigating from one to the next to help them along. The participants went back and forth between group and plenary sessions for three full days. Many High Performance Teams worked through the nights. It was exhausting but exhilarating. The participants expanded the NS exploratory cycle by adding steps relevant to their work:

- The power of a broader mental map was assisted by "*think[ing] public purpose*," "*moving up a value chain of results,*" and "*system mapping*."
- The power of others was assisted by exploring "*weak signals*" and "*points of vulnerability.*"
- The power of citizens was complemented with "*building public support*" and "*citizen-centricity*."

The HPT strategies were presented to Cabinet shortly afterward. It was most rewarding for the participants and for my team that most strategies were approved and only three required additional refinements. A retrospective of this experience was published in 2015.[61]

Canada and Others

The insights from the Master Class in Singapore and from the High Performance Teams in Sarawak were later used to design an Introduction to NS in partnership with the *Institute on Governance* (IOG) in Canada as part of its flagship Executive Leadership Program. An extensive bank of Canadian cases was developed to sustain this effort.[62]

An idea that proves useful in contexts as diverse as Singapore, the State of Sarawak, and Canada is worthy of attention. By the end of 2015, one thousand participants had used the NS framework in some way.[63] In the hands of practitioners, the framework had become a process of discovery, a way to invent solutions to complex problems of concern to society.

The first NS book was written out of a sense of responsibility towards those who had answered my call. The second one imposed itself out of the richness of the lessons learned from a diversity of practice. The *NS Fieldbook* was released in 2017.[64] It was translated into Danish; Denmark is one of the countries that have most constantly explored NS concepts in a variety of domains, ranging from the health sector[65] to municipal management[66] to public service modernization.[67]

Over the years, NS Laboratories were conducted in Australia, Denmark, Finland, Estonia, Norway, and elsewhere. Each event was an opportunity to learn about a country through the eyes of those who have a mission to govern and serve their fellow citizens. It is a rare privilege to be invited to join an inner circle of senior leaders in countries other than one's own. Over the years I learned from Denmark by working with the municipalities of Vejle to build a "resilient city,"[68] Kolding on "Design for Life,"[69] and Fredericia regarding elder care.[70] Denmark's health system is second to none, and yet the efforts of

Figure 16. The two New Synthesis books, *A New Synthesis of Public Administration* (2011, right) and *The New Synthesis of Public Administration Fieldbook* (2017, left).

the Central Denmark Region to invent the health and social ecosystem of the future are unrelenting.[71]

I learned from Finland through my work with their Prime Minister's Office and Department of Finance on futures work, public innovation, and anticipatory governance.[72] The Netherlands has been associated with the NS project since its inception. Their work on a circular economy[73] is groundbreaking. They have one of the most sophisticated foresight processes (Expedition RWS 2050).[74] From Norway, I learned more about innovations in municipal governance and handling cross-cutting issues.[75] Singapore has led a peaceful economic and social revolution. France is an inspiration in skilfully combining prosperity and solidarity, modernity, and heritage.

When one comes to think of it, the New Synthesis Initiative was an incredible gamble, but over the years I have witnessed the difference these ideas can make. In 2023, I received an award from the International Association of Schools and Institutes of Administration (IASIA). The Onkar Prasad Dwivedi Award recognizes an "*outstanding contribution to the public administration and public policy in the world*." The commendation recognized the importance of the New Synthesis initiative.[76] This recognition was totally unexpected and especially important for me as leader of the initiative.

Serving one's country is a privilege and therefore no one should expect other forms of recognition for a job well done. Being recognized by another country, as I was by Australia and France,[77] is a gift that no one entirely deserves, since one gets more out of a relationship than can ever be given. Being recognized by one's peers, people most knowledgeable about the subject matter, is entirely different. People who had contributed to the New Synthesis had catalysed the field of public administration among "scholars and practitioners around the world." What a compliment! This is not a personal achievement, but the achievement of many who dared to explore the new frontiers of public administration. Their achievements deserved to be celebrated, their work deserved to be protected, and the story of this improbable journey deserved to be told. This was one of the incentives behind my decision to prepare my archives for transfer to Library and Archives Canada for safe keeping.

14 Conclusion: Back Where It Began

The documents we have collected and assembled for their transfer to and safe keeping by Library and Archives Canada map out the arc of my professional journey as a public servant in Canada and abroad. The chapters connect my archival documents with the context and ideas that influenced my practice as a public servant, Deputy Minister, Clerk, and Secretary to Cabinet for Canada as well as my research work over the years.

It is fitting that this project brings me back to Canada where it all began when I joined the public service as a student in the summer of 1973. Reviewing the thousands of pages of documents I generated over the years made me more acutely aware of the changes that have taken place in the public service and of the impact of decisions made over time.

Serving and governing is never easy at the best of times. That said, I believe that the second quarter of the twenty-first century is shaping up to be *a more challenging and dangerous time* than what I experienced as Deputy Minister and Clerk. There are turbulent times and strong winds ahead. When the world is in a state of flux, when the future is uncertain, this is when the role of government and public institutions is most important. *We live in such a time.*

People in positions of authority in government will be called upon to steer Canada and the public service through a fast-changing landscape. I believe there is an unprecedented opportunity to shape *an ambitious governing agenda* and *a public sector reform agenda* that would be mutually supportive and reinforcing. Circumstances do not always make this possible. Many of the problems we are facing today have been in the making over a long period of time. Can learning from the past help us to invent a better future? It is with this in mind that I venture to put some ideas forward, knowing full well that those that will matter will be the ones that public officials make their own.

A governing agenda must be owned by the government of the day, and a public service reform agenda must be owned by the people leading it. *This is as it should be.*

A Changing Landscape

There would be much to say about the multiple factors at play and the existential crises looming ahead; international political institutions are breaking down, artificial intelligence is maturing, the planet is warming, and the global population growth rate is collapsing.

Drawing from the previous chapters, I will refer to one of these factors.[1] The protective shield that contributed to a long period of growth and relative peace is breaking down. In the aftermath of the Second World War, international norms, conventions, treaties, and institutions – ranging from the Universal Declaration of Human Rights to the United Nations, the International Court of Justice, the World Trade Organization, and others – progressively wove a "*protective shield*" that benefited developed and developing countries alike. This never amounted to a "universal" system and was never "universally" accepted, but it was sufficiently broadly respected to influence the behaviour of governments.

This international protective shield is breaking down. Today, globalization is moving in reverse, and protectionism is on the rise. We are witnessing the return of *realpolitik*, where countries expand their influence through territorial invasions. Genocides and massacres are showing the weaknesses of common norms when there is no common will to enforce them. The rise of authoritarian regimes and illiberal states is a sign of malaise with the performance of democratic states. A world governed by *realpolitik* is different from a world governed by rules.

Out of necessity, the coming years offer Canada an opportunity to reconnect to the fundamental principles that contributed to its success as a modern democratic society. These include a society governed by the rule of law, democratic equality supported by a social safety net that gives meaning to it, and a balanced approach to governing that strives to reconcile economic prosperity and collective solidarity. As a result, Canada was and remains a magnet for talent. It is in the enviable position of being able to attract some of the best talents in the world. Talent is a powerful comparative advantage for ensuring a country's future prosperity in a turbulent world.

This is an opportune time to bring greater clarity to Canada's strategic interests in ways that strengthen its relationship with its most important allies. Canada will need to reconcile prosperity, solidarity, and fiscal capacity to ensure the sustainability of the common social safety net that gives meaning to being a Canadian citizen. Public sector leaders will need to figure out a way to put an end to Canada's downward economic trend and ensure that an emerging digital economy will get Canadians closer to the aspirations of building a green economy. None of this can be achieved without government, well-performing public institutions and a competent, honest, and efficient professional public service deserving of the trust of Canadians and those they elect.

Rethinking Canada's International Trajectory

Canada's influence in the world has declined in the recent past. And yet, this is an area where there is much potential to align Canada's interest with the interests of its most important allies, including other G7 countries, NATO members, OECD member countries, and other like-minded democratic countries.

Canada is a vital player in the Arctic, North Pacific, and North Atlantic regions. It enjoys strategic assets of great importance for its allies and partners. These include its contribution to Arctic security, minerals and rare earth minerals of critical importance for technological and security reasons, a diversified approach to continental energy security, and the development of renewable energy technologies. A carefully targeted approach in a few strategic areas would do much to improve Canada's influence and help to protect Canada's interests in an increasingly dangerous world.

In the coming years, countries will apply a security lens to public policy decision making. For Canada, this would mean an enhanced focus on national security, defence capabilities, border management, the treatment of refugee claims, technological espionage, money laundering, and the like. Applying a security lens to shaping a *governing agenda* would help to recentre the role of the government of Canada around its primary areas of responsibility, some of which have been neglected over the years. For the public service, this would require careful planning for reallocating resources in support of these missions. A careful rebalancing would open up new avenues for federal-provincial relations – ultimately it is in the interests of all governments to build a better future and to successfully navigate through turbulent times. The interests of all governments are inexorably intertwined.

Rebalancing Canada's Domestic Trajectory

The overall performance of the Canadian economy requires attention. In the summer of 2021, I launched the *Fit for the Future Project* (FFF), tracking Canada's trajectory and preparedness for an accelerating period of change.[2] Canadians like to think of Canada as a G7 country. Indeed, it was the seventh largest economy when it joined this forum in 1976. Today, Canadians need to adjust that perception. In 2021, Canada was the ninth largest economy; today it is tenth. At that time, it was nineteenth in term of GDP per capita, twenty-fourth in term of purchasing power, and on a downward trend since the mid-1980s. The Economic Complexity Index, the Universal Economic Index, and the Global Competitiveness Index were also on downward trends.[3]

In brief, Canadians are getting relatively poorer, and Canada is not well positioned for generating the complex products and services needed to ensure its future prosperity. The challenge for elected and professional officials will be to figure out how to reverse that trend. *No one owes Canada a prosperous future.*

The coming years offer an opportunity to reconcile *economy, technology, and ecology* in new ways to propel Canada forward. A future-oriented economy cannot be achieved by government alone. This requires all hands on deck. It would require private firms investing in leading-edge technologies and innovation, government incentives rewarding the generation of complex goods and services that other countries would find it difficult to emulate, and federal and provincial governments acting synergistically. This is a challenge worthy of the efforts of the best minds in the government and in the country.

Ending a Boom-and-Bust Approach to Fiscal Management

An ambitious governing agenda must be supported by a public administration with the capacity to make it happen and to align resources in support. There is a need to *put an end to a boom-and-bust approach* to fiscal management.

In the 1950s and 1960s, small deficits were followed by small surpluses. This began to change in the early 1970s. The deficit grew from 2 per cent of GDP in 1971 to around 8 per cent of GDP by 1983. The government of Prime Minister Mulroney introduced structural reforms in the mid-1980s (GST, FTA, etc.) and launched numerous expenditure reduction exercises. This period was followed by the program review of 1995, which was in turn followed by a period of expansion. After eleven years of budget surplus, the boom-and-bust cycle started again. Under Prime Minister Harper, the deficit grew to 3.6 per cent of GDP in 2009, due to the combined effect of tax cuts and the 2008 economic crisis; a new expenditure reduction exercise eventually achieved a 0.1 per cent surplus in 2015. Under Prime Minister Justin Trudeau, the deficit grew from marginal in 2016 to 2.1 per cent of GDP in 2024, in part because of the COVID crisis.[4] And so, *a new bust cycle is about to begin again.*

A boom-and-bust approach to fiscal management erodes the institutional capacity to serve Canada and Canadians. In essence, new initiatives are launched by borrowing rather than reallocating fiscal resources, until such time as an expenditure reduction exercise is launched that will cut the level of funding of *pre-existing* programs and services to Canadians. This is done to give visibility to new announcements while limiting the visibility of the cuts that will eventually be necessary. The cuts are invariably presented as "across the board cuts" or actions to "eliminate the fat." The lack of upfront decisions about how new initiatives will be funded over time gives visibility to new announcements and hides the erosion of services to Canadians that the next bust cycle will cause. After years of such practice, two public services co-exist: the public service managing new initiatives where new resources are generously provided, and *the public service left behind* that provides services to citizens with outdated legacy systems and declining resources in spite of increasing demand.

Budgeting is the capacity to align resources and capabilities in support of government priorities and emerging needs. There is a need to learn to do budgeting in a transparent and competent way to reallocate resources in support of emerging priorities. This entails the capacity to make choices, to let go of activities to make room for others, and to reallocate resources on an ongoing basis.

A successful governing agenda requires a government able to set a course and make choices, a Prime Minister and Ministers willing to use the political capital earned through an electoral process to make progress, and a public administration with the institutional, organizational, and individual capability to get things done.

Let Ministers Be Ministers

The governing system of a country is made of many interrelated parts. Changing one element has ramifications for the whole system. Canada has been experimenting with the expansion of a political service for quite some time. The consequences are increasingly visible and should not be ignored.

At first, there were a few political positions to assist ministers with the political activities that a non-partisan public service was prohibited to perform. Today, the original concept has morphed into *a system-wide expansion of the governing political party* in every office of power across the government of Canada. This gives rise to several challenges, including an erosion of ministerial authority, the weakening of a Cabinet system of government, and the breakdown of a policy-making cycle designed to bring together policy formulation and policy implementation. The separation of policy formation from implementation increases the likelihood of poor policy decisions (that do not take account of available evidence) as well as implementation failures maladapted to the reality on the ground. There has been ample evidence of this in recent years.

From a public service perspective, the rapid expansion of a network of political advisors loyal to the governing political party, funded through public funds, and present in every department and agency gives rise to concerns about the political neutrality of the public service. Today, the higher echelons of the public service interact daily with political advisors operating in a perpetual campaigning mode. This makes it difficult for the public service to treat all political parties in an even-handed way and it comes dangerously close to eroding the *principle of political neutrality.*[5]

I realize full well that the view of a former public servant about the role of political staff lacks credibility and can be seen as self-serving. Be that as it may, one way or the other, a conversation is needed if Canada is to continue to be governed by a *Cabinet system of responsible government* where ministers embody authority and accountability to Parliament.

A Unified Public Service

Some decisions have long shadows. It is my view that decisions made many years ago have contributed to some of the weaknesses we are witnessing today.

The creation of the Civil Service Commission (now the Public Service Commission) in 1908 was a historical event. It is from that point on that it became possible to eradicate widespread political patronage and to build a professional non-partisan public service. This project saw the public service as an essential instrument of democratic governance. A professional non-partisan public service was expected to embody the principles of political neutrality, democratic equality, competence, and a commitment to serving the public good and the collective interest above all else. The merit system was designed to ensure that the public service would live up to these principles through competitive examination and impartial assessment for recruitment and promotion. A merit system based on open competition for talent is never perfect, but it has a number of significant advantages. One, it encourages *openness* by making the required qualifications known in advance. Second, it makes it possible for people to *put their names forward* if they believe they meet the requirements. Shutting people out of opportunities for advancement for which they believe they are qualified erodes the drive to excel, even more so when people with less experience and competence are selected without a competitive process.

From the time of the creation of the Public Service Commission till now, there has been a tension between *the need* to build a professional public service as an institution and *the demand* for managerial flexibility. Who should have the last say in appointments? What hierarchy of principles should be used to reconcile conflicting aspirations?

From 1908 to now, the trend has been towards more *managerial flexibility.* Stripped down to the essentials, this is the story running through the Gordon Commission (1946), the Heeney Commission (1959), the Glassco Commission (1962), the Lambert Commission (1979), and the D'Avignon committee (1979), up to and including the Public Service Modernization Act (2003).

This managerial perspective presents a number of risks. For instance, delegation does not guarantee better results and better service to Canadians; these depend on *the capacity of the people* using these tools to fulfil their public mission. Building flexible departmental organizations does not amount to building a professional public service fit for purpose and fit for the time. As an *institution*, the public service must stand for ideas and principles that apply to all public servants irrespective of their domain of activities. It must ensure that it will be able to fulfil its mission in the future and in yet unknown and unforeseen circumstances. The institutional capacity of the public service matters for well-performing public institutions.

Today, the role of the Public Service Commission has been reduced to an audit function. The merit principle is subordinated to managerial considerations and requires neither competitive examination nor impartial assessment. Departments have discretion and delegated authority for classification, staffing, appointment, deployment, and promotion up to the ADM levels. The underlying assumption, for the past fifty years and even more, has been that delegation to departments was the universal remedy for the problems of the public service. This, it was argued, would lead to better results for Canadians, lower costs for taxpayers, and more responsive organizations. Facts do not support this hypothesis.

Canadians have experienced *service failures*, like the long wait for passports and unacceptable delays in processing demands from a whole host of services. They experienced *system failures*. The Phoenix pay system debacle is legendary internationally. *Online services*, the first line of interface for many Canadians, did not keep up with the progress made by other countries. Most concerning of all, there has been an unprecedented number of reported corruption cases. These are *failures* to uphold public sector values of integrity, incorruptibility, probity, and prudence in the use of taxpayers' money.

Today, the public service of Canada is exposed to risks of *politicization* from above. It is at risk of seeing its political *neutrality* being challenged by future governments and at risk of *de-professionalization*. The public service has progressively weakened the focus on excellence and competence that was previously encouraged by an open and competitive search for talent.

An interested observer might be forgiven for asking if the public service of Canada missed a turn along the way. It is time to challenge the hypothesis that delegation is the universal remedy to the problems of the public service; the evidence of the last two decades does not support that claim. Other countries have made different choices. There may be lessons Canada can learn from them.

A balanced approach is needed to *reconcile organizational and institutional capacity* building. Reaffirming the public service commitment to talent, competence, and excellence would be a step in the right direction, and so would be a stronger focus on the importance of service to Canadians. The public service needs talent at all levels and lots of it; fortunately, there is a lot of talent in Canada and in the public service if the system is designed to give people a chance to come forward. An open competitive process is a commitment to talent and competence in the service of Canadians; this helps to foster an environment that encourages excellence.

Assistant Deputy Ministers serve at the highest level of the non-partisan professional public service. They are the future of the public service. Every appointment at that level is of critical importance not only for the department where they serve but for the *public service as an institution.* There is a need to ensure that, as a group, ADMs provide the talent, skills, and experience the public service will need to serve at the highest level in the future. I believe that it would be important to recognize the importance of ADMs and wise for the Public Service Commission to play a more active role in overseeing ADMs' appointments and other appointments at the most senior levels, as is the case in other countries, such as New Zealand and the United Kingdom. It may be wise for the Treasury Board Secretariat to maintain an oversight function over the creation of ADM positions and to limit the use of Order in Council appointments, since this practice increases the risk of politicization.

It is up to a new generation of public sector leaders to reconcile organizational and institutional capacity building and to map the way forward. The coming years offer an opportunity for course corrections and for shaping an ambitious public service reform agenda.

A United Centre of Government

The growth at the centre of government in recent years is disconcerting. Between 2000 and 2024, PCO's budget increased by 250 per cent, TBS's by 540 per cent (partly due to a transfer of responsibilities from the Public Service Commission), and Finance's by 220 per cent.[6] From 2010 to 2024, these agencies increased in population by 24 per cent overall.[7] Furthermore, the extent to which central agencies have successfully exercised their challenge function and their stewardship responsibilities diligently is an open question. For instance, what do recent service and system breakdowns tell us about the role of the centre of government in anticipating and mitigating system-wide risks and introducing course corrections as needed?

Central agencies have been struggling to find their footing in recent times. Added responsibilities have distracted the Treasury Board Secretariat from its core mission as a *Budget Office* and a *Management Board.* This may explain in part the declining attention given to costs, performance, or productivity. The Treasury Board was late in setting service standards, and only half of high-volume services meet basic service standards today. The slow pace of decommissioning of legacy systems has put Canadians at risk.[8]

A well-performing public service needs a well-performing budget office and management board focused on the cost, fitness, and service capacity of the public service as an institution. In the same vein, the voice of the *Employer* in recent years has been conflicted at times. The directions of the most important employer in Canada influence the performance of other public, private, and civic sector employers. The management of the public sector labour force should display at all times a concern for integrity and for generating value for taxpayers' money. Care is needed to avoid creating conditions in the public service that other Canadians cannot aspire to enjoy in other sectors.

The Privy Council Office struggles at times to reconcile responsiveness to the head of government and the responsibility to serve a Cabinet system of responsible government. The role of the Head of the Public Service added to the difficulty.

Some measures would make it easier for the Clerk to fulfil its role as Head of the Public Service. For instance, the obligation to report on the "*State of the Public Service*" could be done every three to five years, as is now done in New Zealand, rather than annually. To make the exercise more meaningful, it could be supported by mandatory reports from the Public Service Commission on the *state of the merit principle*, the Treasury Board Secretariat on the *state of service*, and Finance on the financial planning needed to sustain the *state of public assets*, systems, and infrastructure for critical services. The Office of the Chief Human Resources Officer should report on *the state of the public sector labour force*, including its productivity, demographic profile compared to the Canadian labour force, and critical skills profile. The Deputy Clerk could co-ordinate the preparation of the State of the Public Service report to Parliament. The Minister for PCO may be designated as responsible for the stewardship of the public service, as was done successfully during the program review of 1995 when the Minister for PCO was also responsible for public service renewal. Many avenues are open to make the stewardship of the public service an effective and shared responsibility. A greater danger is for new functions and secretariats to be added to the Privy Council Office whenever government sets new priorities. This should be resisted. A transactional PCO loses the capacity to stay above the fray and is of lesser value in advising the Prime Minister of the strategic decisions ahead.

In recent years, Finance's energy has been consumed with rolling out a steady stream of new initiatives in the context of the COVID crisis and afterward. In some cases, decisions were made with limited interactions with other central agencies and in other cases without the departments or agencies most directly responsible for their implementation. This contributed to some of the policy failures we have witnessed in recent years. What may be justified in exceptional circumstances may not be wise on an ongoing basis. The unrestricted use of omnibus bills has transformed the Department of Finance from one focused on rigorous fiscal management and budgeting to the "*Department of everything*," involved in everything but master of nothing,[9] thus breaking the chain of accountability running through ministers. This erodes the sense of departments' responsibility for decisions in which they were only tangentially involved.

When budgeting becomes transactional, the government loses its capacity to be strategic. This means to set directions and leave it to departments and the

Treasury Board to figure out how best to make it happen. A well-performing country and a well-performing government need a strong Department of Finance responsible for rigorous fiscal management and strategic budgeting to reconcile short-, mid-, and long-term needs.

A *unified centre* is essential to steer the public service through a period of change and to bring the best the public service has to offer in support of the government agenda. Central agencies focused on their core mission and *working as one* are essential for preparing Canada and the public service for what lies ahead.

Reducing the Cost of Compliance

As Alasdair Roberts chronicled well,[10] over the years, there has been an increasing number of independent agencies responsible for "monitoring" the public service and ensuring compliance. On the one hand, the public service is expected to take initiative, innovate, and step in boldly in times of crisis. On the other hand, managers' every move is scrutinized by an ever-increasing number of *watchdogs*. The cost of compliance is increasing, but the real costs are declining trust in government, paralysis since inaction is safer, and an environment favourable to filing complaints or grievances rather than working out solutions at the lowest level.

The first watchdog was the Office of the Auditor General (OAG). The focus was to prevent corruption, the abuse of power, and gross mismanagement. That began to change when the office was given a mandate to judge if government was providing *value for money*. This, in essence, puts the office in a position to second-guess policy makers. Not surprisingly, the style and tone of reports began to change, becoming more aggressive, more controversial, and more newsworthy.

Since the mid-1970s, the list of watchdogs has been increasing, with no end in sight. There is a Privacy Commissioner to oversee compliance with the *Privacy Act*, and an Information Commissioner to oversee compliance with the *Access to Information Act*. A Human Rights Commission receives complaints about discrimination, monitors progress in improving diversity in the public service workforce, and, more recently, ensures compliance with the *Accessible Canada Act*. The Commissioner of the Environment monitors progress on sustainable development goals. The Public Sector Labour Relations and Employment Board investigates employees' complaints and grievances. There is a pay equity commissioner, a National Security and Intelligence Review Agency, a Public Sector Integrity Commissioner … and so on … and so on.

This picture conjures the uncomfortable image of managers being surrounded by a circle of watchdogs ready to go on the offensive at every turn. Who, in these circumstances, will want to be managers in the future? This situation has significant consequences. It builds a public service that is risk-averse rather than innovative, and reactive rather than adaptive.

A compliance system based on distrust and designed to lay blame is different from a compliance system designed to build public confidence that reasonable measures are in place to prevent corruption and misconduct more broadly. A compliance system is important; no one is above the law. It should focus on the fundamentals; zero tolerance for corruption but much tolerance for mistakes and errors, especially when exploring new ways and managing crises.

Multiple crises are looming ahead. It is timely to clarify the concept of compliance the government of Canada wants to promote. It should be possible to consolidate the compliance functions around fewer agencies in ways that would better serve Parliament and reduce the cost of compliance. A well-performing public service must abide by the highest standard, but it must also be *manageable*; without course corrections, we may end up losing on both ends of this proposition.

The Public Service Footprint

One way or the other, the public service of Canada will be asked to reduce its fiscal footprint in the coming years. This is not the most critical public policy issue facing Canada at this time, and yet it is likely to figure prominently on the government agenda irrespective of which political party will form the government after the next federal election. A Liberal government will want fiscal room for new initiatives. A Conservative government will want to cut taxes. Both will need to realign resources to respond to a changing international landscape and to the public security issues that will dominate the international scene.

Unfortunately, this will happen at a time when the perception is that the public service is "bloated." There were six thousand public servants per million Canadians in 1999, eight thousand ten years ago, and nine thousand currently. Canadians find it difficult to reconcile these increases with the services they get. There will be an expectation that it should be possible to reduce government spending without affecting services to citizens. In reality, public-service-wide expenditure reductions affect services to Canadians one way or the other.[11]

By experience, we know that reducing government spending is a political process requiring political decisions at the highest level. We also know that massive exercises to reduce government spending are a sign of failure that result from the inability to make decisions to fund new initiatives and to shed responsibilities on an ongoing basis to make room for emerging needs and priorities. The capacity to adapt and reallocate resources on an ongoing basis *is the central issue that needs to be addressed.*

Expenditure reviews are blind exercises that impact every program and service and erode institutional capacity. It is preferable to end some programs entirely rather than to spread the impact across the whole system. Large-scale expenditure reduction exercises, even when they are well managed, have unintended consequences that appear over a long period of time afterward. Canadians have paid a price to learn about the impact of such practices; this knowledge can be put to productive use. There is a need to think beyond expenditure reviews. *It is possible to do better*.

Canada's deficit, at the time of the 2024 budget, was in the range of 2 per cent of GDP. Despite the risks looming ahead, Canada is in a better fiscal position than most other G7 countries. This is not 1994 all over again when the deficit was 6 per cent of GDP and servicing the debt accounted for one-third of all tax dollars. The situation is serious and requires attention, but *Canada is not yet facing a financial crisis*. This means that there is an opportunity to do things well and to avoid making decisions in a crisis mode.

It is possible to make progress in reallocating resources and reducing the fiscal footprint of the government of Canada while making progress on several fronts at once. There is an opportunity:

- To reconcile prosperity and solidarity with the fiscal capacity of Canadians. Prosperity builds a desirable future; solidarity builds a society worth living in. Fiscality sets the parameters within which a new balance must be found.
- To reconcile economy, technology, and ecology. This is a tall order. Human activities are eroding the biosphere. A new balance is needed to preserve the life-sustaining capacity of the planet, accelerate Canada's economic transition, and ensure that the digital economy will live up to its promise of contributing to building a green economy.
- To recentre to role of the government of Canada around its core responsibilities while recognizing the shared responsibly of governments to work together when the collective interest of Canadians demands it.
- To improve services to Canadians and the value proposition of the public sector to the overall performance of Canada.

These and more may not be the axes that resonate with public officials today, but they illustrate the need for *clarity of purpose*: what problems are we striving to address? What kind of country will result from the proposed changes?

The public service has a choice. Is it to wait to be provided with target cuts (the death by a thousand cuts) that it will implement loyally, or to take charge and bring forward the most powerful ideas it is able to generate? My view is that generating ideas is always the preferable course of action. If nothing else, it *expands the range of options* available for government decisions and it improves the readiness of the public service to provide its best professional advice.

It is the responsibility of government to decide on the best way forward. It is the duty of the professional public service to harness the best available knowledge and ideas to improve government decision making. There is a whole host of possibilities waiting to be invented that could be put in motion. I will mention a few, drawing from past experience in Canada and abroad.

The importance of *prudent fiscal management*. Paul Martin, then Minister of Finance, introduced in the mid-1990s a number of measures worth remembering. They included focusing on spending rather than planned expenditures, using conservative assumptions scrutinized by a Parliamentary committee, building contingency reserves to face unforeseen circumstances, applying increased revenues to reducing the debt, and, above all, launching no new initiatives without a source of funds or a financing plan.

Prudent management does not prevent government from running a sizeable deficit when circumstances demand it, and there is no need for a straitjacket that would force government to balance the budget every year. Government must govern. Prudence brings together fiscal planning by thinking ahead and making decisions.

A lesson from the mid-1980s was that *structural reforms* keep giving. The GST reform has been one of the most significant structural reforms in recent history. Recently, the government of PM Trudeau proposed a modification to the capital gains inclusion rate, and the leader of the opposition, Pierre Poilievre, signalled that this change should be considered in the broader context of a review of the taxation system, promising to launch a task force on tax reform if he became PM.[12] With both signalling an interest in changes to taxation, there may be an opportunity for a review of tax expenditures.

Tax expenditures are money *Canadians leave on the table*. Reducing tax incentives increases revenues. There are hundreds of tax credits, tax deductions, and tax incentives of all kinds and, to my knowledge, they have been excluded from most if not all prior reviews. Who are the main beneficiaries of these tax incentives? What is their true economic and social impact? How are they contributing to Canada's aspirations for increasing productivity, technological and ecological transitions, etc.? Big money is involved. A *tax expenditure review* may yield early results and facilitate the reallocation of resources to support new priorities.

These measures are rather conventional, but they may yield early results and signal a willingness on the part of government to bring discipline. That said, more innovative ideas could be explored.

What about a citizen-centric review? Instead of focusing on costs first, a citizen-centric review would give priority attention to the delivery of services of critical importance for citizens and users. This approach would put citizens at the forefront. I do not entirely subscribe to the imagery of the "poets and plumbers" that Donald Savoie is using,[13] but there is something there. I made a similar point above when I mentioned that there are two public services: one getting resources for new initiatives and the *public service left behind* that is providing services to Canadians with old legacy systems and declining resources in spite of rising demand.

It would be beneficial to identify activities where the public service interfaces directly with Canadians and provides services of critical importance to ensure people's safety and well-being. For one, this would reveal the scale of the service delivery function that is often taken for granted, and second, it would reveal the state of the service delivery capacity in critical areas. It would shed light on what needs to be done to prevent service or system breakdowns, what needs to be done to improve the services Canadians depend on, and how technologies may be used to provide better services to citizens at a lower overall cost for society. It would help to bring together the old and the new, existing services of enduring value and the drive for new initiatives.

A technology review would be a useful companion to a citizen-centric review. This would consider the fitness of public-service-wide technological systems and infrastructures to keep up with the times. What common technological infrastructures would help reduce costs and mitigate risks while improving services? I am less sanguine than most about the benefits of AI and more concerned about the risks; that said, AI, used carefully, could potentially be a low-risk option in reducing overhead costs and reconfiguring corporate services like translation, general communication, finance, accounting, staffing, audit, access to information requests, and the like.

Departments do not need to ask permission or be given targets to undertake *their own program reviews*. Such reviews build the capacity to anticipate, to identify course corrections, and to respond to changing circumstances. The best knowledge about public programs and services rests with the people providing them. They know what works and what does not, what was attempted but did not live up to expectations, what needs to be preserved for the future and what could be stopped.

A departmental review is a process of invention. What would be their most *powerful narrative* if departments were given a free hand to invent how they could fulfil their public mission going forward while contributing to *a collective effort to deploy resources* in support of Canada's most pressing needs and priorities? To departments who dare to launch such a comprehensive review, I would say do not doubt the creativity of the people around you, do not doubt the courage of ministers until you have tested your courage for bringing forward powerful ideas, don't ask permission for what you already have the authority to do; just get on with it. There is no window of opportunity for people or organizations that have nothing to propose.

There is no downside to this work even if departments' ideas are rejected. Departments' ideas reveal where knowledge, past experience, and capacity converge. Successful public policies are those where the political will to bring about change converges with the professional capacity to make it happen.

A word of caution in closing: in a period of instability and high uncertainty it is unwise to destabilize the public administrative arm government depends on. There is a rare opportunity to ensure synergy between a governing agenda and a public reform agenda to improve the likelihood of success of government priorities and to put Canada on a favourable trajectory. Let's not miss that chance.

Governing is a search for balance. The success of government does not rest with the power of individual ideas but with how a mix of ideas, actions, and interventions are woven together to propel a country forward even in the most unpredictable circumstances.

I am not being ironic when I say that this is a good time to be in government. It is not for the faint of heart, but it is a most important time. People serving in the second quarter of the twenty-first century are called upon to serve in a dangerous world and a challenging time. They deserve all the help we can give them. This book is a modest attempt to extend a helpful hand to those who agree to serve their fellow citizens. By drawing from my archives and past experiences, I have tried to explore lessons learned along the way and to raise probing questions that may help public officials and public servants *invent a better future.*

***

This book was sent to University of Toronto Press for publication in the fall of 2024 before the results of the presidential election in the United States of America were known and before the resignation of Prime Minister Trudeau in January 2025.

I chose not to rewrite any of the chapters because the text as written before these events bears an important lesson: many of the challenges Canada is facing in the early days of 2025 have been in the making over a long period of time. A lot was already known that we chose to ignore or that was left unattended. What remained unknown was the scope, scale, and speed of change once a *point of inflexion* is reached.

Now we know.

Other points of inflexion and tipping points of even greater importance will soon be reached. This will be the case for climate change, the impact of AI, other scientific discoveries, population migration, and a shift from global population growth to decline. It is important to manage crises here and now with an eye on the bigger picture and a focus on the future.

In early 2024, I agreed to deliver the Manion Lecture 2025. This is a flagship event for the Canada School of Public Service. While I have been a frequent speaker at international conferences, this will be my first public speech in Canada since leaving the public service of Canada. It will be an opportunity to reflect on the implication of recent events for Canada, the government, and the public service of Canada.[14]

In the midst of the changes that will rock the world in the years ahead, Canada stands out as an island of peace and reason. At the world scale, a modern, democratic, and inclusive country like Canada is a *rare and exceptional achievement*. Canada has the assets, the capacity, and the wherewithal to adapt to changing circumstances and prosper in a turbulent world. The distinctive trajectory that made Canada's success in the past combined aspirations for a better future, a commitment to improved human conditions, and an aspiration for preserving the life-sustaining capacity of the planet. Whatever path Canadians may choose, Canada is worthy of being defended and its future is deserving of the collective efforts of its citizens and their leaders.

To those who make the choice of serving their fellow citizens in turbulent times, I express my gratitude. To fellow public servants I say, it is at times like these that public institutions and public servants are of the most critical importance. Those who serve today should expect that the ones who came before will extend a helpful hand … You can count me in.

Notes

1. Discovering Public Service

1 On leadership, context, and the *Factor-YOU* of public administration, see Jocelyne Bourgon, *The New Synthesis of Public Administration Fieldbook*, 135–7.

2 On public innovation and the chance to invent solutions, see Bourgon, *New Synthesis Fieldbook,* 143–54.

3 More detail can be found in Transport Canada's public history – Transport Canada, "Patterns for change: 1966–1976." Accessed 29 August 2023. https://tc.canada.ca/en/patterns-change-1966-1976.

4 I return to this growth in chapter 10.

5 Kathryn May, "Building a Culture of Public Service on Hybrid Work."

6 In later years, as President of the Canadian Centre for Management Development, I had the Centre alert parliamentarians to events and sessions they might find useful – see Canada, Parliament, House of Commons, Standing Committee on Government Operations and Estimates, 2nd sess., 37th Parliament, Meeting No. 31, 2003. As well, I ran, with former Mulroney Chief of Staff and future Senator Hon. Hugh Segal, an orientation session for new parliamentarians – see Jocelyne Bourgon and Hugh Segal, "Members of Parliament and the Public Service" (PowerPoint, Queen's University, Kingston, ON, 1 February 2001).

2. A Public Service Manager

1 Jocelyne Bourgon and Marcel Lebeau, *Annual Statistical Review of Canadian Fisheries, 1955–1976*, Volume 9.

2 For a particularly direct statement of this idea and those following in the paragraph, see Jocelyne Bourgon, "We Are All Innovators" (speech, Expo Innovation 1994, Ottawa, ON, 16 June 1994).

3 "The employees own the most important resource of the organization – their know-how and their ability to innovate. With all the power in the world, managers cannot command and control creativity and innovation." Jocelyne Bourgon, "Public Service Speaks to One's Soul" (speech, Carleton University, Ottawa, ON, 13 March 1998).

4 The need for room to take risks would come up in my later effort to build up a learning organization. See Jocelyne Bourgon, "A Public Service Learning Organization from Coast to Coast to Coast" (speech, Montreal, QC, 9 May 2000).

5 See also Jocelyne Bourgon, *The New Synthesis of Public Administration Fieldbook*, 96.

6 On the importance of understanding legal constraints and preserving management prerogatives, see Jocelyne Bourgon, "The Middle Manager Today" (speech, Middle Managers' Forum, Ottawa, ON, 27 November 1998).

7 Ever denser, more complex controls may even undermine learning and improvement, rather than serving a core purpose of enabling it; for more on the debate around accountability measures, see Mark D. Jarvis and Paul G. Thomas, "The Limits of Accountability."

8 An issue of concern for some time; at the Canadian Centre for Management Development, I advised new deputy ministers to watch for this. Jocelyne Bourgon, "L'imputabilité des sous-ministres" (presentation, Canadian Centre for Management Development, 10 October 2001).

9 The zone of two hundred nautical miles from Canada's shores in which it has sovereign economic rights per international law, established in 1982.

10 In addition to its relevance to public sector leadership, this insight is tied to the New Synthesis's emphasis on citizen engagement. See Bourgon, *New Synthesis Fieldbook*, 99–124.

11 Managing such long chains is a major element of the New Synthesis; see, e.g., Bourgon, *New Synthesis Fieldbook*, 85–97 on leveraging across boundaries to handle long chains of intermediate results.

12 Michael J.L. Kirby, *Navigating Troubled Waters*, 3.

13 The New Synthesis would later integrate an exploratory process itself. See Bourgon, *New Synthesis Fieldbook*, 69–71.

14 See Jocelyne Bourgon, "Strengthening Our Policy Capacity," 24. As Clerk, I would push for an approach to policy work that involved "greater co-ordination and collaboration across [...] levels of government." Jocelyne Bourgon, *Fifth Annual Report to the Prime Minister on the Public Service of Canada*, 8.

15 Kirby, *Navigating*, 86.

16 Jocelyne Bourgon, "Strengthening Our Policy Capacity," 25–6. More broadly, ideas have to actively be *put* to work – the difference between creativity and innovation detailed in Jocelyne Bourgon, "Innovation and the Public Sector" (speech, 2nd Quality Conference, Copenhagen, Denmark, 3 October 2002).

17 Bourgon, *New Synthesis Fieldbook*, 42–3.

18 See Jocelyne Bourgon, "Future Proofing the State" (speech, ANZSOG Annual Conference, Wellington, New Zealand, July 2012).

19 On a leadership of proximity, see Bourgon, *New Synthesis Fieldbook*, 93.

20 On the formation of DREE and DRIE, see Donald J. Savoie, *Reviewing Canada's Regional Development Efforts*, 153–6.

21 Canada, Department of Regional Industrial Expansion, *Annual Reports 1983–1984*, and *Annual Report 1984–1985*.

22 See Jocelyne Bourgon, "All Aboard!" (speech, Managers' National Professional Development Forum, Banff, AB, 22 April 2002), on the need to build the capacity to deal with unforeseen events – tying it to the need for continuous learning and development. See also Jocelyne Bourgon, *A New Synthesis of Public Administration*, 61–6 on early detection and on emergence in the New Synthesis.

23 For more on commitment, see Johanna Schnabel, "Committed to Coordination?"

24 On federal systems and the need to find ways to act collectively and manage shared responsibilities, see Jocelyne Bourgon, *The Federal Idea*.

25 For more on Mulroney's approach to leadership, see Peter Aucoin, "Organizational Change in the Machinery of Canadian Government."

26 Jocelyne Bourgon, *Program Review*, 13–18.

27 It is also a search for balance between state authority and the collective power of society; see Bourgon, *A New Synthesis of Public Administration*, 46.

28 See Kathryn May, "A Scramble and Scrutiny of the Public Service Not Seen in More Than 20 Years."

29 Jocelyne Bourgon, "Distinctively Public Sector."

3. Becoming Deputy Minister: Consumer and Corporate Affairs

1 For those who served between the 35th and 41st Parliaments, 1993–2015, the average tenure for departing MPs was 8.7 years. James T. Pow, "Amateurs versus Professionals," 647.

2 These lessons stayed with me for years to come. I still have my slides for DM orientation sessions I held as head of the Canadian Centre for Management Development in 2001 and 2003, covering some of these points. Jocelyne Bourgon, "L'imputabilité des sous-ministres" (presentation, Canadian Centre for Management Development, 10 October 2001); Jocelyne Bourgon, "L'imputabilité des sous-ministres" (presentation, Canadian Centre for Management Development, 19 June 2003).

3 Canada, House of Commons Debates, 13 May 1991 (Mr. Schneider, PC). https://parl.canadiana.ca/view/oop.debates_HOC3403_01/12.

4 Canada, Consumer and Corporate Affairs Canada, *The Role of Consumer and Corporate Affairs Canada and Canada's Agenda for Prosperity*, 3.

5 Canada, Consumer and Corporate Affairs Canada, *Annual Report Year-End March 31, 1990* and *Annual Report Year-End March 31, 1991*.

6 CCA, *The Role of Consumer and Corporate Affairs Canada*, 3.
7 Michael E. Porter, *Canada at the Crossroads: The Reality of a New Competitive Environment* (1991), quoted in Consumer and Corporate Affairs Canada, *The Role of Consumer and Corporate Affairs Canada*, 15.
8 See Jocelyne Bourgon, "Strengthening Our Policy Capacity," 26–7; Jocelyne Bourgon, "Strategic Planning, Strategic Thinking, Strategic Governance" (speech, Prague, Czech Republic, 3 March 2017).
9 Martin Bashir, "An Interview with HRH The Princess of Wales."
10 Jonathan Craft, Backrooms and Beyond, 250.
11 Canada, Prime Minister's Office, *Open and Accountable Government.*
12 Ibid.
13 For more detail on this history, see Craft, *Backrooms and Beyond.*
14 Canada, Office of the Conflict of Interest and Ethics Commissioner, *Quarterly Statistical Report 2024–2025: Q2 – July to September 2024.*
15 Mario Dion, *Annual Report 2018–2019, in Respect of the Conflict of Interest Act.*
16 Craft, *Backrooms and Beyond*, 32–40.
17 Canada, Treasury Board Secretariat, *Policies for Ministers' Offices – January 2011.*
18 John Ibbitson, *Stephen Harper*, 294; Jonathan Craft and Paul Wilson, "Policy Analysis and the Central Executive."
19 See, e.g., Mia Rabson, "'Canada's Standing in the World Has Slipped' under Trudeau, Marc Garneau Says in Autobiography."
20 See, e.g., Donald Savoie, *Speaking Truth to Canadians about Their Public Service*, 165.
21 Heath Pickering, Jonathan Craft, and Marleen Brans, "Ministerial Advisers as Power Resources," supplemental data file 2 gives comparative numbers up to 2019; more up-to-date data is not evenly available across countries.
22 Jo-Anna Hagen Schuller and Finn Baker, "Ministers' Private Offices."
23 Terry Moran, "Terry Moran: Time for an Inquiry into the Public Service."
24 Canadian researchers have noted this risk; see Peter Aucoin and Mark D. Jarvis, *Modernizing Government Accountability*, 20.
25 In particular, whether or not ministerial staff can and/or should be called to account for their own actions before parliamentary committees has been widely debated. See Tim Durrant, Nicola Blacklaws, and Ketaki Zodgekar, *Special Advisers and the Johnson Government*, 31–2; Yee-Fui Ng, "Dispelling Myths about Conventions"; Lorraine Finlay, "The McMullan Principle."

4. Canada Is Calling: The Charlottetown Accord

1 Ray Hnatyshyn, "Speech from the Throne to Open the Third Session Thirty-Fourth Parliament of Canada" (speech, House of Commons, Ottawa, ON, 13 May 1991).
2 Gordon Robertson, *Memoirs of a Very Civil Servant*, 352.

3 This is touched upon in Jocelyne Bourgon, "Strengthening Our Policy Capacity"; for further comments on the Cabinet system, ministerial will, and the need to harness knowledge and know-how from across the public service, see Jocelyne Bourgon, "Video for Public Policy Forum (PPF)" (speech outline, PPF Testimonial Dinner Awards, Toronto, ON, 11 April 2013).
4 On thinking ahead and government's anticipative capacity, see Jocelyne Bourgon, *A New Synthesis of Public Administration*, 61–6.
5 25 September, 1 October, and 22–4 October 1991. Testimony starts with Canada, Parliament, Special Joint Committee on a Renewed Canada, *Minutes of Proceedings and Evidence,* 34th Parliament, 3rd Sess., No. 1 (25 September 1991).
6 On these conferences, see James Ross Hurley, *Amending Canada's Constitution*, 122–3; David Milne, "Innovative Constitutional Processes."
7 Julian Beltrame and Joan Bryden, "Natives Join Unity Talks."
8 Hurley, *Amending Canada's Constitution*, 124–5.
9 *Status Report of the Multilateral Meetings on the Constitution, Rolling Draft as at June 11, 1992 – End of Day.*
10 Canadian Press, "Mulroney Invites Premiers to Try Again."
11 "Premiers Tackle Senate Again on Friday, Mulroney Couldn't Be Happier."
12 See Jack Aubry, "The Phantom of July 7."
13 Canadian Press, "Mercredi, Yukon Leader Reject PM's Call."
14 See Don Macdonald, "Federalists Vow to Pack Meeting."
15 Joan Bryden, "Premiers Agree on More Talk."
16 On similar sentiments within Bourassa's party, see Rheal Seguin, "Fight Ahead for Bourassa."
17 Andre Tremblay, quoted in "'On s'est écrasé, c'est tout' – La conversation Wilhelmy-Tremblay."
18 Mulroney said much the same in his memoir (*Memoirs*, ch. 5).
19 Brian Mulroney, speech, August 1984, quoted in Arthur Tremblay, "An Authentically Canadian Deal."
20 On federalism, cooperation within federal systems, and unity, see Jocelyne Bourgon, *The Federal Idea*.

5. From CIDA to Transport

1 Canada, Parliament, House of Commons, Standing Committee on External Affairs and International Trade, Sub-Committee on Development and Human Rights, *Minutes of Proceedings and Evidence,* 34th Parliament, 3rd Sess., No. 42 (27 May 1993).
2 Kim Campbell, *Time and Chance*, ch. 14.
3 Ibid., ch. 15.
4 On working across boundaries, see Bourgon, *New Synthesis Fieldbook,* 90–4.

5 For more on the dangers of reorganization, see Jocelyne Bourgon et al., *Be the Change*, 15, and Bourgon, *A New Synthesis of Public Administration*, 94.

6 Jocelyne Bourgon, *Public Innovation and Public Purpose*, 9.

7 For current official guidance on the caretaker convention, see Canada, Privy Council Office, Guidelines on the Conduct of Ministers, Ministers of State, Exempt Staff and Public Servants during an Election.

8 Canada, Parliament, Senate, Senate Special Committee on the Pearson Airport Agreements, *Report of the Senate Special Committee on the Pearson Airport Agreements*.

9 On the importance of having this policy work ready, see chapter 10 on the Policy Research Initiative.

10 Paul Martin, *Hell or High Water*, 128.

11 A recurring theme in the New Synthesis and surrounding speeches; see, e.g., Jocelyne Bourgon, "The New Synthesis Initiative: Serving in the 21st Century" (speech, Aarhus, Denmark, 17 June 2018).

6. And So ... I Became Clerk

1 A.D.P. Heeney, the first Secretary to the Cabinet, wrote on the formation and importance of the Cabinet Secretariat and the modern PCO. See A.D.P. Heeney, "Cabinet Government in Canada," and Heeney, "Mackenzie King and the Cabinet Secretariat."

2 Alex Smith, *The Roles and Responsibilities of Central Agencies*, 1–2.

3 For more on ministerial responsibility, see Peter Aucoin and Mark D. Jarvis, *Modernizing Government Accountability*, 12–20.

4 See Eddie Goldenberg, *The Way It Works*, 98, on spending decisions being made by the Prime Minister without Cabinet consensus.

5 As was codified under Harper in the 2008 *Policies and Guidelines for Ministers' Offices,* still remaining in today's *Policies for Ministers' Offices* – January 2011. For a recent example, see Bill Morneau's Chief of Staff being selected by the PMO: Bill Morneau, *Where to from Here*, ch. 6.

6 On centralization and growing control of ministers' communications by Prime Ministers' and Premiers' Offices over time, see, for instance, Alex Marland, *Whipped*, 162–5, 169–71.

7 Marland gives a striking anecdote – staff for a provincial minister and their Premier, without notifying the minister, routing media inquiries through the office of the Premier for clearance after an unplanned remark (*Whipped*, 170–1).

8 These are now sections 126 and 127 of the Public Service Employment Act. https://laws-lois.justice.gc.ca/eng/acts/p-33.01/.

9 See also Gordon Robertson's view of the commonalities and differences between the prime ministers he worked with over the years, as well as how they changed in office: Robertson, *Memoirs of a Very Civil Servant*, 375–80.

10 Jean Chrétien, *My Years as Prime Minister,* 16.

11 Chrétien would joke that one of his lead advisors had an "agenda of his own." See ibid., 34.
12 Gordon Robertson, "The Changing Role of the Privy Council Office," 506.
13 On the breadth of ways party platforms have been crafted in Canada, see Greg Flynn, "Rethinking Policy Capacity in Canada."
14 On politics as peaceful conflict resolution, and the challenges ahead for it, see Jocelyne Bourgon, *The New Synthesis of Public Administration Fieldbook*, 176–7.
15 On the dynamics of politics and administration and the cycle of ideas and action, see Jocelyne Bourgon, "The Future of Public Service," 394–5.
16 *Creating Opportunity*, 19.
17 Ibid., 19.
18 Ibid., 20.
19 Note that the centre of government plays a major role in this process. See Jocelyne Bourgon, *A Centre of Government Fit for the Time*, 3.
20 Paul Martin, *Budget Speech* (1994), 1–2.
21 Ibid., 14.
22 Jocelyne Bourgon, *Program Review*, 16.
23 Tim Mau, "Professionalism and Leadership Development," 102; see also Glen Shortliffe, *Public Service 2000*, 11.
24 Bourgon, *Program Review*, 15.
25 Ibid., 8.

7. Regaining Canada's Fiscal Sovereignty

1 On bringing the public service into the process and on the need for a new approach, see Jocelyne Bourgon, "Re-inventing Government" (speech, Industry Canada Management Retreat, Ottawa, ON, 7 June 1994).
2 For the questions, see Jocelyne Bourgon, *Program Review*, 22.
3 Ibid., 26.
4 Jean Chrétien, *My Years as Prime Minister*, 60.
5 Paul Martin gives an account of this decision in his memoir: Martin, *Hell or High Water*, 141–2.
6 Jocelyne Bourgon, "Change and Management in the Public Service" (speech, Association of Professional Executives of the Public Service of Canada, Ottawa, ON, 11 May 1994), 3.
7 See my speech at the retreat: Jocelyne Bourgon, "Government Priorities and Strategic Planning Role" (speech, Deputy Ministers' Retreat, Ottawa, ON, 22 June 1994).
8 Martin includes an account of this event in his memoir; see Martin, *Hell or High Water*, 140. Chrétien recalled using this line on occasion when dealing with resistant ministers – "if the ministers persisted, I sometimes hinted that they seemed to be having difficulty doing the job they had been asked to do." See Chrétien, *My Years as Prime Minister*, 64–5.

9 The 22–3 June DM retreat helped prepare for this ministerial retreat. See Bourgon, "Government Priorities and Strategic Planning Role."
10 Jocelyne Bourgon, "Key Challenges Facing Canada's Public Service" (speech, Public Policy Forum, Ottawa, ON, 13 October 1994), 2.
11 Jocelyne Bourgon, "Beginning the Transformation: A Planning Agenda" (speech, Assistant Deputy Ministers' Forum, Ottawa, ON, 30 November 1994).
12 The *Wall Street Journal* ran a blunt, harsh comparison of Canada and Mexico – "Bankrupt Canada." The *New York Times* also ran a Canada-Mexico comparison, arguing that Canada had a "paler version of the peso crisis." Clyde H. Farnsworth, "Canada's Pale Version of Peso Crisis." Such coverage caused concern; see Martin, *Hell or High Water*, 147–8.
13 On OAS in particular, see Jean Chrétien, *My Years as Prime Minister,* 65–8; and Paul Martin, *Hell or High Water*, 149–53.
14 Jocelyne Bourgon, "Performance Management," 44.
15 On successful public policy and invention, see Jocelyne Bourgon, *A New Synthesis of Public Administration*, 109–10.
16 Regarding implementation, see Jocelyne Bourgon, "New Directions in Public Administration," 316–18.
17 Paul Martin, *Budget Speech* (1995), 4.

8. The 1995 Referendum

1 On the election, see Jean-François Lisée, *Octobre 1995*, 12.
2 Jean Chrétien, *My Years as Prime Minister,* 131.
3 *Des idées pour mon pays*, 5.
4 See, for example, Rhéal Séguin, "Sovereignty Not Tied to Vote."
5 Lisée, *Octobre 1995*, 18.
6 Robert Wright, *The Night Canada Stood Still*, ch. 6.
7 Quebec, National Assembly, *Journal des débats*, 14 March 1995 (Mr. Daniel Johnson, PLQ). https://www.assnat.qc.ca/en/travaux-parlementaires/assemblee-nationale/35-1/journal-debats/19950314/6465.html.
8 Preston Manning, *Think Big: Adventures in Life and Democracy* (Toronto, ON: McClelland & Stewart, 2002). Quoted in Wright, *The Night Canada Stood Still*, ch. 1.
9 Quoted in Anne McIlroy, "Parizeau Drops Demand for Full Sovereignty."
10 Quoted in Philip Authier, "Parizeau Softening Hard Line."
11 Nicholas Bayne, "So Near and Yet So Far," 31.
12 Bill 1, An Act respecting the future of Québec.
13 Wright, *The Night Canada Stood Still*, ch. 7.
14 Chrétien, *My Years as Prime Minister*, 137.
15 "Campaign Rhetoric Hits High Pitch."
16 Jean Chrétien, "'No' Rally at Verdun Auditorium."

17 *Bertrand v. Quebec (Procureur General)*, at para. 67.
18 Patrick J. Monahan, *Cooler Heads Shall Prevail*.
19 Canada, House of Commons Debates, 20 September 1995 (Right Hon. Jean Chrétien, LPC). https://www.ourcommons.ca/Content/House/351/Debates/227/han227-e.pdf.
20 Canada, House of Commons Debates, 20 September 1995 (Right Hon. Jean Chrétien, LPC). https://www.ourcommons.ca/Content/House/351/Debates/227/han227-e.pdf.
21 Jean Chrétien, "Quebec Chamber of Commerce and Industry."
22 Ibid.
23 Chantal Hébert and Jean Lapierre, *The Morning After*, 263.
24 Paul Martin, *Hell or High Water*, 173.
25 Chrétien, *My Years as Prime Minister*, 131.
26 Roméo LeBlanc, "Speech from the Throne to Open the Second Session Thirty-Fifth Parliament of Canada" (speech, House of Commons, Ottawa, ON, 27 February 1996).
27 Clarity Act, SC 2000, c. 26.
28 L-03 – Loi sur la laïcité de l'État, RLRQ, c. L-0,3; Bill 96, An Act respecting French, the official and common language of Québec.
29 Bill 137, The Education (Parents' Bill of Rights) Amendment Act, 2023.
30 Keeping Students in Class Act, S.O. 2022, c. 19.
31 Alexander Quon and Kate McGillivray, "Sask. Says $28M in carbon tax money is 'safe for now' after striking deal with Ottawa," CBC News, 16 July 2024.
32 Alberta Sovereignty within a United Canada Act, SA 2022, c. A-33.8.

9. The Head of the Public Service

1 My thoughts on the roles of the Clerk and the Head of the Public Service have developed over time. One early attempt to distinguish them can be found in Jocelyne Bourgon, "Leadership and the Public Service of Canada" (speech, Canadian Student Leadership Conference, Ottawa, ON, 24 January 1997).
2 Public Service Modernization Act, S.C. 2003, c. 22
3 For some of my contemporary thoughts, from when I was President of the Canadian Centre for Management Development, see Jocelyne Bourgon, "For a Professional, Non-Partisan Public Service: Merit and Learning" (speech, Public Service Commission of Canada, Ottawa, ON, 21 March 2002).
4 This was introduced in 2003's Public Service Modernization Act, and is present in section 30(2) of the Public Service Employment Act.
5 Canada, Public Service Commission, *Public Service Commission of Canada 2015–2016 Annual Report*, 18–19.
6 Australia, Australian Public Service Commission, "Government's Merit and Transparency Policy."

7 Australia, Australian Public Service Commission, "APS Bargaining."
8 New Zealand, Te Kawa Mataaho Public Service Commission, "Ngā pokapū – Central agencies."
9 Public Service Employment Act, S.C. 2003, c. 9, s. 127.
10 See Jocelyne Bourgon, *Third Annual Report to the Prime Minister on the Public Service of Canada*, 1–13.
11 Something I sometimes noted in speeches – e.g., Jocelyne Bourgon, "Ministers, the Public Service and the Future" (speech, Deputy Ministers' Retreat, Ottawa, ON, 28 June 1995).
12 Benefits were highlighted in Jocelyne Bourgon, *Fourth Annual Report to the Prime Minister on the Public Service of Canada*, 32–3.
13 Working across boundaries was a major focus of this period, horizontally and vertically. See, among other speeches, Jocelyne Bourgon, "Strengthening Our Policy Capacity"; Jocelyne Bourgon, "Working Together to Prepare for the Year 2000 and Beyond" (speech, Conference of the Federal Regional Council – Quebec, Saint-Hyacinthe, QC, 4 November 1997); and Jocelyne Bourgon, "Building a Strong Public Policy Capacity" (speech, Policy Research: Creating Linkages Conference, Ottawa, ON, 1 October 1998). It would later be key to the New Synthesis; see Jocelyne Bourgon, *A New Synthesis of Public Administration*, in general; *The New Synthesis of Public Administration Fieldbook*, 90–2.
14 Canada, House of Commons Debates, 7 March 1996 (Mr. Massé, LPC). https://www.ourcommons.ca/documentviewer/en/35-2/house/sitting-8/hansard
15 La Relève Task Force, *First Progress Report on La Relève*, 25–6.
16 Jocelyne Bourgon, *Fourth Annual Report*, 38.
17 *Advisory Committee on Senior Level Retention and Compensation, First Report.*
18 Ibid.
19 On pride and the public service, and the decision to restore awards, see my testimony before the Senate Committee on National Finance: Canada, Parliament, Senate, Standing Senate Committee on National Finance, 1st sess., 36th Parliament, Meeting No. 14, 1998.
20 Jocelyne Bourgon, "The New Synthesis Initiative: Serving in the 21st Century" (speech, Welfare Innovation Day, Denmark, 22 February 2020).
21 A point I emphasized early as Clerk: Jocelyne Bourgon, "The Accomplishments of the Past, the Challenges of the Future" (speech, APEX, Ottawa, ON, 3 May 1995).
22 I explore the 1990s reforms in Canada and internationally in Jocelyne Bourgon, "Public Sector Reform … The Canadian Model" (speech, International Council for Canadian Studies, Ottawa, ON, 25 August 1997). See also, on these general ideas, Bourgon, *A New Synthesis of Public Administration*, 19–30.
23 See Jocelyne Bourgon, *The New Synthesis of Public Administration Fieldbook*, 42–50.

24 On public innovation generally, see Jocelyne Bourgon, "We Are All Innovators" (speech, Expo Innovation 1994, Ottawa, ON, 16 June 1994); Bourgon, *The New Synthesis Fieldbook*, 143–54.
25 Alasdair Roberts, "Public Management," 318.
26 Jocelyne Bourgon, "Key Challenges Facing Canada's Public Service" (speech, Public Policy Forum, Ottawa, ON, 13 October 1994), 4.
27 The PCO published a final report on the DM Task Force process in December 1996, summarizing the findings of all nine: Canada, Privy Council Office, *Deputy Minister Task Forces*.
28 The Task Force on Service Delivery Models produced a four-volume report. Task Force on Service Delivery Models, *Service Delivery Models*.
29 Task Force on a Planning Tool for Thinking about the Future of the Public Service, *A Planning Tool for Thinking about the Future of the Public Service*.
30 Task Force on Overhead Services, *Management of Overhead Services*.
31 Task Force on Values and Ethics, *Discussion Paper on Values and Ethics in the Public Service*.
32 Task Force on Managing Horizontal Policy Issues, *Managing Horizontal Policy Issues*.
33 Task Force on Strengthening Policy Capacity, *Strengthening Our Policy Capacity*.

10. A Public Service Reform Agenda

1 Jocelyne Bourgon, "The Many Faces of Alternative Service Delivery" (speech, Deputy Ministers' Retreat, Ottawa, ON, 13 June 1996).
2 As opposed to the private sector's focus on customers; see Jocelyne Bourgon, *Fourth Annual Report*, 24.
3 See, in particular, Jocelyne Bourgon, "Public Management Framework for Service Delivery: Culture, Context, Circumstance and Capacity" (speech, CAPAM National Seminar, Entebbe, Uganda, 19 November 2001).
4 Task Force on Service Delivery Models, *Service Delivery Models*.
5 This became a major part of the New Synthesis, particularly in the application/workshop phase. See Bourgon, *The New Synthesis Fieldbook*, 101–7; Jocelyne Bourgon, Rachael Calleja, Rishanthi Pattiarachchi, and Queena Li, *Enforcement and Safety*, 12; Jocelyne Bourgon and Rachael Calleja, *The New Synthesis in Action*.
6 Bourgon, *Third Annual Report*, 40–1. The language in the 1995 annual report is that of *clients*; the Smith task force recommended the language of *citizens* a year later. See Task Force on Service Delivery Models, *Discussion Paper*, 1:19–21. This would be reflected in later annual reports.
7 Jocelyne Bourgon, "La Relève: Our Greatest Challenge" (speech, Human Resources Centre of Canada Conference, Cornwall, ON, 6 November 1996).

8 For a general overview, see Corin Tentchoff, *Modernizing Service Delivery*, 6–8.

9 Canada, Office of the Auditor General, "Involving Others in Governing," 23–13.

10 Roméo LeBlanc, "Speech from the Throne to Open the First Session Thirty-Sixth Parliament of Canada" (speech, House of Commons, Ottawa, ON, 23 September 1997).

11 Ibid.

12 See "Canada On-Line: Community Access Program," Connecting Canadians, archived 10 March 2000 at the Wayback Machine, https://web.archive.org/web/20000310045252/http://connect.gc.ca/en/240-e.htm. I highlighted these programs in speeches at the time; e.g., Jocelyne Bourgon, "Connecting Canadians: Public Service in the Information Age" (speech, Technology in Government Week, Ottawa, ON, 20 October 1997).

13 Chris Cobb, "Cyberschool."

14 Canada, Industry Canada, *Performance Report for the Period Ending March 31, 1999*, 17.

15 United Nations, Department of Economic and Social Affairs, *Benchmarking E-Government*, 36.

16 United Nations, Department of Economic and Social Affairs, *E-Government Survey 2024*, 173.

17 For more on the CCSN and the ICCS, see Brian Marson and Ralph Heintzman, *From Research to Results*.

18 See Jocelyne Bourgon, "Building a Strong Public Policy Capacity" (speech, Policy Research: Creating Linkages Conference, Ottawa, ON, 1 October 1998); Jocelyne Bourgon, untitled speech (speech, Statistics Canada, Gatineau, QC, 18 November 2002).

19 See Jocelyne Bourgon, "New Directions in Public Administration," 316–18, 324.

20 Task Force on Managing Horizontal Policy Issues, *Managing Horizontal Policy Issues*.

21 Task Force on Strengthening Policy Capacity, *Strengthening Our Policy Capacity*.

22 Canada, Policy Research Initiative, *Overview*.

23 For a summary of the report, see Canada, Policy Research Initiative, *Canada 2005*.

24 For more on the Policy Research Initiative, see Corin Tentchoff, *Developing Policy Capacity and the Policy Research Initiative*.

25 For information on Voyer's leadership, see Jean-Pierre Voyer, "Policy Analysis in the Federal Government."

26 Canada, Policy Horizons Canada, *Disruptions on the Horizon*.

27 See the Committee for the Future web page: https://www.eduskunta.fi/EN/valiokunnat/tulevaisuusvaliokunta/Pages/default.aspx.

28 Jocelyne Bourgon, "Change and Management in the Public Service" (speech, APEX, Ottawa, ON, 11 May 1994).

29 Jocelyne Bourgon, "Reform in the Public Service of Canada: Human Resources Management and Partnerships" (speech, Assistant Deputy Ministers' Forum, Ottawa, ON, 25 June 1996).
30 Jocelyne Bourgon, "La Relève: Our Greatest Challenge" (speech, Human Resources Centre of Canada Conference, Cornwall, ON, 6 November 1996).
31 Jocelyne Bourgon, *Fourth Annual Report to the Prime Minister on the Public Service of Canada*, 38.
32 La Relève Task Force, *First Progress Report on La Relève*.
33 Bourgon, *Fourth Annual Report*, 48–9.
34 La Relève Task Force, *First Progress Report on La Relève*, 28–9.
35 Canada, the Leadership Network, *Performance Report for the Period Ending March 31, 1999*, 3.
36 Bob Chartier, email message to Public Governance International, 29 July 2023.
37 For more on La Relève and the Leadership Network, also covering my time at the Canadian Centre for Management Development, see Corin Tentchoff, *La Relève, the Leadership Network, and the Formation of the Canada School of Public Service*.
38 Canada, Treasury Board Secretariat, *Employment Statistics for the Federal Public Service: April 1, 1999, to March 31, 2000*, 23.
39 Canada, Treasury Board Secretariat, "Population of the Federal Public Service," 11 July 2024.

11. Moving On: The Canadian Centre for Management Development

1 Rosemary Speirs, "Thin Ranks of PM's Female Aides Now Thinner."
2 My own accompanying announcement placed my move to CCMD in continuity with La Relève: Jocelyne Bourgon, "Letter from the Clerk of the Privy Council and Secretary to the Cabinet to All Employees of the Public Service of Canada."
3 On the Pearson case, see chapter 5.
4 Jean Chrétien, "Challenges for the Canadian Centre for Management Development for the New Millennium."
5 Roméo LeBlanc, "Speech from the Throne to Open the First Session Thirty-Sixth Parliament of Canada" (speech, House of Commons, Ottawa, ON, 23 September 1997); Adrienne Clarkson, "Speech from the Throne to Open the Second Session Thirty-Sixth Parliament of Canada" (speech, House of Commons, Ottawa, ON, 12 October 1999).
6 A number of speeches from 1999 and on cover this topic; e.g., Jocelyne Bourgon, "Canada's Public Service – Looking to the Future" (speech, Montreal, QC, 11 February 1999); Jocelyne Bourgon, "Citizens, Government, Democracy: A New Deal?" (speech, International Summit on Public Service Reform, Winnipeg, MB, 11 June 1999).

7 B. Guy Peters and Donald J. Savoie, eds., *Governance in the Twenty-First Century*.

8 The report was released in two parts: a *Policy Discussion Paper* and *Directions for the Future*.

9 Jocelyne Bourgon, "Colour Me Management: Learning, Doing, Amazing" (speech, Conference of Senior Federal Public Servants of Quebec, Trois-Rivières, QC, 30 November 2000).

10 Ibid.

11 Canada, Canadian Centre for Management Development, Learning and Development Committee, *A Public Service Learning Organization*.

12 Jocelyne Bourgon, "Management Reform Agenda: 2001–2010" (speech, Association for Public Policy Analysis and Management, Seattle, WA, 3 November 2000), 2.

13 Canada, Canadian Centre for Management Development, "Canadian Centre for Management Development Announces Revitalized Fellows Program and Announces Two Appointments"; Canada, Canadian Centre for Management Development, "Fellows."

14 See Canada, Canadian Centre for Management Development, Partnership for International Cooperation, "The Partnership."

15 Canada, Prime Minister's Office, "Prime Minister Announces Formation of Task Force on Modernizing Human Resources Management in the Public Service."

16 This quote has been attributed to various systems thinkers, including W. Edwards Deming, Don Berwick, and Paul Batalden. Batalden says it was a variation on an insight from Arthur Jones: "All organizations are perfectly designed to get the results they get!" See Paul Batalden and Earl Conway, "Like Magic?"

17 Jocelyne Bourgon, "For a Professional, Non-Partisan Public Service: Merit and Learning" (speech, Public Service Commission of Canada, Ottawa Congress Centre, Ottawa, ON, 21 March 2002).

18 For an account of this change, including its rationale and the debate around it, see Luc Juillet and Ken Rasmussen, *Defending a Contested Ideal*, 212–18.

19 For a summary, see Margaret Smith, *Legislative Summary: Bill C-25*.

20 Canada, Canadian Centre for Management Development, *CCMD 5 Year Review – Canadian Centre for Management Development Report to Parliament December 2001*, 54–6.

21 Canada, Parliament, House of Commons, Standing Committee on Government Operations and Estimates. 2nd sess., 37th Parliament, Meeting No. 31, 2003.

22 For more on the creation of the CSPS and my time at CCMD, see Corin Tentchoff, *La Relève, the Leadership Network, and the Formation of the Canada School of Public Service*.

12. The International Public Servant

1 Jocelyne Bourgon, untitled speech (speech, Statistics Canada, Gatineau, QC, 18 November 2002), 1.
2 Jocelyne Bourgon, "Public Sector Reform … the Canadian Model" (speech, International Council for Canadian Studies, Ottawa, ON, 25 August 1997).
3 Jocelyne Bourgon, *Fifth Annual Report to the Prime Minister on the Public Service of Canada,* 1–5.
4 Jocelyne Bourgon, "The Canadian Model of Public Sector Reform" (speech, Commonwealth Conference in Public Administration, Meech Lake, QC, 22 April 1998).
5 Jocelyne Bourgon, "Public Sector Reform in Canada" (speech, Civil Service College, Singapore, 10 September 1998).
6 Peter Aucoin, "The Public Service as a Learning Organization."
7 "Canada's New Spirit."
8 Klaus Schwab calls this the "fourth industrial revolution"; see Schwab, *The Fourth Industrial Revolution.*
9 Jocelyne Bourgon, "21st Century Public Services – Learning from the Front Line" (speech, Public Service Reform Conference 2007, London, UK, 27 March 2007), 8.
10 Jocelyne Bourgon, "Citizens, Government, Democracy: A New Deal?" (speech, International Summit on Public Service Reform, Winnipeg, MB, 11 June 1999).
11 Jocelyne Bourgon, "Redesigning the Public Service for the Future" (speech, Fourth National Civil Service Conference, Kuala Lumpur, Malaysia, 17 July 1999).
12 Jocelyne Bourgon, "Serving in the Knowledge Age: A Commitment to Lifelong Learning" (speech, Seventh Annual Technology in Government Week, Ottawa, ON, 19 October 1999).
13 John Kamensky, "A Brief History."
14 Jocelyne Bourgon, "Management Reform Agenda: 2001–2010" (speech, Association for Public Policy Analysis and Management, Seattle, WA, 3 November 2000).
15 Ibid., 2.
16 Jocelyne Bourgon, "Public Service Leadership in the Knowledge Age" (speech, 2001 Conference on Governance and Public Administration in the 21st Century, Athens, Greece, 10 July 2001).
17 Jocelyne Bourgon, "Different Circumstances … Common Challenges, Common Purpose" (speech, Public Sector Leadership Forum 2001, Singapore, 28 August 2001).
18 Jocelyne Bourgon, "Public Management Framework for Service Delivery: Culture, Context, Circumstance and Capacity" (speech, CAPAM National Seminar, Entebbe, Uganda, 19 November 2001).

19 See Bourgon, "Different Circumstances …," 5.

20 Ibid., 7.

21 Commonwealth Expert Group on Development and Democracy, *Making Democracy Work for Pro-Poor Development*, 6.

22 Ibid.

23 See in particular Jocelyne Bourgon, *The New Synthesis of Public Administration Fieldbook*, 73–84 on positioning.

24 Commonwealth Expert Group on Development and Democracy, *Making Democracy Work for Pro-Poor Development*, 42–3.

25 United Nations, Committee of Experts on Public Administration, *Report on the Fifth Session.*

26 United Nations, Committee of Experts on Public Administration, *Report on the Sixth Session.*

27 United Nations, Committee of Experts on Public Administration, *Report on the Seventh Session.*

28 United Nations, Committee of Experts on Public Administration, *Report on the Eighth Session.*

29 Jocelyne Bourgon, "Unlocking the Human Potential for Public Sector Performance – Challenges and Trends" (speech, Ad-Hoc Expert Group Meeting, Florence, Italy, 6 May 2004).

30 Ibid., 3.

31 Jocelyne Bourgon, "Introductory Report" (speech, IIAS Second International Regional Conference, Yaoundé, Cameroon, 15 July 2003), 5.

32 Ibid., 7.

33 Ibid., 9.

34 Jocelyne Bourgon, "Introduction."

35 Jocelyne Bourgon, "In Praise of an Unusual Organization" (speech, OECD Council, Paris, France, 20 March 2007).

36 See Jocelyne Bourgon, *Reform and Modernization of the OECD*.

13. A New Synthesis of Public Administration

1 Jocelyne Bourgon, "Responsive, Responsible and Respected Government," 9.

2 Kurt Lewin, *Field Theory in Social Science*.

3 Bourgon, "Responsive, Responsible, and Respected Government," 9.

4 On the growth of exempt staff, see chapter 3.

5 Christopher Pollitt, "'Towards a New Public Administration Theory,'" 37.

6 Christopher Pollitt, "Mini-Symposium on 'Towards a New Public Administration theory': Editor's Introduction," 5.

7 Donald F. Kettl., *The Transformation of Governance*.

8 Speech in 2006, published in 2007: Jocelyne Bourgon, "Responsive, Responsible and Respected Government."

9 *Literature Scan no. 1: On the Need for a New Synthesis of Public Administration* (Ottawa, ON: New Synthesis Network, 2009); republished in *Compilation of Literature Scans.*

10 *Literature Scan no. 2: Complexity Theories: What Are They and What Do They Tell Us about Public Administration in the 21st Century*? (Ottawa, ON: New Synthesis Network, 2009), republished in *Compilation of Literature Scans*.

11 The distinction between difficult, complicated, and complex is covered in both the 2011 New Synthesis book and the 2017 *Fieldbook.* Jocelyne Bourgon, *A New Synthesis of Public Administration*, 20–2; Jocelyne Bourgon, *The New Synthesis of Public Administration Fieldbook*, 31–2.

12 *Literature Scan no. 3: Resilience: Key Concepts and Themes and Their Implications for Public Administration* (Ottawa, ON: New Synthesis Network, 2009), republished in *Compilation of Literature Scans.*

13 C.S. Holling, "Understanding the Complexity of Economic, Ecological, and Social Systems."

14 Ann S. Masten and Jelena Obradović, "Disaster Preparation and Recovery."

15 *Literature Scan no. 4: Collective Intelligence: What Is It and How Can It Be Tapped?* (Ottawa, ON: New Synthesis Network, 2009), republished in *Compilation of Literature Scans.*

16 *Literature Scan no. 5: Disentangling Performance Management Systems from Control Mechanisms* (New Synthesis Network, 2010), included in *Compilation of Literature Scans.*

17 *Compilation of Literature Scans*, 125.

18 *Compilation of Literature Scans*, 127.

19 Several such scandals, most famously the Enron accounting scandal that brought down audit and consulting multinational Arthur Andersen, led the United States to enact the Sarbanes-Oxley Act in 2002. The act, among other things, restricted the simultaneous provision of compliance-focused audit and performance-focused consulting services. See Michael W. Peregrine and Charles W. Elson, "The Important Legacy of the Sarbanes Oxley Act."

20 See also Jocelyne Bourgon, "Performance Management."

21 *Literature Scan no. 6: Applications of Complex Adaptive Systems Theories in Governance, Public Administration and Public Policy* (New Synthesis Network, 2010), included in *Compilation of Literature Scans*.

22 Tony Bovaird, "Emergent Strategic Management and Planning Mechanisms in Complex Adaptive Systems."

23 Walter Buckley, "Society as a Complex Adaptive System."

24 Andreas Duit and Victor Galaz, "Governance and Complexity – Emerging Issues for Governance Theory."

25 Thomas Homer-Dixon, *The Upside of Down.*

26 Eve Mitleton-Kelly, "Ten Principles of Complexity and Enabling Infrastructures."

27 Elements of the NS four-quadrant diagram can be seen as early as June 2008: Jocelyne Bourgon, "The Future of Public Service," 391.
28 Jocelyne Bourgon, "Understanding the Public Leadership Environment: Preparing People to Serve People in the 21st Century" (speech, CAPAM, Kuala Lumpur, Malaysia, 22 June 2009).
29 June 2009 speech, published as Jocelyne Bourgon, "Serving beyond the Predictable."
30 Jocelyne Bourgon, "Building the Capacity for Public Results: The History and Future of Nation-Building" (speech, IIAS, Helsinki, Finland, 7 July 2009).
31 Jocelyne Bourgon, "Public Purpose, Government Authority and Collective Power" (speech, XIV International Congress of CLAD, Salvador de Bahia, Brazil, 29 October 2009).
32 Jocelyne Bourgon, "New Directions in Public Administration: Serving beyond the Predictable" (speech, 2008 PAC Conference, York, UK, 1 September 2008).
33 Jocelyne Bourgon, "The Future of Public Service."
34 Ibid.
35 For more on the Sam Richardson Award, see the IPAA website: "Sam Richardson Award," Institute of Public Administration Australia, accessed 18 June 2024, https://www.ipaa.org.au/national-awards/sam-richardson-award/.
36 *Compilation of Literature Scans*.
37 Jocelyne Bourgon, *A New Synthesis of Public Administration*, 255–60.
38 Through my work with CAPAM, I was also actively working with Commonwealth countries in Africa and the Caribbean. Insights from these countries enriched the New Synthesis as well.
39 Their counterpart to Canada's Clerk of the Privy Council.
40 Bourgon, *A New Synthesis of Public Administration,* 262–4.
41 *Resilience and Emergence in Public Administration.*
42 Ibid., 42–4.
43 *Achieving Public Results*.
44 Ibid., 15–17. Andrew Graham's homelessness strategy case study was included in the 2011 book: Bourgon, *A New Synthesis of Public Administration*, 167–81. Don Lenihan's labour mobility case study was published on its own: Lenihan, *Collaborative Federalism*.
45 *Governance in the 21st Century*.
46 Bourgon, *A New Synthesis of Public Administration*, 155.
47 Jocelyne Bourgon, *The New Synthesis of Public Administration Fieldbook*, 18.
48 *Preparing Government to Serve beyond the Predictable*.
49 Bourgon, *A New Synthesis of Public Administration*, 267.
50 See *Preparing Government to Serve beyond the Predictable*, 18–19, as well as the opening remarks and closing rapporteurs' presentation from the roundtable.
51 Bourgon, *A New Synthesis of Public Administration*, 267–9.
52 *A Public Service Renewal Agenda for the 21st Century*.

53 Bourgon, *A New Synthesis of Public Administration,* 269.
54 See Jocelyne Bourgon, "The History and Future of Nation-Building? Building Capacity for Public Results" (speech, IIAS, Helsinki, Finland, 7 July 2009).
55 Randall Russell, "The New Synthesis Project."
56 Jocelyne Bourgon, *NS-Lab.*
57 *A Self-Help Guide for Practitioners.*
58 Jocelyne Bourgon, *A Summary of Learning of the First NS Master Class Program Held in Singapore in March–May 2013.*
59 Jocelyne Bourgon and Rishanthi Pattiarachchi, *Rule of Law, Citizenship and Enforcement Strategies.*
60 "Reading Material (NS World Examples)," in the PGI archives.
61 Jocelyne Bourgon, Rachael Calleja, Rishanthi Pattiarachchi, and Queena Li, *Enforcement and Safety.*
62 For some of the New Synthesis cases from around the world, see https://pgionline.com/joining-the-ns-initiative/multiyear-partnerships/.
63 Jocelyne Bourgon, *A User's Guide for Practitioners*, v.
64 Jocelyne Bourgon, *The New Synthesis of Public Administration Fieldbook.*
65 E.g., a one-day NS workshop in June 2018; see Jocelyne Bourgon, "NS Lab for Central Region Denmark" (workshop, Aarhus, Denmark, 18 June 2018).
66 Jocelyne Bourgon, "Learning from the Coronavirus Pandemic: A New Synthesis Perspective" (speech, National Conference – Association of Municipalities, Vejle, Denmark, 18 August 2020).
67 Jocelyne Bourgon, "The New Synthesis Initiative: Serving in the 21st Century" (speech, Copenhagen, Denmark, 20 June 2018).
68 Jonas Kroustrup and Rachael Calleja, *NS Live Case Series 2017: The Vejle Resilience Strategy.*
69 Ulrik Jungersen and Rachael Calleja, *NS Live Case Series 2017: Kolding – We Design for Life.*
70 *NS Live Case Series 2017: Elder Care in Frederica, Denmark.*
71 Jocelyne Bourgon, "Leadership Summit 2022 – Central Denmark Region" (speech, Leadership Summit 2022, Aarhus, Denmark, 16 May 2022).
72 See, e.g., Jocelyne Bourgon, "Finland: From Success to Sustained Success" (speech, Finland, 26 June 2010); Jocelyne Bourgon, "From Process to Outcome: A Contribution to the Self-Evaluation of the Government-Wide Strategic Policy-Making Process" (speech, Helsinki, Finland, 12 October 2016).
73 See Susan Stuebing and Cees Anton de Vries, *Governance for the Circular Economy: Leadership observations* (Maarn, The Netherlands: Quadrahhuis Press, 2018).
74 Jocelyne Bourgon, "Expedition 2050: Building the Future of Netherlands" (speech, the Netherlands, 15 October 2020).
75 Jocelyne Bourgon, "The New Synthesis Initiative: Serving in the 21st Century" (speech, Future of Municipalities Conference, Norway, 4 June 2020).

76 Najat Zarrouk, letter to Jocelyne Bourgon, 3 August 2023.
77 France made me a Chevalier de l'Ordre nationale du Mérite in 2013.

14. Conclusion: Back Where It Began

1 See, as well my recent keynote speech in Singapore, Jocelyne Bourgon, *Serving in 2025 and Beyond.*
2 Nisrine Dandache and Jocelyne Bourgon, *Is Canada Fit for the Future?*
3 See the *Fit for the Future* report for 2021 data and trends.
4 Per the *Annual Financial Reports of the Government of Canada.*
5 See also Peter Aucoin, "New Political Governance in Westminster Systems."
6 Based on the Estimates for 2000–1 and 2024–5.
7 Per Treasury Board numbers: https://www.canada.ca/en/treasury-board-secretariat/services/innovation/human-resources-statistics/population-federal-public-service-department.html.
8 Catherine Morrison, "Just Over Half of 'High-Volume' Government Services Met Standards Last Year."
9 An idea previously captured by the Hon. Mitchell Sharp, observing the role's growth since his time as Minister of Finance; see Eddie Goldenberg, *The Way It Works*, 131.
10 See Alasdair Roberts, *The Adaptable Country*, 110–16.
11 For more on these issues, see Jocelyne Bourgon, "Expenditure Management Redefined: Serving Canada and Canadians" (PowerPoint, Shared Services Canada, Ottawa, ON, 27 November 2024).
12 Canada, House of Commons Debates, 11 June 2024 (Mr. Poilievre, CPC). https://www.ourcommons.ca/DocumentViewer/en/44-1/house/sitting-329/hansard.
13 Donald Savoie, *Speaking Truth to Canadians about Their Public Service*, 64–82.
14 Since writing this section, I delivered the lecture. An extended version has now been published: Jocelyne Bourgon, *Serving Canada in 2025 – Au service du Canada en 2025.*

Bibliography

Unpublished Material

This manuscript was written while I was preparing my records for transfer to Library and Archives Canada, in part to give context to these records. Several of the sources cited – in particular, many of the underlying speeches – have not been published.

The Library and Archives Canada collection can be found under the label *Jocelyne Bourgon fonds*, archival reference no. R18904, MIKAN 6652689.

Published Material

Achieving Public Results: Societal and Civic: The New Synthesis Project – Canada Roundtable Report. Edited by Jocelyne Bourgon. Ottawa, ON: Public Governance International, 2010.

Advisory Committee on Senior Level Retention and Compensation, First Report. Ottawa, ON: Treasury Board Secretariat, 1998. https://www.tbs-sct.canada.ca/rp/adcm1-eng.asp.

Alberta Sovereignty within a United Canada Act, SA 2022, c. A-33.8

Aubry, Jack. "The Phantom of July 7: Premiers Thought They Had Clear Picture of What Bourassa Wanted in a Deal." *Ottawa Citizen* (Ottawa, ON), 17 August 1992.

Aucoin, Peter. "New Political Governance in Westminster Systems: Impartial Public Administration and Management Performance at Risk." *Governance* 25, no. 2 (2012): 177–99. https://doi.org/10.1111/j.1468-0491.2012.01569.x.

– "Organizational Change in the Machinery of Canadian Government: From Rational Management to Brokerage Politics." *Canadian Journal of Political Science* 19, no. 1 (1986): 3–27.

– "The Public Service as a Learning Organization: Maintaining the Momentum in Public Service Reform." In *Modernizing Governance: A Preliminary Exploration*,

147–84. Ottawa, ON: Canadian Centre for Management Development, 2000. https://publications.gc.ca/Collection/SC94-75-2000E.pdf.

Aucoin, Peter, and Mark D. Jarvis. *Modernizing Government Accountability: A Framework for Reform*. Ottawa, ON: Canada School of Public Service, 2005.

Australia. Australian Public Service Commission. "APS Bargaining." 6 February 2024. https://www.apsc.gov.au/apsbargaining.

– "Government's Merit and Transparency Policy." 11 December 2020. https://www.apsc.gov.au/working-aps/governments-merit-and-transparency-policy.

Authier, Philip. "Parizeau Softening Hard Line; He Won't Rule Out Links to Canada." *Montreal Gazette* (Montreal, QC), 20 April 1995.

"Bankrupt Canada." *Wall Street Journal* (New York, NY), 12 January 1995.

Bashir, Martin, interviewer. "An Interview with HRH The Princess of Wales." "Panorama." Season 43, episode 35, BBC 1. 20 November 1995.

Batalden, Paul, and Earl Conway. "Like Magic?" PSQH Blog. Patient Safety & Quality Healthcare. 3 August 2015. Archived 21 September 2015, at the Wayback Machine, https://web.archive.org/web/20150921105724/http://psqh.com/psqh-blog/like-magic.

Bayne, Nicholas. "So Near and Yet So Far: The 1995 Quebec Referendum in Perspective." *London Journal of Canadian Studies* 32, no. 1 (2017): 25–41. https://doi.org/10.14324/111.444.ljcs.2017v32.004.

Beltrame, Julian, and Joan Bryden. "Natives Join Unity Talks; May 31 Target Set for Offer to Quebec." *Ottawa Citizen* (Ottawa, ON), 13 March 1992.

Bertrand v. Quebec (Procureur General), 1995 CanLII 11036 (QC CS).

Bill 1, An Act respecting the future of Québec. 1st Session, 35th Legislature, Quebec, 1995 (first reading).

Bill 96, An Act respecting French, the official and common language of Québec, 1st Session, 42nd Legislature, Quebec, 2021

Bill 137, The Education (Parents' Bill of Rights) Amendment Act, 2023, 3rd Session, 29th Legislature, Saskatchewan, 2023.

Bourgon, Jocelyne. *A Centre of Government Fit for the Time: Acting as One, Serving as One, Learning as One*. Ottawa, ON: Public Governance International, 2014.

– *Distinctively Public Sector: The Case for a New Synthesis of Public Administration.* Ottawa, ON: Public Governance International, 2015.

– *The Federal Idea.* Ottawa, ON: Public Governance International, 2015.

– *Fifth Annual Report to the Prime Minister on the Public Service of Canada.* Ottawa, ON: Privy Council Office, 1998.

– *Fourth Annual Report to the Prime Minister on the Public Service of Canada.* Ottawa, ON: Privy Council Office, 1997.

– "The Future of Public Service: A Search for a New Balance." *Australian Journal of Public Administration* 67, no. 4 (2008): 390–404.

– "Introduction." *International Review of Administrative Sciences* 70, no. 3 (2004): 435–7.

– "Letter from the Clerk of the Privy Council and Secretary to the Cabinet to All Employees of the Public Service of Canada" (Ottawa, ON: Privy Council Office, 14 December 1998), archived 25 January 2000 at the Wayback Machine, https://web.archive.org/web/20000125030218/http://www.pco-bcp.gc.ca:80/ClerkSP-JB/message_e.htm.

– "New Directions in Public Administration: Serving beyond the Predictable." *Public Policy and Administration* 24, no. 3 (2009): 309–30.

– *A New Synthesis of Public Administration: Serving in the 21st Century*. Kingston, ON: McGill-Queen's University Press, 2011.

– *The New Synthesis of Public Administration Fieldbook*. Copenhagen, Denmark: Dansk Psykologisk Forlag A/S, 2017.

– *NS-Lab: A New Synthesis Laboratory for Master Practitioners*. Ottawa, ON: Public Governance International, 2013.

– "Performance Management: It's the Results That Count." *Asia Pacific Journal of Public Administration* 30, no. 1 (2008): 41–58.

– *Program Review: The Government of Canada's Experience Eliminating the Deficit, 1994–99: A Canadian Case Study*. London, UK: Institute for Government, 2009.

– *Public Innovation and Public Purpose*. Ottawa, ON: Public Governance International, 2015.

– *Reform and Modernization of the OECD*. Waterloo, ON: Centre for International Governance Innovation, 2009.

– "Responsive, Responsible and Respected Government: Towards a New Public Administration Theory." *International Review of Administrative Sciences* 73, no. 1 (2007): 7–26.

– "Serving beyond the Predictable." *ETHOS*, December 2009.

– *Serving Canada in 2025 – Au service du Canada en 2025*. Ottawa, ON: Public Governance International, 2025.

– *Serving in 2025 and Beyond*. Ottawa, ON: Public Governance International, 2024.

– "Strengthening Our Policy Capacity." In Canadian Centre for Management Development, *Rethinking Policy: Strengthening Policy Capacity: Conference Proceedings*. Ottawa, ON: Canadian Centre for Management Development, 1996.

– *A Summary of Learning of the First NS Master Class Program Held in Singapore in March–May 2013*. Ottawa, ON: Public Governance International, 2013.

– *Third Annual Report to the Prime Minister on the Public Service of Canada*. Ottawa, ON: Privy Council Office, 1995.

– *A User's Guide for Practitioners*. Ottawa, ON: Public Governance International, 2016.

Bourgon, Jocelyne, et al. *Be the Change: Peer Review Report of the Cabinet Office Role in Modernizing Government*. London, UK: Cabinet Office, 2000.

Bourgon, Jocelyne, and Rachael Calleja. *NS Live Case Series 2017: Kolding – We Design for Life*. Ottawa, ON: Public Governance International, 2017.

– *NS Live Case Series 2017: The Vejle Resilience Strategy*. Ottawa, ON: Public Governance International, 2017.

– *The New Synthesis in Action: A Retrospective of the NS Labs Conducted in 2013–2014 Based on Singapore's Experience*. Ottawa, ON: Public Governance International, 2014.

Bourgon, Jocelyne, Rachael Calleja, Rishanthi Pattiarachchi, and Queena Li. *Enforcement and Safety: A Retrospective of the Sarawak Civil Service High Performance Team (HPT) Retreat 2015*. Ottawa, ON: Public Governance International; Malaysia: Government of Sarawak, 2015.

Bourgon, Jocelyne, and Marcel Lebeau. *Annual Statistical Review of Canadian Fisheries, 1955–1976*, Volume 9. Ottawa, ON: Fisheries and Environment Canada, 1977.

Bourgon, Jocelyne, and Rishanthi Pattiarachchi. *Rule of Law, Citizenship and Enforcement Strategies*. Ottawa, ON: Public Governance International, 2015.

Bovaird, Tony. "Emergent Strategic Management and Planning Mechanisms in Complex Adaptive Systems." *Public Management Review* 10, no. 3 (2008): 319–40. https://doi.org/10.1080/14719030802002741.

Bryden, Joan. "Premiers Agree on More Talk." *Calgary Herald* (Calgary, AB), 11 August 1992.

Buckley, Walter. "Society as a Complex Adaptive System." *Emergence: Complexity and Organization* 10, no. 3 (2008): 86–112.

"Campaign Rhetoric Hits High Pitch: Sovereigntist Leader Bouchard Warns against Repeating 1980." *Vancouver Sun* (Vancouver, BC), 25 September 1995.

Campbell, Kim. *Time and Chance: The Political Memoirs of Canada's First Woman Prime Minister*. Toronto, ON: Doubleday Canada, 1996.

Canada. Canadian Centre for Management Development. "Canadian Centre for Management Development Announces Revitalized Fellows Program and Announces Two Appointments." 29 November 1999. Archived 11 March 2004 at the Wayback Machine, https://web.archive.org/web/20040311190847/http://www.ccmd-ccg.gc.ca/about/newsroom/release/newsrel3_e.html.

– *CCMD 5 Year Review – Canadian Centre for Management Development Report to Parliament December 2001*. Ottawa, ON: CCMD, 2001.

– "Fellows." Archived 21 February 2004 at the Wayback Machine, https://web.archive.org/web/20040221114630/http://www.ccmd-ccg.gc.ca/about/fellows/index_e.html.

– Learning and Development Committee. *A Public Service Learning Organization: From Coast to Coast to Coast: Directions for the Future*. Ottawa, ON: Canadian Centre for Management Development, 2000.

– Partnership for International Cooperation, "The Partnership." Archived 6 January 2002 at the Wayback Machine, https://web.archive.org/web/20020106184359/http://international.gc.ca/public/2_1_about_us.asp.

Canada. Consumer and Corporate Affairs Canada. *Annual Report Year-End March 31, 1990*. Ottawa, ON: Consumer and Corporate Affairs Canada, 1990.

– *Annual Report Year-End March 31, 1991*. Ottawa, ON: Consumer and Corporate Affairs Canada, 1991.

– *The Role of Consumer and Corporate Affairs Canada and Canada's Agenda for Prosperity*. Ottawa, ON: Consumer and Corporate Affairs Canada, 1991.

Canada. Department of Regional Industrial Expansion. *Annual Reports 1983–1984*. Ottawa, ON: Regional Industrial Expansion, 1985.

– *Annual Report 1984–1985*. Ottawa, ON: Regional Industrial Expansion, 1986.

Canada. Industry Canada. *Performance Report for the Period Ending March 31, 1999*. Ottawa, ON: Industry Canada, 1999.

Canada. The Leadership Network. *Performance Report For the period ending March 31, 1999*. Ottawa, ON: Leadership Network, 1999.

Canada. Office of the Auditor General. "Involving Others in Governing: Accountability at Risk." In *Report of the Auditor General of Canada*. Ottawa, ON: Office of the Auditor General, 1999.

Canada. Office of the Conflict of Interest and Ethics Commissioner. *Quarterly Statistical Report 2024–2025: Q2 – July to September 2024*. Ottawa, ON: Office of the Conflict of Interest and Ethics Commissioner, 2024.

Canada. Parliament. Senate. Senate Special Committee on the Pearson Airport Agreements. *Report of the Senate Special Committee on the Pearson Airport Agreements*. 1st sess., 35th Parliament.

Canada. Policy Horizons Canada. *Disruptions on the Horizon*. Ottawa, ON: Policy Horizons Canada, 2024.

Canada. Policy Research Initiative. *Canada 2005: Global Challenges and Opportunities – Overview*. Ottawa, ON: Policy Research Initiative, 1997. Archived 14 September 2000 at the Wayback Machine, https://web.archive.org/web/20000914061032/http://policyresearch.schoolnet.ca:80/keydocs/overview/global-e.htm.

– *Overview: Report on Growth, Human Development, and Social Cohesion*. Ottawa, ON: Policy Research Initiative, 1996. Archived 14 September 2000 at the Wayback Machine, https://web.archive.org/web/20000914061039/http://policyresearch.schoolnet.ca/keydocs/overview/growth-e.htm.

Canada. Prime Minister's Advisory Committee on the Public Service. *Second Report of the Prime Minister's Advisory Committee on the Public Service*. Ottawa, ON: Privy Council Office, 2008.

Canada. Prime Minister's Office. *Open and Accountable Government*. https://www.pm.gc.ca/en/news/backgrounders/2015/11/27/open-and-accountable-government.

– "Prime Minister Announces Formation of Task Force on Modernizing Human Resources Management in the Public Service." 3 April 2001. Archived 26 April 2001 at the Wayback Machine, https://web.archive.org/web/20010426081736/

http://pm.gc.ca/default.asp?Language=E&page=newsroom&sub=newsreleases&doc =managmenttaskforce.20010403_e.htm.

Canada. Privy Council Office. *Deputy Minister Task Forces: From Studies to Action*. Ottawa, ON: Privy Council Office, 1996.

– *Deputy Ministers' Task Team on Values and Ethics Report to the Clerk of the Privy Council*. Ottawa, ON: Privy Council Office, 2023.

– Guidelines on the Conduct of Ministers, Ministers of State, Exempt Staff and Public Servants during an Election. https://www.canada.ca/en/privy-council/services /publications/guidelines-conduct-ministers-state-exempt-staff-public-servants -election.html.

Canada. Public Service Commission. *Public Service Commission of Canada 2015–2016 Annual Report*. Ottawa, ON: Public Service Commission, 2016.

Canada. Treasury Board Secretariat. *Employment Statistics for the Federal Public Service: April 1, 1999, to March 31, 2000*. Ottawa, ON: Treasury Board Secretariat, 2000.

– *Policies for Ministers' Offices – January 2011*. https://www.canada.ca/en/treasury -board-secretariat/services/policies-ministers-offices-january-2011.html.

– "Population of the Federal Public Service." 11 July 2024. https://www.canada.ca/en /treasury-board-secretariat/services/innovation/human-resources-statistics /population-federal-public-service.html.

Canada. Public Service Commission. *Fiscal Year 2022 to 2023 Annual Report: Building Tomorrow's Public Service Today*. Ottawa, ON: Public Service Commission, 2023.

"Canada's New Spirit." *Economist*, September 2003.

Canadian Press. "Mercredi, Yukon Leader Reject PM's Call; Native Group Plans to Protest Exclusion from First Ministers' Meetings." *Edmonton Journal* (Edmonton, AB), 5 August 1992.

– "Mulroney Invites Premiers to Try Again; But PM Imposes July 15 Deal Deadline and Warns He'll Go It Alone after That." *Daily News* (Halifax, NS), 25 June 1992.

Chrétien, Jean. "Challenges for the Canadian Centre for Management Development for the New Millennium." Speech, CCMD Open House, Ottawa, ON, 10 February 1999. Transcript archived 22 January 2001 at the Wayback Machine, https://web .archive.org/web/20010122014200/http://www.ccmd-ccg.gc.ca/newsroom/speeches /challenge.html.

– *My Years as Prime Minister*. Paperback edition. Toronto, ON: Vintage Canada, 2008.

– "'No' Rally at Verdun Auditorium." Speech, Montreal, QC, 24 October 1995. https://web.archive.org/web/19970624014743/http://pm.gc.ca/english/pmo /pm_speech/rally12a.htm.

– "Quebec Chamber of Commerce and Industry." Speech, Quebec City, QC, 18 October 1995. https://web.archive.org/web/19970624014806/http://pm.gc.ca /english/pmo/pm_speech/quebec_9.htm.

Clarity Act. SC 2000.

Clarkson, Adrienne. “Speech from the Throne to Open the Second Session Thirty-Sixth Parliament of Canada.” Speech, House of Commons, Ottawa, ON, 12 October 1999.

Cobb, Chris. “Cyberschool: Canada Leads the World with an On-Line Educational Network Called Schoolnet.” *Ottawa Citizen* (Ottawa, ON), 26 November 1995.

Commonwealth Expert Group on Development and Democracy. *Making Democracy Work for Pro-Poor Development*. London, UK: Commonwealth Secretariat, 2003.

Compilation of Literature Scans. Ottawa, ON: Public Governance International, 2010.

Craft, Jonathan. *Backrooms and Beyond: Partisan Advisers and the Politics of Policy Work in Canada*. Toronto, ON: University of Toronto Press, 2016. https://doi.org/10.3138/9781442617636.

Craft, Jonathan, and Paul Wilson. “Policy Analysis and the Central Executive.” In *Policy Analysis in Canada*, edited by Laurent Dobuzinskis and Michael Howlett, 147–63. Bristol, UK: Policy Press, 2018. https://doi.org/10.2307/j.ctt22rbkbb.

Creating Opportunity: The Liberal Plan for Canada. Ottawa, ON: Liberal Party of Canada, 1993.

Dandache, Nisrine, and Jocelyne Bourgon. *Is Canada Fit for the Future? A PGI Working Paper*. Ottawa, ON: Public Governance International, 2021.

Des idées pour mon pays: Programme du Parti Québécois. Montreal, QC: Parti Québécois, 1994.

Dion, Mario. *Annual Report 2018–2019, in Respect of the Conflict of Interest Act*. Ottawa, ON: Office of the Conflict of Interest and Ethics Commissioner, 2016.

Duit, Andreas, and Victor Galaz. “Governance and Complexity – Emerging Issues for Governance Theory.” *Governance: An International Journal of Policy, Administration, and Institutions* 21, no. 3 (2008): 311–35. https://doi.org/10.1111/j.1468-0491.2008.00402.x.

Durrant, Tim, Nicola Blacklaws, and Ketaki Zodgekar. *Special Advisers and the Johnson Government*. London, UK: Institute for Government, 2020.

Farnsworth, Clyde H. “Canada’s Pale Version of Peso Crisis.” *New York Times* (New York, NY), 24 January 1995.

Finlay, Lorraine. “The McMullan Principle: Ministerial Advisors and Parliamentary Committees.” *University of Tasmania Law Review* 35, no. 1 (2016): 69–94.

Flynn, Greg. “Rethinking Policy Capacity in Canada: The Role of Parties and Election Platforms in Government Policy-Making.” *Canadian Public Administration* 54, no. 2 (2011): 235–53. https://doi.org/10.1111/j.1754-7121.2011.00172.x.

Goldenberg, Eddie. *The Way It Works: Inside Ottawa*. Toronto, ON: McClelland & Stewart, 2007.

Governance in the 21st Century: Using Government Authority and Collective Power: The New Synthesis Project – Brazil Roundtable Report. Edited by Jocelyne Bourgon. Ottawa, ON: Public Governance International, 2010.

Hagen Schuller, Jo-Anna, and Finn Baker. "Ministers' Private Offices." Institute for Government, 21 October 2020. https://www.instituteforgovernment.org.uk/explainer/ministers-private-offices.

Hannaford, John. "Message from the Clerk: Bringing Our Values and Ethics to Life in Our Changing Environment." *Maple Leaf*, 18 September 2023. https://www.canada.ca/en/department-national-defence/maple-leaf/defence/2023/09/bringing-values-ethics-life-changing-environment.html.

Hébert, Chantal, and Jean Lapierre. *The Morning After: The 1995 Quebec Referendum and the Day That Almost Was*. Toronto, ON: Knopf Canada, 2014.

Heeney, A.D.P. "Cabinet Government in Canada: Some Recent Developments in the Machinery of the Central Executive." *Canadian Journal of Economics and Political Science* 12, no. 3 (1946): 282–301. https://doi.org/10.2307/137283.

– "Mackenzie King and the Cabinet Secretariat." *Canadian Public Administration* 10, no. 3 (1967): 366–75.

Hnatyshyn, Ray. "Speech from the Throne to Open the Third Session Thirty-Fourth Parliament of Canada." Speech, House of Commons, Ottawa, ON, 13 May 1991.

Holling, C.S. "Understanding the Complexity of Economic, Ecological, and Social Systems." *Ecosystems* 4, no. 5 (2001): 390–405. https://doi.org/10.1007/s10021-001-0101-5.

Homer-Dixon, Thomas. *The Upside of Down: Catastrophe, Creativity and the Renewal of Civilization*. Toronto, ON: Vintage Canada, 2007.

Hurley, James Ross. *Amending Canada's Constitution: History, Processes, Problems and Prospects*. Ottawa, ON: Canada Communication Group Publishing, 1996.

Ibbitson, John. *Stephen Harper*. Toronto, ON: McClelland & Stewart, 2015.

Jarvis, Mark D., and Paul G. Thomas. "The Limits of Accountability: What Can and Cannot Be Accomplished in the Dialectics of Accountability?" In *From New Public Management to New Political Governance: Essays in Honour of Peter C. Aucoin*, edited by Herman Bakvis and Mark D. Jarvis, 271–313. Kingston, ON: McGill-Queen's University Press, 2012. https://doi.org/10.1515/9780773587229.

Juillet, Luc, and Ken Rasmussen. *Defending a Contested Ideal: Merit and the PSC of Canada, 1908–2008*. Ottawa, ON: University of Ottawa Press, 2008. https://doi.org/10.2307/j.ctt1ckpgdd.

Jungersen, Ulrik, and Rachael Calleja. *NS Live Case Series 2017: Kolding – We Design for Life*. Ottawa, ON: Public Governance International, 2017.

Kamensky, John. "A Brief History." National Partnership for Reinventing Government, January 1999. https://govinfo.library.unt.edu/npr/whoweare/history2.html.

Keeping Students in Class Act, S.O. 2022.

Kettl, Donald F. *The Transformation of Governance: Public Administration for Twenty-First-Century America*. Baltimore, MD: Johns Hopkins University Press, 2002.

Kirby, Michael J.L. *Navigating Troubled Waters: A New Policy for the Atlantic Fisheries: Highlights and Recommendations*. Ottawa, ON: Task Force on Atlantic Fisheries, 1982.

Kroustrup, Jonas, and Rachael Calleja. *NS Live Case Series 2017: The Vejle Resilience Strategy*. Ottawa, ON: Public Governance International, 2017.

L-03 – Loi sur la laïcité de l'État, RLRQ, c. L-0,3.

La Relève Task Force. *First Progress Report on La Relève: Overview*. Ottawa, ON: Privy Council Office, 1998.

– *La Relève: A Commitment to Action*. Ottawa, ON: Privy Council Office, 1997.

LeBlanc, Roméo. "Speech from the Throne to Open the First Session Thirty-Sixth Parliament of Canada." Speech, House of Commons, Ottawa, ON, 27 February 1997. https://lop.parl.ca/sites/ParlInfo/default/en_CA/Parliament/throneSpeech/speech361.

– "Speech from the Throne to Open the Second Session Thirty-Fifth Parliament of Canada." Speech, House of Commons, Ottawa, ON, 27 February 1996. https://lop.parl.ca/sites/ParlInfo/default/en_CA/Parliament/throneSpeech/speech352.

Lenihan, Don. *Collaborative Federalism: How Labour Mobility and Foreign Qualification Recognition Are Changing Canada's Intergovernmental Landscape*. Ottawa, ON: Public Governance International, 2012.

Lewin, Kurt. *Field Theory in Social Science*. New York, NY: Harper & Row, 1951.

Lisée, Jean-François. *Octobre 1995: Tous les espoirs, tous les chagrins*. Montreal, QC: Québec Amérique, 2015.

Macdonald, Don. "Federalists Vow to Pack Meeting." *Gazette* (Montreal, QC), 28 August 1992.

Marland, Alex. *Whipped: Party Discipline in Canada*. Vancouver, BC: UBC Press, 2020. https://doi.org/10.59962/9780774864985.

Marson, Brian, and Ralph Heintzman. *From Research to Results: A Decade of Results-Based Service Improvement in Canada*. Toronto, ON: Institute of Public Administration of Canada, 2009.

Martin, Paul. *The Budget Speech*. Ottawa, ON: Department of Finance, 1994.

– *The Budget Speech*. Ottawa, ON: Department of Finance, 1995.

– *Hell or High Water: My Life in and out of Politics*. Emblem edition. Toronto, ON: McClelland & Stewart, 2009.

Masten, Ann S., and Jelena Obradović. "Disaster Preparation and Recovery: Lessons from Research on Resilience in Human Development." *Ecology & Society* 13, no. 1 (2008). http://www.ecologyandsociety.org/vol13/iss1/art9/.

Mau, Tim. "Professionalism and Leadership Development." *CSL Leadership Review* 1, no. 2 (2006).

May, Kathryn. "Building a Culture of Public Service on Hybrid Work." *Policy Options*, 16 May 2024. https://policyoptions.irpp.org/magazines/may-2024/public-service-remote/.

– "A Scramble and Scrutiny of the Public Service Not Seen in More Than 20 Years." *Policy Options*, 28 March 2024. https://policyoptions.irpp.org/magazines/march-2024/overbilling-fraud-public-service/.

McIlroy, Anne. "Parizeau Drops Demand for Full Sovereignty; Panel Report Gives Premier Chance to Alter Position." *Ottawa Citizen* (Ottawa, ON), 20 April 1995.

Milne, David. "Innovative Constitutional Processes: Renewal of Canada Conferences, January–March 1992." In *Canada: The State of the Federation 1992*, edited by Douglas Brown and Robert Young, 27–51. Kingston, ON: Institute of Intergovernmental Relations, 1992.

Mitleton-Kelly, Eve. "Ten Principles of Complexity and Enabling Infrastructures." In *Complex Systems and Evolutionary Perspectives of Organisations: The Application of Complexity Theory to Organisations*, edited by Eve Mitleton-Kelly. Amsterdam, Netherlands: Elsevier, 2003.

Monahan, Patrick J. *Cooler Heads Shall Prevail: Assessing the Costs and the Consequences of Quebec Separation*. C.D. Howe Institute Commentary 65. Toronto, ON: C.D. Howe Institute, 1995.

Moran, Terry. "Terry Moran: Time for an Inquiry into the Public Service." *The Conversation*, 31 October 2012. https://theconversation.com/terry-moran-time-for-an-inquiry-into-the-public-service-10277.

Morneau, Bill. *Where to from Here: A Path to Canadian Prosperity*. Toronto, ON: ECW Press, 2023.

Morrison, Catherine. "Just Over Half of 'High-Volume' Government Services Met Standards Last Year." *Ottawa Citizen* (Ottawa, ON), 4 January 2025.

Mulroney, Brian. *Memoirs*. Toronto, ON: McClelland & Stewart, 2011.

New Zealand. Te Kawa Mataaho Public Service Commission. "Ngā pokapū – Central agencies." n.d. https://www.publicservice.govt.nz/system/public-service-sectors/central-agencies.

Ng, Yee-Fui. "Dispelling Myths about Conventions: Ministerial Advisers and Parliamentary Committees." *Australian Journal of Political Science* 51, no. 3 (2016): 512–29. https://doi.org/10.1080/10361146.2016.1190808.

NS Live Case Series 2017. Elder Care in Frederica, Denmark. Ottawa, ON: Public Governance International, 2017.

"'On s'est écrasé, c'est tout' – La conversation Wilhelmy-Tremblay." *La Presse* (Montreal, QC), 1 October 1992.

Peregrine, Michael W., and Charles W. Elson. "The Important Legacy of the Sarbanes Oxley Act." *Harvard Law School Forum on Corporate Governance*, 30 August 2022. https://corpgov.law.harvard.edu/2022/08/30/the-important-legacy-of-the-sarbanes-oxley-act/.

Peters, B. Guy, and Donald J. Savoie, editors. *Governance in the Twenty-First Century: Revitalizing the Public Service*. Kingston, ON: McGill-Queen's University Press, 2000. https://doi.org/10.1515/9780773568884.

Pickering, Heath, Jonathan Craft, and Marleen Brans. "Ministerial Advisers as Power Resources: Exploring Expansion, Stability and Contraction in Westminster Ministers' Offices." *Parliamentary Affairs* 77, no. 2 (2024): 305–27. https://doi.org/10.1093/pa/gsad005.

Pollitt, Christopher. "Mini-Symposium on 'Towards a New Public Administration Theory': Editor's Introduction." *International Review of Administrative Sciences* 73, no. 1 (2007): 5–6. https://doi.org/10.1177/0020852307075685.

– "'Towards a New Public Administration Theory': Some Comments on Jocelyne Bourgon's 5th Braibant Lecture." *International Review of Administrative Sciences* 73, no. 1 (2007): 37–41.

Pow, James T. "Amateurs versus Professionals: Explaining the Political (In) Experience of Canadian Members of Parliament." *Parliamentary Affairs* 71, no. 3 (2018): 633–55. https://doi.org/10.1093/pa/gsx082.

"Premiers Tackle Senate Again on Friday, Mulroney Couldn't Be Happier." *Hamilton Spectator* (Hamilton, ON), 30 June 1992.

Preparing Government to Serve beyond the Predictable: The New Synthesis Project – Singapore Roundtable Report, edited by Jocelyne Bourgon. Ottawa, ON: Public Governance International, 2010.

Public Service Employment Act, S.C. 2003.

Public Service Modernization Act, S.C. 2003.

A Public Service Renewal Agenda for the 21st Century: The New Synthesis Project – United Kingdom Roundtable Report. Edited by Jocelyne Bourgon. Ottawa, ON: Public Governance International, 2011.

Quon, Alexander, and Kate McGillivray. "Sask. Says $28M in Carbon Tax Money Is 'Safe for Now' after Striking Deal with Ottawa." CBC News, 16 July 2024. https://www.cbc.ca/news/canada/saskatchewan/sask-carbon-tax-cra-dispute-1.7264919.

Rabson, Mia. "'Canada's Standing in the World Has Slipped' under Trudeau, Marc Garneau Says in Autobiography." CBC News, 5 July 2024. https://www.cbc.ca/news/politics/marc-garneau-trudeau-canada-reputation-suffering-1.7255120.

Resilience and Emergence in Public Administration: The New Synthesis Project – The Netherlands Roundtable Report. Edited by Jocelyne Bourgon. Ottawa, ON: Public Governance International, 2010.

Roberts, Alasdair. *The Adaptable Country: How Canada Can Survive the Twenty-First Century*. Kingston, ON: McGill-Queen's University Press, 2024.

– "Public Management: A Flawed Kind of Statecraft." In Brint Milward et al., "Roundtable – Is Public Management Neglecting the State?" *Governance: An International Journal of Policy, Administrations and Institutions* 29, no. 3 (2016): 311–34.

– Robertson, Gordon. "The Changing Role of the Privy Council Office." *Canadian Public Administration* 14, no. 4 (1971): 487–508.

– *Memoirs of a Very Civil Servant: Mackenzie King to Pierre Trudeau*. Toronto, ON: University of Toronto Press, 2000. https://doi.org/10.3138/9781442677203.

Russell, Randall. "The New Synthesis Project: A Laboratory for Master Practitioners." Canadian Government Executive, 2013. https://canadiangovernmentexecutive.ca/the-new-synthesis-project-a-laboratory-for-master-practitioners/.

Savoie, Donald J. *Reviewing Canada's Regional Development Efforts*. St. John's, NL: Royal Commission on Renewing and Strengthening Our Place in Canada, 2003.

– *Speaking Truth to Canadians about Their Public Service*. Kingston, ON: McGill-Queen's University Press, 2024.

Schnabel, Johanna. "Committed to Coordination? Intergovernmental Councils as a Federal Safeguard." *Swiss Political Science Review* 23, no. 2 (2017): 191–206. https://doi.org/10.1111/spsr.12248.

Schwab, Klaus. *The Fourth Industrial Revolution*. New York, NY: Crown Business, 2017.

Séguin, Rhéal. "Fight Ahead for Bourassa." *Globe and Mail* (Toronto, ON), 24 August 1994.

– "Sovereignty Not Tied to Vote: Parizeau: Referendum Call Would Come Later." *Globe and Mail* (Toronto, ON), 9 May 1994.

A Self-Help Guide for Practitioners. Ottawa, ON: Public Governance International, 2013.

Senge, Peter M. *The Fifth Discipline: The Art and Practice of the Learning Organization*. New York, NY: Doubleday/Currency, 1990.

Shortliffe, Glen. *Public Service 2000: Second Annual Report to the Prime Minister on the Public Service of Canada*. Ottawa, ON: Privy Council Office, 1994.

Smith, Alex. *The Roles and Responsibilities of Central Agencies*. Revised edition. Ottawa, ON: Library of Parliament, 2015.

Smith, Margaret. *Legislative Summary: Bill C-25: The Public Service Modernization Act*. Ottawa, ON: Library of Parliament, 2003. https://lop.parl.ca/staticfiles/PublicWebsite/Home/ResearchPublications/LegislativeSummaries/PDF/37-2/c25-e.pdf.

Speirs, Rosemary. "Thin Ranks of PM's Female Aides Now Thinner." *Toronto Star* (Toronto, ON), 17 December 1998.

Status Report of the Multilateral Meetings on the Constitution, Rolling Draft as at June 11, 1992 – End of Day. Ottawa, ON: 1992. https://www.solon.org/Constitutions/Canada/English/Proposals/19920611_cad.html.

Steubing, Susan, and Cees Anton de Vries. *Governance for the Circular Economy: Leadership Observations*. Maarn, The Netherlands: Quadrahhuis Press, 2018.

Task Force on Managing Horizontal Policy Issues. *Managing Horizontal Policy Issues*. Ottawa, ON: CCMD, 1996.

Task Force on Overhead Services. *Management of Overhead Services*. Ottawa, ON: CCMD, 1996.

Task Force on a Planning Tool for Thinking about the Future of the Public Service. *A Planning Tool for Thinking about the Future of the Public Service*. Ottawa, ON: CCMD, 1996.

Task Force on Service Delivery Models. *Service Delivery Models*. Ottawa, ON: CCMD, 1996.

Task Force on Strengthening Policy Capacity. *Strengthening Our Policy Capacity*. Ottawa, ON: CCMD, 1996.

Task Force on Values and Ethics. *Discussion Paper on Values and Ethics in the Public Service*. Ottawa, ON: CCMD, 1996.

Tentchoff, Corin. *Developing Policy Capacity and the Policy Research Initiative: An Overview*. Ottawa, ON: Public Governance International, 2024.

– *La Relève, the Leadership Network, and the Formation of the Canada School of Public Service: An Overview*. Ottawa, ON: Public Governance International, 2024.

– *Modernizing Service Delivery: An Overview*. Ottawa, ON: Public Governance International, 2024.

Tremblay, Arthur. "An Authentically Canadian Deal." *Canadian Parliamentary Review* 12, no. 4 (1989).

United Nations. Committee of Experts on Public Administration. *Report on the Fifth Session*. E/2006/44-E/C.16/2006/6. 27–31 March 2006. https://undocs.org/en/E/2006/44(SUPP).

– *Report on the Sixth Session*. E/2007/44-E/C.16/2007/6. 10–13 April 2007. https://docs.un.org/en/E/2007/44(SUPP).

– *Report on the Seventh Session*. E/2008/44 E/C.16/2008/6. 14–18 April 2008. https://undocs.org/en/E/2008/44(SUPP).

– *Report on the Eighth Session*. E/2009/44 E/C.16/2009/5. 30 March–3 April 2009. https://docs.un.org/en/E/2009/44(SUPP).

United Nations. Department of Economic and Social Affairs. *Benchmarking E-Government: A Global Perspective*. New York, NY: United Nations, 2002.

– *E-Government Survey 2024: Accelerating Digital Transformation for Sustainable Development*. New York, NY: United Nations, 2024.

Voyer, Jean-Pierre. "Policy Analysis in the Federal Government: Building the Forward-Thinking Policy Research Capacity." In *Policy Analysis in Canada: The State of the Art*, edited by Laurent Dobuzinskis, Michael Howlett, and David Laycock, 217–37. Toronto, ON: University of Toronto Press, 2007. https://doi.org/10.3138/9781442685529.

Wright, Robert. *The Night Canada Stood Still*. Toronto, ON: HarperCollins, 2014.

Index

THE INSTITUTE OF PUBLIC ADMINISTRATION OF CANADA
SERIES IN PUBLIC MANAGEMENT AND GOVERNANCE

Networks of Knowledge: Collaborative Innovation in International Learning, Janice Stein, Richard Stren, Joy Fitzgibbon, and Melissa Maclean

The National Research Council in the Innovative Policy Era: Changing Hierarchies, Networks, and Markets, G. Bruce Doern and Richard Levesque

Beyond Service: State Workers, Public Policy, and the Prospects for Democratic Administration, Greg McElligott

A Law unto *Itself: How the Ontario Municipal Board Has Developed and Applied Land Use Planning Policy*, John G. Chipman

Health Care, Entitlement, and Citizenship, Candace Redden

Between Colliding Worlds: The Ambiguous Existence of Government Agencies for Aboriginal and Women's Policy, Jonathan Malloy

The Politics of Public Management: The HRDC Audit of Grants and Contributions, David A. Good

Dream No Little Dreams: A Biography of the Douglas Government of Saskatchewan, 1944–1961, Albert W. Johnson

Governing Education, Ben Levin

Executive Styles in Canada: Cabinet Structures and Leadership Practices in Canadian Government, edited by Luc Bernier, Keith Brownsey, and Michael Howlett

The Roles of Public Opinion Research in Canadian Government, Christopher Page

The Politics of CANDU Exports, Duane Bratt

Policy Analysis in Canada: The State of the Art, edited by Laurent Dobuzinskis, Michael Howlett, and David Laycock

Digital State at the Leading Edge: Lessons from Canada, Sanford Borins, Kenneth Kernaghan, David Brown, Nick Bontis, Perri 6, and Fred Thompson

The Politics of Public Money: Spenders, Guardians, Priority Setters, and Financial Watchdogs inside the Canadian Government, David A. Good

Court Government and the Collapse of Accountability in Canada and the U.K., Donald Savoie

Professionalism and Public Service: Essays in Honour of Kenneth Kernaghan, edited by David Siegel and Ken Rasmussen

Searching for Leadership: Secretaries to Cabinet in Canada, edited by Patrice Dutil

Foundations of Governance: Municipal Government in Canada's Provinces, edited by Andrew Sancton and Robert Young

Provincial and Territorial Ombudsman Offices in Canada, edited by Stewart Hyson

Local Government in a Global World: Australia and Canada in Comparative Perspective, edited by Emmanuel Brunet-Jailly and John F. Martin

Behind the Scenes: The Life and Work of William Clifford Clark, Robert A.Wardhaugh

The Guardian: Perspectives on the Ministry of Finance of Ontario, edited by Patrice Dutil

Making Medicare: New Perspectives on the History of Medicare in Canada, edited by Gregory P. Marchildon

Overpromising and Underperforming? Understanding and Evaluating New Intergovernmental Accountability Regimes, edited by Peter Graefe, Julie M. Simmons, and Linda A. White

Governance in Northern Ontario: Economic Development and Policy Making, edited by Charles Conteh and Bob Segsworth

Off and Running: The Prospects and Pitfalls of Government Transitions in Canada, David Zussman

Deputy Ministers in Canada: Comparative and Jurisdictional Perspectives, edited by Jacques Bourgault and Christopher Dunn

The Politics of Public Money, Second Edition, David A. Good

Commissions of Inquiry and Policy Change: A Comparative Analysis, edited by Gregory J. Inwood and Carolyn M. Johns

Leaders in the Shadows: The Leadership Qualities of Municipal Chief Administrative Officers, David Siegel

Funding Policies and the Nonprofit Sector in Western Canada: Evolving Relationships in a Changing Environment, edited by Peter R. Elson

Backrooms and Beyond: Partisan Advisers and the Politics of Policy Work in Canada, Jonathan Craft

Fields of Authority: Special Purpose Governance in Ontario, 1815–2015, Jack Lucas

A Quiet Evolution: The Emergence of Indigenous–Local Intergovernmental Partnerships in Canada, Christopher Alcantara and Jen Nelles

Canada's Department of External Affairs, Volume 3, Innovation and Adaptation, 1968–1984, John Hilliker, Mary Halloran, and Greg Donaghy

Federalism in Action: The Devolution of Canada's Public Employment Service, 1995–2015, Donna E. Wood

Distributed Democracy: Health Care Governance in Ontario, Carey Doberstein

Top Secret Canada: Understanding the Canadian Intelligence and National Security Community, edited by Stephanie Carvin, Thomas Juneau, and Craig Forcese

The Four Lenses of Population Aging: Planning for the Future in Canada's Provinces, Patrik Marier

Statecraft: Canada's Prime Ministers and their Cabinets, edited by Stephen Azzi and Patrice Dutil

A Public Servant's Voice: Through the Words of the First Woman Clerk for the Privy Council of Canada, Jocelyne Bourgon